The True Story Of Wainfleet . . . With Lies By William Thomas
Guys: Not Real Bright and Damn Proud Of It!
The Cat Rules (Everything, Including the Dog)
Never Hitchhike on the Road Less Travelled
The Dog Rules (Damn Near Everything!)
Margaret and Me
Malcolm and Me: Life in the Litterbox
Hey! Is That Guy Dead or is He the Skip?
The Tabloid Zone: Dancing with the Four-Armed Man

WILLIAM THOMAS

The Legend of ZIPPY CHIPPY

LIFE LESSONS FROM HORSE RACING'S MOST LOVABLE LOSER

McCLELLAND
& STEWART

Library and Archives Canada Cataloguing in Publication data is available upon request.

Tony Kornheiser's primer on "footie football" (page 14) was reprinted with permission of the author.

ISBN: 978-0-7710-8159-0

Cover design by CS Richardson
Cover image: © Bob Mccaffrey / EyeEm / Getty Images
Text design by Andrew Roberts

Printed and bound in the United States of America

Published in North America by McClelland & Stewart,
a division of Penguin Random House Canada Limited,
a Penguin Random House Company

www.penguinrandomhouse.ca

10 9 8 7 6 5 4 3 2 1

Penguin
Random
House

*For Monica Rose, who worked so long and hard
at reading, typing, and shaping the manuscript of this book
that she deserves a co-author credit.
She won't get one, but dammit, she should!*

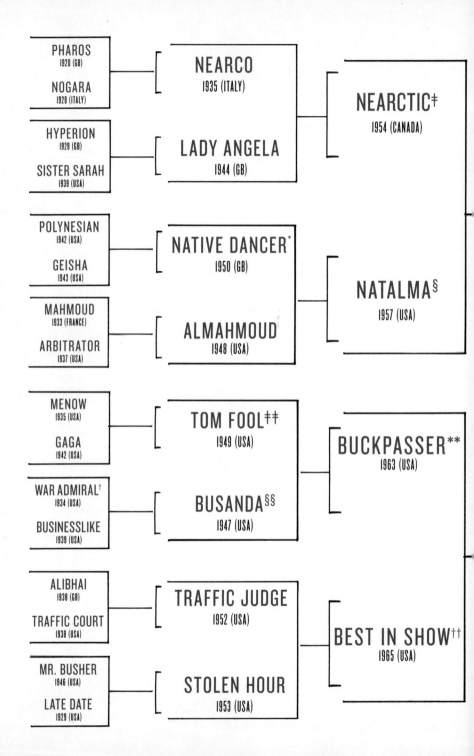

PATRILINEAL TREE

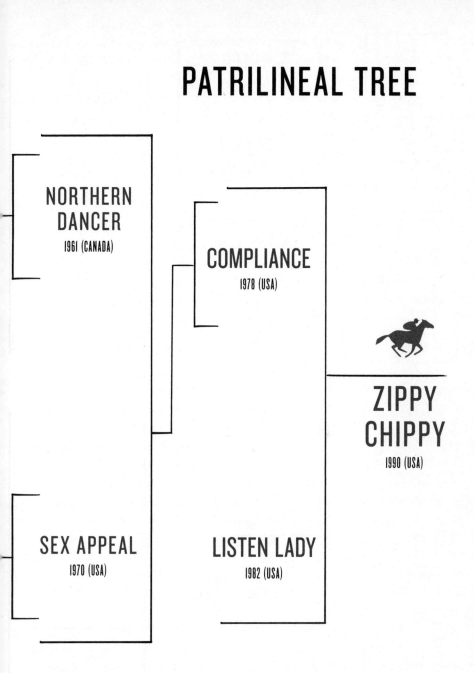

NORTHERN DANCER
1961 (CANADA)

COMPLIANCE
1978 (USA)

SEX APPEAL
1970 (USA)

LISTEN LADY
1982 (USA)

ZIPPY CHIPPY
1990 (USA)

*NATIVE DANCER: Triple Crown Winner (1953), Won 21 of 22 races; † WAR ADMIRAL Triple Crown Winner, *Blood-Horse* Magazine #1 Horse of All Time; ‡ NEARCTIC: Canadian Horse of the Year; § NATALMA: Canadian Racing Hall of Fame; ** BUCKPASSER: Horse of the Year; †† BEST IN SHOW: Broodmare of the Year; ‡‡ TOM FOOL: Horse of the Year; §§ BUSANDA: Winner, Saratoga Cup

MATRILINEAL TREE

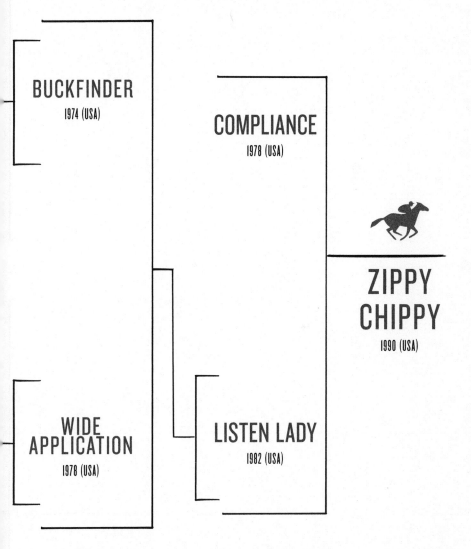

BUCKFINDER
1974 (USA)

COMPLIANCE
1978 (USA)

ZIPPY CHIPPY
1990 (USA)

WIDE APPLICATION
1978 (USA)

LISTEN LADY
1982 (USA)

*NATIVE DANCER: Triple Crown Winner (1953), Won 21 of 22 races; † BOLD RULER: Preakness Stakes Winner, sire of Secretariat; ‡ ROUND TABLE: Considered to be the greatest American turf horse; § BUCKPASSER: Horse of the Year; ** TOM FOOL: Horse of the Year; †† WHAT A PLEASURE: Top Sire in 1975 and 1976; ‡‡ WAR ADMIRAL Triple Crown Winner, *Blood-Horse* Magazine #1 Horse of All Time

PROLOGUE

The Curse: "Winning isn't everything;
it's the only thing."

Like a runaway, riderless horse on the track, deceit is running circles around professional sports today, while corruption in everyday life has honesty and decency beat by two and a half lengths. And everything duplicitous and immoral is acceptable – unless of course you get caught. The scandals in sports and society are coming so fast and so frequent, we North Americans have lost our capacity to be shamed: where once we gasped or cursed under our breaths, now we shrug.

Cyclist Lance Armstrong, the closest we've come to watching a real-life Superman in action, systematically set out to bully and destroy the reputation of whistle-blower Betsy Andreu, desperate to keep the lid on all the lies he told about using performance-enhancing drugs. New England Patriots quarterback Tom Brady, a fabulous athlete, felt the need to deflate footballs in order to gain an unfair advantage over his opponent.

What in hell's name was the team from Spain thinking at the 2000 Paralympics in Sydney, Australia, when they bypassed tests in order to send out fifteen perfectly abled athletes to beat young people from other countries suffering mental and physical disabilities?

Yeah, Spanish athletes pretended to be handicapped in order to steal medals from amputees and kids with Down syndrome!

And who can forget Tonya Harding (though many of us have tried)? Tonya won the 1994 U.S. Figure Skating Championships in Detroit, Michigan, after some doofus from her camp wielding a metal baton kneecapped Nancy Kerrigan, her chief rival. (Not being the sharpest blade in the skate rack, I swear the first thing Harding would have done if she had ever won an Olympic gold medal would have been to . . . have it bronzed!)

What exactly has inspired such reprehensible conduct by people who still stand proudly as their national anthem is played? Winning at all costs. Take no prisoners. Just bring home the gold. Period. "Winning isn't everything; it's the only thing." First attributed to UCLA Bruins football coach Henry "Red" Sanders and often repeated by the legendary Green Bay Packers, Vince Lombardi, that edict has seriously damaged professional sports and, by extension, degraded the ethics of North American society since the 1960s. Before players adopted this near-suicidal attitude, they helped each other up after a hard hit and scolded a teammate for taking a cheap shot. Strategy, not trash, was the topic of talk. Players respected the game and knew full well that it was bigger than any one of them. In the last half century professional sports has gotten bigger but not better, and uglier. Team owners have become media moguls instead of community leaders, and players are now brands instead of true teammates. There used to be a thing called "fan allegiance" whereby you lived and died with your favorite team, be they great, awful, or ordinary. Today a struggling team like the Toronto Maple Leafs can expect to be roundly booed by their fans, who then toss their team jerseys onto the ice like so much expensive litter.

Every time professional sports crank it up a notch with more intensity, more violence, and more blind will to win, they use the mantra "Winning isn't everything; it's the only thing" to sell their juiced-up product. Over time that quote has become an easy excuse for abhorrent and dangerous behavior.

With sports our metaphor for life, ordinary citizens have become, by osmosis, much like the professional athletes they pay too much to watch. As long as results are attained, cheating is okay. Sabotaging a colleague is smart strategy, and greed really has become "Wall Street good." The means justify the end, and the means – drugs, lip readers, bullies badgering their own teammates, bounties paid to injure an opponent, concussions, suicides – really are mean. If "Kill or be killed in order to win" is the curse, then a quote by Cassius Longinus might lead us to the cure. "In great attempts," said the Greek philosopher, "it is glorious even to fail." Trying and striving and persevering – those are the elements that spell true success in the field of sports and in the game of living. Winning is a welcome reward, but losing ought not to be a life-or-death consequence.

Stupendously, at the turn of this century, a racehorse by the name of Zippy Chippy became America's greatest "attempter." Glorious was this horse in failure, tireless in the trying game. There was no winning, no cheating, no million-dollar contract for this remarkable athlete, because when all was said and done and put out to pasture, he was the great Zippy Chippy – a record-setting, always-struggling, full-striding scoundrel who became the best thoroughbred in professional racing at stealing people's hearts.

TRULY A ONE-OF-A-KIND KINDA HORSE

There are a few spectacular racehorses – Secretariat, Man o' War, Citation, Kelso, Count Fleet, Native Dancer, and now American Pharoah. There are many great racehorses – Affirmed, Seattle Slew, Dr. Fager, War Admiral, Seabiscuit, and Whirlaway. There are terrific horses that you can't help falling in love with – Smarty Jones, John Henry, Ferdinand, Northern Dancer, Funny Cide, Tom Fool, and beautiful Barbaro.

Running their little hearts out at only a few days old and winning races well before they turn three, each of these highly bred horses must have instinctively aspired to run in the greatest race of all: the Kentucky Derby at Churchill Downs in Louisville, Kentucky. The Derby is the first leg and signature race of the Triple Crown, the Holy Grail of horse racing.

As the oldest continuous sporting event in American history, dating back to May 17, 1875, the Kentucky Derby is the Super Bowl of horse racing, the Stanley Cup for thoroughbreds. The Kentucky Derby and Louisville are to horse racing what the Masters and Augusta, Georgia, are to golf. The Derby is such a classy event, that even the lead ponies have their own lead ponies. This single race attracts so much wealth that people who attend the race are actually required to purchase an old Kentucky home before they're allowed to sing "My Old Kentucky Home." Every trainer in North America fantasizes about someday running his best horse at Churchill Downs; every jockey yearns to hear the paddock judge yell, "Riders up!" on Derby day, followed by the crowd, as one, shouting, "They're off!"

There isn't a racehorse in all of North America that did not dream of one day being saddled up for the legendary "Run for the Roses." But only the amazing Zippy Chippy stopped to smell those flowers . . . usually while coming around the clubhouse turn. While winning was great and blue-blooded breeding was important, Zippy wasn't much of a racetrack social climber. He mostly followed his heart — and, okay, all of the other horses in most races — but still, he preferred his own individuality to trying to keep up with the Smarty Joneses.

ONE

A champion runner doesn't even know he's in the race.
He runs because he loves it.

Anonymous

ippy Chippy was bred to be a champion. He was procreatively designed not just to keep pace with other racehorses but to verily blow them all away coming down the homestretch. He was conceived by two half-ton horses rutting for money at the end of a long lineup of remarkable heritage. Sparked by spectacular bloodlines and infused with expensive sperm, Zippy Chippy's pedigree was steeped in high-stakes success.

Zippy was the great-great-grandson of Native Dancer, the dominant "Gray Ghost" who lost only once in his career of twenty-two races. Zippy was also the great-great-grandson of Bold Ruler, the father of Secretariat, the greatest thoroughbred of them all. He was a direct descendent of Triple Crown winner War Admiral, who won twenty-one of twenty-six starts, nosing out Seabiscuit to become Horse of the Year in 1937. War Admiral was the son of Man o' War, the horse who smashed world records and won races by as much as one hundred lengths on his way to winning twenty-one of his twenty-two starts. Count Fleet, the 1943 Kentucky Derby winner who captured the Triple Crown by twenty-five lengths in the Belmont Stakes, also contributed to Zippy's DNA chart.

Zippy Chippy was the grandson of none other than the great Northern Dancer, the little Canadian colt that was passed over at his 1962 yearling auction, forcing corporate tycoon E.P. Taylor and Windfields Farm to keep him.

The runt of the 1961 litter that stable hands joked looked like a golden retriever was not small but low, stocky, and powerful. Built like a military tank, Northern Dancer was fearless, unyielding, and above all, feisty. This muscular colt had more than a will to win; he had an unnatural hatred of losing. The "Pocket Battleship" seemed to have something to prove to his doubters every time he went to post. And he did.

In a brief two-year career, the bonny bay colt had fourteen victories in eighteen trips around the track, never once finishing out of the money. His short, choppy strides worked like the pistons of a powerful V8 engine. Detroit could not manufacture the horsepower Northern Dancer naturally possessed.

In 1964 Northern Dancer won the Kentucky Derby in a jaw-dropping time of two minutes flat, breaking an eighty-nine-year-old record. He then won the Preakness and Canada's Queen's Plate, the oldest continuously run sports event in North America. His earnings of $32,258 per start would soon pale in comparison to the money he'd make for a one-night stand with an ovulating mare.

Cited by the National Thoroughbred Racing Association as "one of the most influential sires in thoroughbred history," Northern Dancer was, simply, the most magnificent stud in the history of thoroughbred racing. His initial stud fee of $10,000 was higher than any Canadian horse before him and it quickly skyrocketed as his first crop of youngsters started piling up victories. In 1970 his son, Nijinksy II, became the first horse in thirty-five years to win the English Triple Crown. In the early eighties, servicing up to forty mares a season, his stud fee was $300,000 and his annual income was $12 million. In 1981, ten of Northern Dancer's offspring sold at an auction for $13,335,000; the sire himself had been passed over at $25,000. Soon he was earning $1 million for one regal roll in the hay. (Although technically, that's not how it's done.) In the spring of 1982, Windfields Farm's syndicate of shareholders, led by Charles Taylor, turned down an offer from a French consortium to buy the horse for $40 million. Northern Dancer was twenty-six years old at the time; the life expectancy of a thoroughbred is twenty-five to thirty years. Still, with great riches came low humor. When Taylor asked his right-hand man how an afternoon's breeding session had gone, stable manager Joe Thomas replied, "Perfectly. Except he spilled about half a million dollars' worth on the floor."

By the time of his death in 1990, Northern Dancer was genetically responsible for one thousand stakes-race winners; his progeny of 295 winning horses amassed career earnings of $183 million. In the 2015 Kentucky Derby, a full twenty-eight years after Northern Dancer bred his last mare, every one of the eighteen horses entered in the race often called "the two most exciting minutes in sports" boasted this stud's name on the sire side of their charts. That's more than strong genes; that's Kryptonite DNA delivered by bullets.

When aficionados of horse racing hear the names Northern Dancer, Man o' War, Count Fleet, Bold Ruler, Native Dancer, or War Admiral – all ancestors of Zippy Chippy – they put their hands together and look to the heavens. Zippy's blue-blooded ancestry was royalty at its absolute richest! You have to go back to King Solomon to strike gold that glitters more brightly than Zippy Chippy's natal star. This planned production was akin to breeding a Princess Grace of Monaco with a King Juan Carlos of Spain and . . . unfortunately coming up with a Prince Harry. Look, it's not an exact science, okay?

It didn't take long at all — kind of a "Wham! Bam! Thank you, Listen Lady." She would be Zippy's mom; Compliance was his dad. Odd that the mother of Compliance was a mare called Sex Appeal and the grandfather of Listen Lady was a stallion named What a Pleasure. Stud services rarely come with this sort of civility.

Eleven months after the romp in the rutting barn, on April 20, 1991, a slime-soaked little foal slipped out of dam Listen Lady and onto the soft straw floor in a stall at Capritaur Farm in upstate New York. This dozy, all-brown baby with his big head, spindly legs, and a tiny white pyramid imprinted on his forehead struggled to his feet, took two steps forward, and stopped.

He was not hesitating at the shock of his new and unfamiliar surroundings, because even back then, Zippy Chippy was fearless. He was not hesitating at the uncertainty of his physical capabilities, because really, he would develop into an "iron horse" of sorts, making a mockery of the statistic that the average thoroughbred makes about fifteen starts.

At only a few minutes old, Zippy Chippy came to a full stop in order to look around and get a handle on things. He took his sweet time gazing off into the distance at nothing in particular, or possibly a cloud formation in the shape of a bunch of carrots. Taking his time and daydreaming – this would be his style and his philosophy of life. And really, who are we to judge a dreamer as being less relevant than a doer?

So this cute little unstable fellow stood his ground in that barn on that spring day so many years ago, and his body language verily screamed, *Hell no, I won't go!* But nobody listened to him, so he lay down and had a nap.

Men seldom do listen. They refuse to stop and ask for directions when they're lost, which prompted comedian Roseanne Barr to say that only a man can read a map because only a man can imagine that one inch equals ten miles.

Men never listen when it comes to horses, either, believing that they know best when it comes to how to breed 'em and bet 'em, how to train 'em and ride 'em. They also don't listen to their horses – the very reason we have "horse whisperers" but not "human whisperers," although a certain former U.S. president sure could have used one: "No, Bill, hit that thing with a gavel or something. Nobody's going to believe that intern is coming to the Oval Office to deliver a pizza!"

Somewhere from the back of the small crowd straining to peek into the stall, a voice, maybe that of a seasoned trainer or a wizened stable boy, said, "He's on his feet and lookin' good!" And based on that assessment, Zippy Chippy was destined for a career as a racehorse. Every race day his handlers would haul him out of his comfortable stable and lead him onto a track, where he got his shoes all dirty; if it had been raining, the muck would splash all over his chest and sometimes right in his face. Along with a healthy appetite, Zippy Chippy's quirkiness was established at birth.

There is little doubt that Zippy wanted to run . . . east to the Adirondack Mountains, where he'd do a bum slide across a frozen Lake Placid, or north up to Canada, where he would seek refuge as a "track dodger" and score a sweet healthcare package. Running free over grassy knolls with your mane being combed by the wind – that's what horses were meant to do. He just didn't want to run in a race with other horses. That was demeaning, and too confrontational. Being saddled in leather and then decorated with silks of bright, tacky colors – good gawd. Was there no trainer in North America who had ever heard of soft tones, like camel or even taupe?

And these creepy jockeys with frilly, silky outfits who straddled you tightly with both legs, all the while spanking you with a riding crop. What the hell was that about? I mean, that was strange even for Kentucky, where owners of horses wore plaid pants with red blazers, and women, to their credit, refrained from pointing and laughing out loud. Then again, maybe the women couldn't actually see the men for all that Derby hat.

And that ghastly starting gate – it was one long line of tiny little jail cells, and once you were locked in there they would scare the crap out of you with that unbearable bell. RINGGGGGGGG!

Even when you knew it was coming, that thing was frightening, and Zippy Chippy would need a moment or two to compose himself and get his bearings, and, well, in horse racing, where trainers are often seen draped over fences staring at stopwatches, these are known as very valuable seconds.

Native Dancer and Northern Dancer be damned! They were Zippy's ancestors and they were great racehorses, but really, where does greatness stop? He may have been just a gangly little foal, but Zippy inherently knew a few things to be true: to compete against those deemed better than you, to challenge for the lead and hold it, to thrive and drive and whirl away and find another gear – those were the dreams of his forebearers, not his. He had smaller dreams that played in slow motion, and these did not include being fawned over by the owner's family in the winner's circles of American tracks, having his picture taken by the official photographer, or having blankets of roses draped round his neck. A quick glance at his stats tells you that Zippy may in fact have been allergic to flowers and felt that jockeys who came in first all the time were just showing off.

No, not everybody dreams in color or yearns to finish first or takes losing to heart. Zippy would go on to have fun and frivolity in his career as a racehorse — something that, if you've ever seen the movie *Seabiscuit*, you know that horse never had. All that blood and guts and the lower-body injuries — man, give it a rest! Chill would have been an excellent name for this gamboling, devil-may-care four-footer. His casual gait and wandering mind spelled **RELAX** in caps and boldface. "Stop and smell the fumes that little filly Heart's Desire is giving off down the row" — that was Zippy's motto.

No, Zippy Chippy would not go on to become what sports writers call a "phenom," an exceptional athlete who defies the odds by surprising everyone with a series of eye-popping victories. The only thing Zippy Chippy and Secretariat had in common was that they ate from food buckets and randomly soiled the straw in their stalls. Yet Zippy would go on to defy everything and everybody, especially those people who handled him. And in the end, what he accomplished was nothing short of phenomenal. Very few thoroughbred horses ever run one hundred races, and none ever accomplished that feat with the zeal and admiration, the aplomb and the arrogance, the style and the dash of the Zipster. (Okay, *dash* may have been a bad choice of words.) Secretariat may have set the racing world on its ear establishing track records at will, but he never once lunged at his closest competitor and bit him in the ear!

Oh, Zippy Chippy would run, alright, at a time and place and pace of his choosing, but he would never bide a harness willingly or bear a saddle kindly. Leather straps and blindfolds, time trials and claiming races — that was the stuff of trainers and track masters, handicappers and long-shot bettors. He was neither a speedster nor a steeplechaser, not a long-haul closer or a railside racer.

He was Zippy Chippy, a free spirit at large and far from the grind of greatness, not sweating but celebrating the small stuff of life. He was at all times a professional racehorse, thriving, indeed rejoicing, in a quirky little world of his own. They broke the mold when they made the Zipster —to which many, particularly people who bet on horses to win, would say quite frankly, "Thank God."

And what was his reward for showing such rugged individualism and singular focus early on in his career? They cut his nuts off, that's what they did. No warning, no consent form, no "It's your last night as a real stud so we left a stable door open for you. Heart's Desire. Third on the left." No, it was four swipes of the scalpel, and two prairie oysters hit the stainless steel surgical dish. Oh yeah, this is not a pretty story. But still, I think it's a pretty good one.

SIMPLIFY! CLARIFY!
WHAT DOES ALL THIS NONSENSE MEAN?

Maidens and stakers, stables and rakers, starting gates and handicap weights. Program hawkers, railside gawkers, betting touts, and workout clockers. I know what you're thinking – this horse racing stuff is way too complicated. No, not really.

When soccer and the World Cup first came to the United States in 1994, Americans were confused by the strange rules and unusual terminology of this sport that the rest of the world was madly in love with. So the brilliant Tony Kornheiser, then a columnist with the *Washington Post,* wrote a primer explaining "footie football" to the uninitiated.

> *Don't call it a game, it's a "match." Don't call it a field, it's a "pitch."* . . . *You don't get a penalty, you get "booked."* . . . *Referees give out a yellow card for a cautionary penalty. If you get two yellow cards in one game, or commit a blatant foul, you get a red card, which means immediate ejection from that game, and the next game as well. If you get a green card, you can work at 7-Eleven. If you get a gold card you can charge all your purchases at 7-Eleven."*

And sports fans embraced it all with gusto – "Okay, got it. Blow the whistle, drop the ball, and pass me a cold tallboy."

From a weanling to a yearling to a rambunctious young colt, a male foal grows into a stallion. Same with a filly until she is five; then she's a mare, and sometimes a broodmare, raising her own little hellion.

A horse wearing blinkers can still see the track, while trailing in the field or leading the pack. He prefers the jockey's hand ride without the whip, but if it'll help them win, then he'll respond to the clip.

A handicapped horse is not in any trouble. You can bet him to win or put him in the double.

A horse can lead, stay close, or bring up the rear. He can lose and get claimed or become Horse of the Year. He can struggle to hold the lead as the finish line nears, but the real champions switch to even higher gears.

While a light ride given to a horse is a hack, the equipment of the rider is known as tack. A length is a measuring of eight or nine feet. The leader at the stretch, that's the horse to beat. Horses in a pack are all in the fight; while the sprinters rush to lead, the champions sit tight. A horse can win by a nose or lose by a head. When they finish in a photo, the results hang by a thread.

A furlong is not too far to run, for a rider and a horse weighing half a ton. A gelding can never be a sire, and a speedster wins leading wire to wire. They run on grass, they run in mud; horses eat hay, cows chew cud.

The speedster is the rabbit the rest of them chase. The closer is a winner coming from far and away. More than just speed, pace makes the race. And somebody — as the song goes — always bets on the bay.

TWO

Money, horse racing, and women — three things
the boys just can't figure out.
Will Rogers

Not a lot is known about the early days of Zippy Chippy's career, because apparently nobody wants to take the blame for it. Born with great promise on that spring day at Capritaur Farm in upstate New York, Zippy had impeccable bloodlines, which included La Troienne, the greatest brood mare of the twentieth century.

As a foal Zippy was allowed to romp and roll around with other newborns on the farm, occasionally being hand-walked for a little formal exercise when he was two or three months old. Although he was probably teased and called a "weenie" by the other foals on the farm, he was technically a "weanling" until his first birthday, when he was separated from his dam, Listen Lady. Between the ages of one and two, Zippy's training gradually got more serious, with circle walks on a lead and wide rotations followed by tight turns, all directed by voice commands and a lunge line to keep him out and away from the trainer. Slowly he got used to a bit in his mouth and a saddle on his back. Then on gangly legs he was allowed to "hack" or run at his leisure across the fenced-in countryside, getting a sense of his own strength and speed. One day a rider began carefully lying across his back with his belly over the saddle so the horse could feel the weight of a person on him. The rider patiently let Zippy tire himself out from all the physical protesting. The saddling and mounting procedures became easier with each outing as the young colt got used to the routine. Soon the rider started to actually mount him, left foot into the stirrup and right leg over the top.

From "Rider up!" it was only a matter of time before Zippy was galloping with a jockey on board, slowly at first, alone and then with other horses his age. Soon Zippy was ready to assume the title of professional racehorse. Even as a youngster he was a bit of a comedian – always sticking his tongue out at people, smiling for strangers with cameras, and tear-assing off in the opposite direction of his pack of one-year-old pals. Yet with a few rehearsal races under his belt, the son of Compliance and Listen Lady was off to the races to make a name for himself. And that he would do in spades, but not like any other thoroughbred ever had, not like any of his handlers had ever planned.

Charles "Bill" Frysinger, an oil and gas executive from Ohio with a passing interest in racehorses and a not-so-keen eye for investing, became Zippy Chippy's first owner, by proxy. He met a New York financial track manager who created thoroughbred investment packages for moneyed men like himself. Everything from the purchase of the horse to the training, boarding, and racing schedule was handled by the manager. All Frysinger had to do was provide the cash and watch his investment grow. Except anything to do with racehorses is a huge gamble, and though Bill couldn't have known it at the time, Zippy Chippy would go on to a great career of disappointing bettors. He was to gamblers what carpal tunnel syndrome is to a little old lady addicted to slot machines.

Much like Zippy Chippy, Belmont Park was the product of blue blood and high breeding. August Belmont II built a European-style racecourse on 650 acres of prime New York real estate at Elmont, the "Gateway of Long Island." This property already included a stunning and turreted Tudor Gothic mansion, which later became the track's exclusive Turf and Field Club. On May 4, 1905, forty thousand racing fans made a muddy mess of the narrow dirt road leading up from New York City, and most missed the first race, in which August Belmont's Blandy held off the 100–1 shot Oliver Cromwell to win the $1,500 Belmont Inaugural, a princely sum of a purse back then.

Five years later, Wilbur and Orville Wright drew 150,000 spectators to their international air show at Belmont Park. The "Back the Attack" war-bond promotion held there in 1943 raised nearly $30 million in a single day.

Belmont Park hosts the third jewel in racing's Triple Crown, a unique honor bestowed upon a horse who has already won the Kentucky Derby at Churchill Downs and the Preakness Stakes at Baltimore's Pimlico Race Course. So rare is a Triple Crown winner, Belmont Park has witnessed this grand finale only twelve times in its 111-year history. This crucial race, the longest of the three at a mile and a half and known as the "Test of Champions," has crowned some of the finest racehorses that ever entered a starting gate, from Sir Barton in 1919 to Gallant Fox, Omaha, and War Admiral in the 1930s; Whirlaway, Count Fleet, Assault, and Citation in the 1940s; Secretariat in 1973, Seattle Slew in 1977, Affirmed in 1978, and now American Pharoah in 2015. It was here in 2007 that Rags to Riches beat Curlin to become the first filly in 102 years to win the Belmont Stakes. Whereas most of his royal relatives triumphed regularly at historic Belmont Park, one of America's classiest tracks,

Zippy Chippy would put up numbers that showed he had no sense of history.

For his very first professional race, on September 13, 1994, three-year-old Zippy Chippy was naturally nervous. Opening days, first dates, and debuts are perilously unpredictable. At best it's a crapshoot, at worst a pratfall. Even people paid to analyze such events seldom predict how a "first ever" will actually unfold.

On that warm fall day, the Belmont Park dirt track was fast, and the field of maidens were all anxious to put their very first win up on the board. Jockey Julio Pezua would have had no reason to expect great things from Zippy Chippy, who went off at a long but reasonable odds of 15–1. The rookie racehorse broke from the gate's sixth pole position only to lag the whole way round and finish eighth in the six-and-a-half-furlong test. With Zippy well out of the money, it was a most forgettable coming-out party. For an athlete of his breeding, there should have been a crowd of fans, or at least a good luck banner. Instead, a few thousand people watched a young horse with a funny name come in eighth in a field of ten horses. Life is seldom fair, for horses and humans alike.

Not one of the horses that finished ahead of him had Zippy's precious pedigree. Disheartening was the fact that he got beat by D'Moment, a loser by forty-seven lengths in his first four races. Retired after only six races, D'Moment won just one race in his career – this one. And for this first race, Zippy earned nothing. By contrast, Funny Cide, a Kentucky Derby winner who would one day share a retirement home with Zippy, earned $25,800 for his debut win and $93,000 for every outing after that. More awful than auspicious was this debut of Northern Dancer's grandson.

Back at the same Belmont track ten days later, under an overcast sky and on a muddy oval with Julio Pezua aboard again, there was reason for the owner to be encouraged. Zippy struggled from tenth at the start to fifth down the stretch, and finished third behind Mantequilla and But Anyway. Frysinger pocketed $3,360 from the $28,000 purse for Zippy's third-place finish. Not bad.

Eight days after that race, on October 1, with a new jockey named Robbie Davis aboard, Zippy took wide turns in a lackluster performance over just more than a mile on dirt, disappointing his bettors by coming in fourth. Thinking grass might be more to his liking, trainer Carl Domino entered Zippy in a one-mile race on turf. On only five days' rest, Zippy broke from the gate well and held strong to hit the wire third. Jose Santos, a very capable rider who would one day win the Kentucky Derby with Funny Cide, had given Zippy every chance to win the race. Still, with Zippy finishing only three lengths behind the winner, Lord Basil, third place showed some promise. He earned $3,600. Zippy was knocking on the door of success but not showing any real desire to come in and join the party.

Ten days later, with the talented Mike Smith on his back, Zippy Chippy finished twenty-eight lengths behind the winner, Captain Bainbridge, consequently decamping from the classy track of Belmont Park out of gas and out of the money. When a wealthy owner attaches himself to an aristocratic racetrack that's all about money, he expects his horse to contribute to the equation. Zippy, so far, was having none of it. What seemed odd to his owner and trainer was the fact that despite five straight losses, Zippy was still eager to run, accepting the saddling-up session with gusto. When Belmont Park closed in mid-October, Carl Domino moved Zippy and the rest of his stable of horses from Long Island to the "Big A" in Queens, New York.

Aqueduct Racetrack opened its turnstiles in 1894 under the directors of the Queens County Jockey Club. Horse racing had flourished in North America in the nineteenth century, with the city of Toronto boasting no less than six dirt racetracks, where the grounds were shabby, the rules were fuzzy, and some results were highly suspicious. However it wasn't unusual at the admission price of twenty-five cents to have eight thousand spectators attend a day of racing in that city. The sport crashed in the late 1800s when widespread corruption kept the crowds away from small tracks. Massive racing enterprises like Belmont and Aqueduct marked a great cleansing of thoroughbred racing on the continent. Though Aqueduct lacks the great architecture and rich history of Belmont Park, spectacular horses like Seattle Slew, Nashua, Excelsior, and Count Fleet have brought it great prestige. It also boasted one of the largest restaurants in New York City. Crowds of over seventy thousand spectators came here to watch thorough-breds like Cigar win his first two races, the beginning of an amazing sixteen-race winning streak. In 1973, the incomparable Secretariat was publicly retired here. Pope John Paul II said mass to seventy-five thousand believers at Aqueduct on October 6, 1995, including dozens of heathens who had misunderstood the phrase "From your lips to God's ear" and showed up hoping for insider tips on long shots.

On October 28, two weeks after he arrived at Aqueduct, Zippy was entered in the second race of the day on a firm track, along with eleven other horses also looking for their first win. With Robbie Davis up, Zippy got off to a good start, keeping pace with the leaders around the first half mile of turf. Then he hit the stretch and, as it turned out, the proverbial wall. He tired and finished ninth, twenty lengths behind the winner, Crosskate, who finally shook off the label of "maiden."

Nineteen days later and back on dirt, Zippy lagged badly and finished eighth in an eight-horse field, an incredible fifty-four lengths and a neck behind the winner, Viva La Flag. Even worse, he finished fifty-four lengths behind the second horse, which was named Sixfeetunder. That's when you know you're in way over your head.

This last disastrous outing marked the end of Zippy Chippy racing at class tracks for five-figure purses. Except for two brief appearances at Aqueduct the following year that resulted in unremarkable seventh- and tenth-place finishes, Zippy was dropped from major-league racing for his failure to crack the winner's circle. In his last appearance at Aqueduct he did, however, add a little comic relief to the afternoon program. It was eight days into the new year of 1995, with Richard Migliore on the whip, when Zippy created a match race out of a miserable finish. Even though nine of the horses had crossed the finish line, a real nail-biter broke out in front of the grandstand, and you could hear the excitement in the track announcer's voice: "It's Zippy Chippy and Witchcraft Star, Witchcraft Star and Zippy Chippy as they come neck and neck to the wire!" Appreciating the slapstick, the fans cheered wildly. In a brutal and personal duel down the last eighth mile of dirt, Zippy clipped Witchcraft by a neck at the finish line . . . thereby coming in tenth in an eleven-horse race. Although a real crowd-pleaser, it was the kind of performance that had handicappers imagining these two horses eventually pulling tourist carriages in Central Park.

Zippy Chippy was subsequently demoted to the minor leagues and motored down the New York State Thruway to a small track in Farmington, a half-hour drive south of Rochester. Basic and built in the early sixties, today Finger Lakes Gaming and Racetrack survives on the money it pulls in from off-track betting and the cavernous casino where hundreds of bettors play the slots, oblivious to the horses racing on the track out back. In the 1920s there were no less than 300 thoroughbred racetracks

like Finger Lakes operating in North America. Today there are 54 tracks and 1,560 casinos, with 10,000 racehorses competing for gaming dollars against 50,000 slot machines. These days the local fairgrounds can't sustain a weekend racing card, but the local charity can host "Casino Night" a dozen times a year. As many tracks battle bankruptcy, often there are more horses in the barns than spectators in the seats out front. It's a diehard demographic that still comes to watch the ponies. Yet the cigar-smoking, beer-before-noon crowd of eccentrics cannot save the sport. The horses are eager, their handlers are willing but the crowds just don't come anymore. On most afternoons as few as fifty people watch the races from grandstands built for five and ten thousand. Today, the Finger Lakes Racetrack in Farmington, New York, is a great place to watch the ponies . . . if you like to be alone.

Great jockeys like Angel Cordero, Pat Day, and Bill Shoemaker have ridden at Finger Lakes, as has female pioneer Julie Krone. Its greatest moment was Independence Day in 2007, when the track doubled its normal purse to $100,000 for the Wadsworth Memorial Handicap in order to attract Funny Cide, winner of the Kentucky Derby, as well as the Preakness. A record crowd of twelve thousand fans came out to watch this handsome chestnut gelding win while barely breaking a sweat.

Early on, Funny Cide was gelded because he was a ridgling, meaning he suffered from an undescended testicle that made it painful for him to run. Zippy Chippy had no such excuse for his early failings. On November 26, 1994, the track was fast, the weather was cloudy, and each contestant was looking for his first career win. The $6,000 purse offered for race five was a full $24,000 less than Zippy had been used to, reflecting the drop in class of the horses he was now running against.

With the benefit of a new trainer, Ralph D'Alessandro, as well as a new jockey and a bunch of slower horses to run against, Zippy's Farmington debut was not nearly as disastrous as his coming-out party at Belmont Park had been. Kevin Whitley gave Zippy a good ride and kept him comfortably in third spot halfway around the oval. But Zippy "flattened out," according to the race footnotes, finishing fourth and thereby collecting just $300 for his effort.

On thirteen days' rest, Zippy did a little better in his next start at Finger Lakes. D'Alessandro had even talked Finger Lakes legend Leslie Hulet into riding his gelding. The winningest jockey ever at the Farmington oval, Hulet earned almost $18 million in purse money for the owners of his mounts. After stumbling from the number one position to seventh, Hulet did manage to bring Zippy up to the number two spot for most of the race and a solid third at the wire. Zippy finished just three lengths behind the winner, Byby Fran's Kitchen, and he earned $570.

Four days later Zippy took a lackadaisical five-and-a-half-furlong lap around the dirt track, bringing home $183 for coming in fifth, with David Gordon in the saddle. "Late again," read the footnote on the results chart. Astarforevermore he was not; that horse came in third. He finished just two lengths behind winner Enchanted Mind, and Zippy was definitely in the hunt as the crowd of horses rushed to the wire. From last to fifth in the race for home, Zippy had, at the very least, shown some late speed and tenacity.

On the move again, as the Zipster's purses were going south, he was headed east to Beantown.

A STUD WHO TOOK
HIS JOB SERIOUSLY

Much like his grandson Zippy Chippy, the great Northern Dancer could be an ornery critter. During his career, the horse's home was Barn 7A at Woodbine Racetrack on the northwest outskirts of Toronto. Nobody dared get into Northern Dancer's space except for his handlers and his flamboyant Argentine-born trainer, Horatio Luro. From the horse's steady stream of fan mail came a letter from a blind boy in Brantford, Ontario, who hoped one day to meet The Dancer. Weeks later a limousine pulled up to the barn, and out stepped Mrs. E.P. Taylor, the queen of Toronto's socialite scene, with the little guy in tow. It's safe to say that "Winnie," who often entertained royalty at Windfields Estate in Toronto and their gated mansion in Lyford Cay in the Bahamas, had never been in Northern Dancer's stall.

Meanwhile, back at the barn, the horse was in such a foul mood that Luro couldn't get a halter on him. When he did finally manage to get him strapped, Northern Dancer turned on the trainer, who desperately scrambled out of the stall, under the webbing, with hooves flailing and teeth gnashing at his heels.

With peppermints in her purse, Winnie arrived on the shed row calling out, "Where's my baby?" Northern Dancer went still. As she gently talked to her horse at the stall and guided the boy's hands to the horse's forelock, Northern Dancer obliged like a pet puppy. Witnesses to the event said the transformation from aggressive colt to lap dog was nothing short of incredible.

E.P. Taylor's prized stakes winner began breeding at Windfields' Oshawa farm before being shipped out to the Maryland farm, and Northern Dancer took to "studding" eagerly and often.

If a trailer pulled up to the barn filled with hay or equipment, Northern Dancer never batted an eye. But if a trailer pulled up transporting a mare, the horse would try to kick his way out of the stall to get at her. Eventually his handlers moved him to a stall in the back where there was less distraction.

In the midst of his busy breeding schedule at the Oshawa farm, The Dancer was brought by E.P. Taylor to Woodbine for a final farewell, a much anticipated victory lap for his legion of devoted fans. As he arrived at the track he got confused and assumed he was being led to the breeding shed, also known as the "love shack." Well, afternoon delight!

That's when Northern Dancer, as they say at the track, "dropped his manhood." The dapper Horatio Luro, trainer to the wealthy and friend to Hollywood stars, almost died of embarrassment. For his last public and oh-so-memorable appearance on a fall afternoon in 1969 at Woodbine Racetrack, Northern Dancer greeted his many fans with a full erection. Thank God in those days there was no such thing as "selfies"! Lewd, but given his current profession, quite fitting. Like a baseball slugger saying goodbye to the crowd with a grand slam. There were many reasons why Zippy Chippy was gelded, and now we can add this one to the list.

THREE

Horse sense is the thing a horse has which
keeps it from betting on people.
W.C. Fields

Since 1935, Suffolk Downs in East Boston, Massachusetts, has always been a blue-collar track, where a charity event called the Hot Dog Safari drew more spectators than the races. Owned for a time by the wonderfully entertaining Bill Veeck (as in *wreck*), a P.T. Barnum wannabe, the venue once held twenty-four thousand Beatles fans attending a late-summer concert in 1966, the largest crowd ever to fill the stands. Cigar and Whirlaway have both won on this one-mile dirt oval, and in 1937, a capacity crowd of forty thousand watched Seabiscuit and the legendary John "Red" Pollard smash yet another record to win $70,530 and the Massachusetts Handicap. A Canadian hard-luck kid, Pollard, who rode Seabiscuit to eighteen major victories, was blind in one eye and didn't tell anyone until he retired.

On a cold and rainy winter's day, January 23, 1995, the four-year-old Zippy Chippy made his thirteenth professional appearance, with a new jockey in Jorge Vargas and a new trainer in Sherryl Meade, the latter having been brought in to break the horse's habit of losing. Still owned by Bill Frysinger, Zippy appeared to be up to his old tricks, none of which involved outdistancing other racehorses. Because he was no longer running with the elite, Zippy should have found the high ground against horses like Upbeat Music, Campo's Legend, and Atlanta Gold, the usual suspects who lurked at the back of the pack.

An optimist might characterize Zippy's first race at Suffolk as encouraging. Starting from the number one pole position, Zippy dropped back to the rear of the race and floundered in ninth spot until the homestretch, where without warning he decided to crank it up and outdistance half the field. It was a valiant effort in a losing cause. From a healthy purse of $11,000, he came away with $330 for coming in fifth on a muddy six-furlong track. Far from encouraging was the fact that Zippy finished a glaring twenty-six-and-a-quarter lengths behind the winner, Frank's Return. To put that in perspective, the lineups for tickets by the crowd of 22,169 fans who came to watch Cigar win his fifteenth race in a row at Suffolk Downs in 1996 were not quite as long as twenty-six-and-a-quarter lengths.

As for the horses Zippy managed to beat? Well . . . He's Been Lucky wasn't. I'mjumpinjackflash didn't. And Brave and Crafty looked kind of timid and dull. Roberto's Shadow frightened himself back into ninth place. But still, Zippy had dispatched half the pack of ten and earned a little prancing-around money. Things could have been worse.

And pretty soon they were, because on February 15, Zippy finished dead last in a field of a dozen four- and five-year-old thoroughbreds. Frysinger and Meade must have thought their horse's performance to this point was Beyond All Reason, the horse that finished seven places ahead of him.

Seven days later, as he raced through rain and over mud, Zippy dashed any hope of sustaining a pattern of improvement. From the ninth and worst pole position, Zippy took off out of the gate like a rocket and led the field well into the first turn. After a stiff challenge from Military Band and Field Game, Zippy flatlined his way to the finish line.

Undeterred, surprisingly enough, Zippy came charging out of the gate a month later, on March 10, a clear and dry day at Suffolk Downs, only to finish eighth and last. "Outrun" was an understatement in describing the horse that broke bad to finish eighteen lengths behind the victorious Irrawaddy. Eight out of eight by eighteen lengths – there was some weird mathematical retrogression going on here.

"When you fall off a horse that goes that slow," yelled one disgruntled fan, summing up Zippy's performance and taunting jockey Jorge Vargas at the same time, "at least you can't get hurt!"

On April 12, Zippy broke his habit of coming in last by finishing fourth in a field of six maidens, again with Jorge Vargas aboard. The Lion Wins won. Randy First came in third. The effort by Shininlikediamonds (where in the hell do they get these names?) was tarnished with a second-place finish. Zippy collected $550 for his improved outing.

In his last Boston contest, on April 28, 1995, Zippy used a late rally from sixth position at the halfway mark to finish in third place. While the winner, Military Band, was described as going "all out," Zippy was all done at Suffolk Downs and going home. Jorge Vargas had proved to be his loyal rider or, as some would say, a masochist. In a half-dozen races against horses that had also never actually won a race, Zippy had finished an astonishing combined total of ninety-two lengths behind the winners, shying away from the finish line like he was afraid he might trip over it.

Looking way back to when the redcoats gathered on Boston Common, it's safe to say that if Paul Revere had mounted Zippy Chippy instead of Brown Beauty for his midnight ride to warn of the impending British attack, Americans today would be drinking warm beer with their bangers and mash and Hank Aaron would hold the record for 715 career broken wickets.

Zippy Chippy distinguished himself at Suffolk Downs with routine efforts clocked at humdrum speeds, but nobody told the horse he was in a rut. No guidance counselor came to his pen to discuss alternative career choices. Zippy approached each race with a professional air and a keenness to compete. No slouching, no sadness in the eyes – *Let's get it started*. Zippy's people were now completely flummoxed. Whereas most horses would get depressed or stressed after eighteen career losses, Zippy remained sound and sane. Most losing horses would report to work listless and exhibiting the body language of defeat. Not Zippy. On race day he came to the paddock stoked and returned to his stable triumphant. It was only during the actual race that he looked less like a real winner.

So after starting eighteen times on well-regarded tracks like Belmont, Aqueduct, and Suffolk Downs, Zippy Chippy had six third-place finishes and three second-place finishes to show for his best efforts. That's no wins and a few close calls, but still to come, as luck would have it, was a double-wide horse van full of second chances. Zippy, though nobody could understand why, lived for his next big race.

Worrisome was the fact that in that last outing, an exasperated Frysinger had entered Zippy Chippy in a claiming race, which meant anybody with a track license and a fat wallet could take ownership of him. In each case there were no takers at $5,000, the claiming price hanging over Zippy's head. But the message was clear from the owner of the horse the media had dubbed "the Zipless Wonder" – *I've had it, he's yours, show me some money.*

The greatest danger in claiming a racehorse is that any damn fool can do it. Take my nephew David, for example. Having spent a good part of his college days at the races, he and two fellow ne'er-do-wells decided to make a move up the track ladder from losing bettors to thoroughbred owners. So one day they walked into the administration office at the Fort Erie Race Track, just across the Canadian border from Buffalo, New York, and told the clerk that they wanted to claim a horse.

"She looked at us like we were high on crack," David later recalled. Undaunted, they talked to a track guy who knew another guy who had a license, and $2,000 later they were the proud owners of a professional racehorse.

"Yeah, we named him Threeguysonthesauce." (You see now why the crack was unnecessary?) So there they were, three college kids strutting around the paddock like a trio of Kentucky straw-hat dandies and coming this close to speaking with a southern drawl. "A syndicate of investors" was what they preferred to call themselves.

All went well, and the girls were impressed – until the first vet bill came in at $1,000, along with a monthly $500 tab for room and board. A sobering experience, that. Soon thereafter, the ungifted horse became a "regift" and went off to be a jumper at a show farm. The boys gave up sipping Kentucky bourbon and went back to being two-dollar, beer-swilling hunch bettors.

In the longest shot on the board of life, my nephew went on to become a responsible and successful human being. Today he lives in Atlanta, creates training programs for a living, and oversees a staff of eight people, who I hope never read this book.

SERIOUSLY, WHO NAMES A HORSE
TAKIN' UP SPACE?

When it comes to naming a racehorse, why do so many owners employ a really warped sense of humor? Forget for a moment the obscene names that never got by the censors, like Arfur Foulkesaycke, Oil Beef Hooked, Pee Nesenvy, and Wear the Fox Hat. Think about an honest horse somebody named Sham, a healthy horse called Ivegotabadliver, or a perfectly innocent colt registered as Ohnoitsmymotherinlaw. I understand Deweycheatumnhowe to be a crooked salute to the legal community, but Odor in the Court? And Toss the Rider doesn't exactly get your horse and his jockey off to a rollicking start.

British soccer star Wayne Rooney once tried to name his two thoroughbreds Hoof Hearted and Norfolk Enchants. Profane but clever. And remember, the track announcer has to yell these names out loud over the public address system. Another Horse did sneak past the naming officials, so that whenever he was in the lead, the track announcer had to say, "Another Horse has taken the lead." Confusing? You want confusing? Try Olivia Loves Jesus for the name of a racehorse!

Another British owner had the name Big Tits rejected by the English racing authorities, so he had it registered in France, where it doesn't translate. Similarly, in her last career victory at Aqueduct, Bodacious Tatas beat A Wink and a Nod by almost three lengths. Dick Face, Harry Azzol, and Ivanna Humpalot never stood a chance of censorship approval, although Passing Wind made it through. They look fine on paper, but try saying them out loud. Sofa Can Fast actually won approval by the censors. I can imagine the track announcer calling in sick when he saw that horse on the next day's program.

Worse than these names are the ones that stigmatize the horses as real losers even before they've run a race. Zippy Chippy ran against horses named Sixfeetunder, Dearly Dunce, Takin' Up Space, and Imgonnabiteyourass. At Finger Lakes he shared the backside with Stinky Dinky. Thank goodness he never appeared in a program with Bag o' Bones, Born Loser, Three Legs and a Prayer, Horse-Apples, Whipping Post, or (okay, this one has a certain cachet) Nag Nag Nag. As does Fiftyshadesofhay. I can't imagine what name his owners would have given Zippy Chippy after they'd seen him run a few times. Maybe a real long one like We'rewaitingonzippychippytofinish-inordertodeclarethisraceofficiallyover.

Weird names make for strange coincidences. In two years, 1919 and 1920, the magnificent Man o' War won an unimaginable twenty of his twenty-one high-stakes races. The only horse ever to beat the champion of champions was a horse named . . . Upset.

Very unusual are many of the names given to thoroughbred horses by their owners. And yes, Very Unusual is one of them.

FOUR

It were not best that we should all think alike;
it is difference of opinion that makes horse races.
Mark Twain

t the end of Zippy's unproductive stint at Boston's Suffolk Downs, Charles "Bill" Frysinger unloaded his horse after eighteen winless starts, never having met him or even seen him race. By selling his once-prized possession for $2,500, he took a loss of $6,500.

Any hopes the new owner, Michael Barbarita, and his trainer, Ralph D'Alessandro, had of turning Zippy into a winner were dashed by two subpar fourth-place finishes at Finger Lakes, so they too disowned the enigmatic gelding. Zippy was being passed around like a bottle of malt liquor on skid row because his bottom line was shrinking, even if his self-esteem was not.

While his owners were feeling the pinch of expenses not covered by earnings, Zippy Chippy was not feeling their love. "I once had the misfortune of owning that dog" is how Frysinger looked back on those days. Stats men all of them, they were not a bit impressed by Zippy's endearing personality or his comical behavior of eating the hats of passersby, or goosing backside workers from behind. Zippy once ate a pizza while it was still in the box.

By the time this New York–bred four-year-old racked up twenty losses, he had gone through two owners, three trainers, and eleven jockeys. Generally speaking, a used car will go through fewer owners and mechanics over that period of time. Many racehorses break down and are summarily retired after such an unpromising start, but Zippy seemed to take losing in stride. Indeed, he loved racing almost as much as he loved his postgame shower and meal. Even in those very early years, Zippy Chippy seemed to assume the Iron Man role. While half of the thirty-seven thousand thoroughbreds foaled each year in North America never even get to race once, Zippy had already answered the call to post twenty times and was chomping at the bit for more.

At this point a groom and vagabond named Louis somehow acquired Zippy Chippy. It's likely Louis bought the horse using Michael Barbarita's name and license to do the deal or else accepted the horse on a "hand-off," in which case no money was involved. The immediate savings in stabling, food, and vet bills are substantial whenever an owner rids himself of a horse not consistently finishing in the money.

Louis's boss at Finger Lakes Racetrack was a horseman named Felix Monserrate, a fifty-two-year-old trainer with a stable of five thoroughbreds, a few of which he owned himself. A compact, round-faced, bronze-skinned man, he had come to America from Puerto Rico as a twenty-year-old exercise boy, first galloping thoroughbreds in South Florida, and later at Belmont Park. He was no stranger to losing; neither Felix nor Finger Lakes was considered the best in the field of racing horses. In Zippy, Felix saw a lot of himself – not too big, not running in rich circles, but a hard worker and one that didn't quit. Zippy liked to fool around a lot; Felix liked to tour the backside with a beer. Zippy was not shaken by losing. Felix just loved the life of a horseman.

But even Felix had never before come face-to-face with a zero-for-twenty starter. It stands to reason that if you're a thoroughbred that runs often enough, you will eventually find yourself in a race in which the other horses are stressed, stiff, sore, in a bad mood, worried about the implications of starting a union, or pissed off about the food being served in the backside buckets. And on that day, odds are you will win. Zippy Chippy was unique in that he was destined to defy those odds. Unique? When you look up the word *unique* in *Horse Racing for Dummies*, you'll see just an empty picture frame where Zippy failed to show up for his photo session that day.

Shortly after he took possession of Zippy Chippy and without ever having raced him, Louis decided to relocate from the snowbelt of the Finger Lakes to Florida, where the tracks have palm trees and hand-squeezed juice bars. But before he headed south, Louis had to dispose of his horse. Sadly, a horse who can't earn enough to pay for his food is dead meat in the racing business. And there's no such thing as a pet at a racing stable; even the dog in the barn is there to calm the horses, and the cat earns his keep by catching the mice.

When he heard his groom's plan, the trainer went berserk. "Kill the Zippy horse!" screamed Felix. "No way, Jose!" This was both magnanimous of the man as well as an obvious mistake, since, as I mentioned, the groom's name was Louis.

Louis needed $5,000 to purchase a vehicle for the trip. Felix didn't have $5,000, but he did have an old truck. Thus, the kind of barter deal that usually involves a recently paroled brother-in-law was struck. When it comes to the term *horse trading*, this swap, a 1988 Ford truck for a horse who avoided the finish line like it was an electric fence, both defines the phrase and serves as its best example. The dirty white truck, which had been used to cart horses all over the country, had 188,000 miles on it. Zippy, as Felix would find out much later, ran like he had more. "That guy," recalled Felix, "he push him around and say bad things about him, so yeah, he got the truck and I got a friend."

From this moment on, Zippy Chippy, possibly the most stubborn and cantankerous horse ever to enter a starting gate, would be forever entwined with Felix Monserrate, the most stubborn, patient, and optimistic trainer ever to clean his boots off with a stick. With Zippy Chippy, Felix was accepting the challenge of his life, a baffling but battling no-win wonder. With Felix Monserrate, Zippy was moving from an owner to a family of horse lovers, which included the trainer's partner, Emily Schoeneman, and their kids, Marisa and Jared. All would go on to spend the rest of their lives on horse farms and the backsides of the racetracks. It's all they know; it's all they love.

The most successful horsemen approach thoroughbred racing as a business, a tough trade of buying and selling, racing the best and unloading the worst. Remaining emotionally detached from the animals is a given. By contrast, the Monserrates did not deal in racehorses; they doted on them. They cared deeply for their purebred racetrack brood, waiting on them hand and hoof.

"Better not love a horse" was the mantra of trainers and owners who had seen their horses sold, traded, injured, shipped off to stud farms, and euthanized on the track.

After waving goodbye to his groom and his van, Felix went into the barn as the new and proud owner of Zippy Chippy, a horse that had nowhere to go but up. By way of offering his opinion of the trade, the horse immediately bit him. Just like that. Not exactly the "Felix, I think this is the beginning of a beautiful friendship" kind of moment you see in movies. But it was memorable; Felix still has the scar on his back today.

Felix figured Zippy Chippy's problem resulted from a personality clash between the horse and his previous trainers. Zippy didn't much care for the training sessions, which were hard and frequent. Consequently, when he got mad, which for this horse was his normal temperament, he would simply ignore the trainer.

During his perfect stretch of no wins in twenty outings, Zippy had earned the reputation of a badass racehorse, difficult to handle and impossible to motivate. Yet with those doe-like eyes and a penchant for finding trouble in the unlikeliest places, to those who knew him and worked with him, Zippy Chippy had become a lovable scamp.

Just for kicks, when he had nothing better to do, Zippy would beat the hell out of his stall and boot his water bucket around like it was a soccer ball. His favorite trick was to snatch anything from the hands and heads of handlers walking by his stall and then to return them partly chewed. Even the backsiders who kept a healthy distance from him admired this character of comedy begrudgingly. Although they remained alert while working with him, they had not a clue as to what he might do next. As thoroughbreds go, Zippy had become a scoundrel of professional proportions. A life-of-the-party kind of horse, he would have looked good running a race with a lampshade on his head. In the serious business of racing horses, Zippy Chippy seemed to be honing his skills and relishing his role as the track clown.

Felix was certain he could change all that. Emily wasn't so sure. "I mean, just look at him," she said. "He's a miserable, ugly-looking horse, and he's poopy brown in color." In fairness, the horse is quite unremarkable to look at, blotchy brown from stockings to mane, with a tail to match. Only a white marking on his forehead the size of a silver dollar gives any relief to the dark dullness of his physique.

"He looks like a donkey with those big ears. He's got a big butt and a little neck. He's just homely." Okay, okay, okay, Emily — so he looks more like Had the Biscuit than Seabiscuit — we get the picture. (Note: One thing you will not see at the end of this book is a footnote revealing that Emily Schoeneman eventually left the horse racing business and went into public relations.)

Emily still shakes her head at the thought that Felix would take on the role of owner and trainer of a horse that was frustrating and failing race fans everywhere, a horse that was dropping from A-list tracks to second-rate ovals faster than . . . well, faster than just about every horse he ever raced against. But Felix had earned the reputation of a Father Flanagan figure around Finger Lakes: a soft-hearted, humane man, a loyal friend, an absolute believer in a sport full of skeptics. "Felix always believed he could turn Zippy Chippy into a star someday," Emily said, with great wonder.

Felix, like the other owners before him, had obviously been dazzled by Zippy's aristocratic roots. Blinded by the possibility of success this horse had inherited and oddly enamored by their new and awkward relationship, Felix was unaware that he was crossing a line trainers clearly drew in the dirt of racetracks everywhere. They bred, trained, and raced horses for money and, just maybe, fame. Period. This unwritten law was so clearly embraced by trainers it hardly needed posting. NO PETS ALLOWED!

Emily, of course, would come to love Zippy Chippy as much as Felix — that is, as much as Felix loved the horse, and, as a matter of fact, still does. They both do. It's complicated. But nobody loved that horse more than little Marisa, their daughter with the big eyes and a heart devoted to abandoned animals. While most little girls were getting sticky with Betty Crocker's Easy-Bake Oven, Marisa was taking care of horses sixteen hands high and twenty times her weight. "Zippy was really my horse," she said. "They just didn't know that yet."

And although it would take a few more bite marks, a couple of bruises shaped like a horse hoof, and a career record full of zeros, one day Zippy Chippy would be a star. It's hard to understand what the man saw in the horse, especially when the man was always running around the barn two strides ahead of the horse, which was quite often trying to kill him. The fact that Felix Monserrate was still alive at the end of Zippy Chippy's career is a major victory in and of itself. But what a ride it was between the horse trade and the transformation of Zippy Chippy to a high-stakes winner in the end.

HORSE
TRADING

Due to the difficulty of evaluating the merits of an equine animal, be it a plough horse or a thoroughbred, horse trading has always been a little dicey. Hence, all such tricky deals that involve hard bargaining – from used car swaps to vote mongering – have come to be called horse trading.

No other milieu generates better or stranger horse trades than the world of sports. In 1989 the Reno Silver Sox, a minor-league baseball club, traded Tom Fortugno to the Milwaukee Brewers for $2,500 and a bag of baseballs. The Calgary Vipers once traded pitcher John Odom to the Laredo Broncos for a bag of bats. The Pacific Suns traded Ken Krahenbuhl to the Greenville Bluesmen for ten pounds of catfish. Not amused, Krahenbuhl went to the mound a week later and pitched a perfect game. In a schizophrenic swap, the 2005 Toronto Blue Jays sent infielder John McDonald to the Detroit Tigers for . . . John McDonald, who returned to Toronto at the end of the season.

Eddie Shore, the wily owner of the American Hockey League's Springfield Indians franchise, prided himself on always screwing the other owners in trades. In one deal, the owner of a Pacific coast franchise could not wait to hear Shore rant and rave at receiving a player who was about to arrive at his Massachusetts office with his arm broken and in a sling. The same West Coast owner was not so anxious to hear from Shore when the traded Springfield player walked back into his office with his leg broken and in a cast.

In what many sports fans consider the worst trade ever, Boston Red Sox owner and theatrical producer Harry Frazee sent the great

Babe Ruth to the New York Yankees for . . . a musical? Although Frazee said little at the time, it is believed he took cash from the Yankees in order to stage the Broadway play *No, No, Nanette*. Enough to make a dark horse blush, this trade precipitated the "Curse of the Bambino," which, according to superstition, kept the Red Sox from winning a World Series for eighty-six consecutive years, starting in 1918 when the deal was sealed.

What might be the strangest trade in sports history took place at the 1973 New York Yankees spring training camp in Florida, in which players Fritz Peterson and Mike Kekich swapped spouses, kids, cars, and houses. Yeah, they traded lives, with wives and everything else, including two kitchen sinks. Only spouses Susanne and Marilyn know for sure who got the best performer in that deal.

But Babe Ruth traded for a girly play! And Zippy Chippy exchanged for an '88 Ford truck that was already seven years old? Wouldn't you love to see the beady-eyed accountant at the IRS trying to figure out who made something taxable in all these deals?

FIVE

Success consists of going from failure to
failure without losing enthusiasm.
Winston Churchill

n those first twenty races before Felix Monserrate acquired Zippy Chippy for a pre-owned vehicle with rust spots, the horse had lost on dirt and grass and muddy tracks, under skies that were clear, cloudy, sunny, and rainy. The horse had failed to win with three different Davids in the saddle, two Joses, a Gerry, a Richard, a Mike, a Julio, a Jorge, a Carlos, and a Leslie, as well as a Robbie and a Bobbie. He lost going outside on Inside News, and on another occasion he managed to slip away from Eileen's Embrace. Then he got beat by an Angry Cop. He earned two thumbs down for finishing behind Two Chums Up, and he lost to Nine Years, though Zippy himself was only four. In all those trips to the track, the officials' footnotes described him as "baring out," "swinging wide," "drawing off," "showing little," "fading fast," "weakening," and at best making a "mild bid between foes" to come in third. Zippy Chippy was once even described as "failing to menace" a horse named Shadow Lark, ridden by a guy named Dennis!

Alas, the seasons changed, but Zippy Chippy did not. The losses piled up like bales of hay in the barns out back, one disappointment atop another. The best results the Zippy and Felix team produced were two unexciting third-place finishes in their first seven races together. In both cases, with David Rivera aboard, Zippy had rallied well in the stretch but was too late to overtake the winners.

No matter what the new plan was, Zippy Chippy went out and proved it wasn't the right one. But then suddenly the sun would break through the dark clouds hanging over Zippy's career, and he would show signs of brilliance. In the first race of the day at Finger Lakes on September 23, 1995, the track was muddy and the purse was a paltry $3,700, to be divided up between eight horses, maidens every one. Zippy got off to a good start but then tapered off to sixth place at the first turn, where to Felix it looked like business as usual. But into the backstretch Zippy surprised everybody by pulling ahead of London Lucky and Me Native Buddie to take sole position of fourth.

Slowly and with confidence, Zippy passed the pack, moving from fourth to third to second and finally to first by a head at the far pole and driving hard. Coming into the homestretch, a real donnybrook broke out between Zippy and Ginger's Appeal for first place. Shoulder to shoulder, they came pounding down the dirt track, two geldings who had never caught the whiff of victory, each believing his time had come. The race caller's voice took on an edge of excitement while fans of long shots and underdogs rushed to the rail to get a closer look.

Jorge Hiraldo used the whip on Zippy while Pedro Castillo hand-rode Ginger's Appeal a half length into the lead. Neither horse faded; both barreled down to the wire at full speed, and when they hit it, Ginger's Appeal won by a nose! A nose! One bloody foot, from eyelash to flaring nostril. One length represents one-fifth of a second in speed. A nose means Zippy lost the race by the blink of an eye, one-fortieth of a second.

The finish-line photo showed two dark noses, one touching the wire and the other, the nose with the star at the top, close to the first horse's ear. Zippy had been wrong-footed. By the luck of the stride, if Zippy had been leaning in and the other horse recoiling, they would have switched places on the results board, with Zippy breaking his losing streak at number twenty-eight. But for the length of one sweat-soaked snout, Felix would look like the genius who had decoded the Zippy Chippy enigma machine, and his horse would shake off a rash of bad outings as well as all the taunting and criticism that came with it.

Zippy the bridesmaid earned $740, which was $1,480 less than the winner. Incredibly, Ginger's Appeal would be retired after twenty-four races with one single win in his entire career: his victory over Zippy Chippy.

Zippy had given it his best shot, Hiraldo had given him a good ride, and Felix, a man who gratefully accepted the small surprises his job offered up, was pleased with both of them. He affectionately slapped the sweaty neck of his favorite horse. "Real close today. Real close. Tomorrow we be closer," he said with a smile.

Felix held that happy face for a full ten days, and on October 3, on the same track but at a slightly shorter distance, Zippy turned his trainer's facial expression into an all-out grin. With only a furlong left to go in the race, the two horses challenging for the win could not have been further apart. Boardwalk Runner had led the entire way around the track, and Zippy had held down sole position of last place all the way into the homestretch. In an amazing burst of late speed, with the sharp clip of his riding crop, Jorge Hiraldo had Zippy Chippy closing in on the leader like a runaway train in a Denzel Washington movie. From ninth place and behind by five lengths at the top of the stretch, Zippy sped past seven horses on the outside to almost, but not quite, catch

Boardwalk Runner at the finish line. He closed with a rush to beat the third horse, Doctorraisedwell, handily.

Finishing faster than ever before, Zippy was short of a win by a neck! A neck! Fully extended, that's about a quarter of a length! Two feet, for godsake. First a nose and now a neck! Good lord. Zippy was running out of body parts used to measure his near wins, and if he kept this up he might become the first racehorse in history to lose a race by a groin. Felix dined out on those two Herculean efforts by the pet favorite of his stable. "Backa tabacka!" he would say to the press and horse people alike in his soft Ricky Ricardo accent. "My horse, he comes second twice in a row!"

After those two oh-so-close calls, Zippy suffered long stretches of really bad losses, agonizing slumps of six, nine, and seventeen races in a row. These dismal performances caused great grief for the trainer. Once buoyed by two excellent efforts, Felix now grew more disillusioned with each new outing. But – and with the horse with the oversized ass, there was always a butt – Zippy still thought of himself as the prize in the Cracker Jack box. Before each race his head bobbed sharply and resolutely. *Put me in, Felix, I'm ready to run.* After each race his head nodded in confidence and his tail arched high in triumph. In his mind he had won.

Felix tried every trick in the manual to make Zippy Chippy a winner. Although not the most successful trainer at Finger Lakes, Felix was not used to having a horse that lost continually. After all, he had trained Carrie's Turn to eight first-place finishes, earning her owner about $100,000 in purse money. As he watched the horse that beat Zippy have his picture taken in the winner's circle, Felix, mashing yet another metaphor, said to his daughter Marisa more than once: "The victor gets spoiled."

So, in order to change things up, Felix tried different jockeys, shorter races, longer workouts, more days off. When that didn't work, exercise riders were switched, saddles were changed, and routines were altered. He mixed up Zippy's feed bucket — always oats, sometimes with corn, then sweet feed one week and bran the next. Firing off ideas in all directions, Felix was in a bit of a fog, strategy-wise. The tactics sounded like they came from Lewis Grizzard's book *Shoot Low, Boys — They're Ridin' Shetland Ponies.*

About thirty months and almost fifty losses later, in the early spring of 1998, without warning or any noticeable improvement in training or tactics, Zippy decided to put a little streak together. On April 14, on a fast track under cloudy skies at Finger Lakes, Zippy Chippy was a slow fifth out of the gate for the short five-furlong test, but quickly closed to third and then second at the far pole. This time it was a horse named Sir Hillard Lewis that caught Zippy's fancy.

With his sights on the leader, Zippy was now challenging instead of sniffing a bunch of bums down the backstretch. The horses moved head to head down the dirt track in front of the grandstand. Zippy's jockey, Benny Afanador, was wearing the green and white silks of trainer Felix Monserrate, as well as a very surprised look on his face. As he moved into the homestretch, Zippy boldly dueled with Sir Hillard Lewis, who looked like he might be tiring. Alas, nearing the end of the short trip, Zippy's opponent proved to have more in the tank than him, finishing first by a length and a half.

On just six days' rest, Zippy had finished a respectable second, earning a whopping (for him) $1,020 in purse money. Comments listed on the results page regarding Zippy's almost-excellent performance included "held his place" and "broke in air," which caused some people familiar with the horse's off-track antics to assume that Zippy had somehow gotten into some bad curry the night before.

Eleven days later, on the same track at the same distance, Afanador took an awkward turn in the saddle when Zippy broke badly from the gate's number one position. Athousandthunders was out first and Zippy was last as the herd left the gate and pounded down the back stretch in a flurry of drifting dust.

Steadily gaining ground on the rest, Afanador moved Zippy up nicely into the third spot at the far pole. He held that spot all the way down into the homestretch, where he made a valiant move to nail Rings of a Angle at the wire. A tad late, but still gaining ground on Rings, Zippy finished second by a single length, again earning $1,020 for his second-place finish. Totaling $2,040 for his last two races, Zippy was unaccustomed to such extravagance.

The owner of the winner, Edward Perdue, had a champ as well as a problem with grammar on his hands – not Wings of an Angel or even Rings of an Angel, but Rings of a Angle? This might be the only horse ever to win a race with both a jockey and a typo on his back – except, of course, for American Pharoah, whose misspelled name was talked about so much that the horse started wearing ear plugs. (Honest – he wore ear plugs!).

Nonetheless, Zippy was on a roll. Missing by a length and a half and then just a length showed great improvement on his performance chart. Two close calls usually meant a horse was about to strike gold the next time out and – in horse racing par-lance – finally "break his cherry." Handicappers would expect him to impress even more moving forward.

"Yeah, he run real constant here," said Felix. Constant? For Zippy Chippy, two second-place finishes in a row was like captur-ing the Derby and the Preakness.

"For a while there he run pretty good," said a beaming Felix, a man who could see the positive side of the earth taking a direct hit from another, bigger planet. It only took the odd "backa tabacka" to put the spring back in this trainer's step.

By not winning in those hair-raising efforts, Zippy missed out on his very own "Donut Day." In this quaint backside tradition, whenever a horse wins a race, the next morning that jockey's agent or the jockey himself must show up with a box of donuts and muffins, enough for the half-dozen people working in that particular barn. Zippy had a habit of ruining Donut Day by turning it into the Breakfast Club for One. Never mind that he snagged Emily's muffin or Felix's black walnut square — if he got close enough to the guy carrying the box, well, I suppose cardboard could taste good if it had enough Krispy Kreme stuck to it.

"It was his favorite day of the week," remembered Marisa. "I mean, we'd give him one anyway, but that was like a teaser." While most racehorses turn up their noses at human treats the way a cat will ignore bread, Zippy was a snackaholic. With the exception of sugar cubes and raw carrots, most horses stick to whatever's in the feed bag. Zippy, on the other hand, loved everything that was sticky: cupcakes, ice cream, candy canes, chips, popcorn, chocolate bars, pizza, and peanuts, shells and all.

"Pop-Tarts, brown sugar and cinnamon flavor, that was his favorite," recalled Marisa. She was a sweet kid who adored her dad but still had great difficulty with the fact that although she could not have hard candy, her dad always had a pocketful of peppermints for Zippy. Pop-Tarts may have been his favorite when Marisa was around, but a bag of Doritos and a cold bottle of beer was the number one snack combo Zippy shared with Felix.

Had Zippy Chippy fully understood the reason behind Donut Day, I'm convinced he would have won a race or two. Three, if Felix had hung a dozen chocolate-frosted along the finish line.

Zippy had accomplished the rare and somewhat twisted feat of seventy-six losses in a row, and his popularity was wreaking havoc on the tote board. It was now obvious to Finger Lakes officials that the horse was attracting a large following of fans. And boy, were they betting on him! If Zippy had gone off at realistic odds of 35–1, he would have returned about forty dollars to the two-dollar, second-place bettor. Instead, in his last race he had paid only $4.90 to place. The track stewards were grateful that Zippy Chippy was filling up empty seats, but they were puzzled as to why anybody would bet on him.

Compared to the nearly $5,000 he'd made in his two second-place streaks, Zippy usually settled for the chump change of fourth- or fifth-place finishes. Returning to his stable, however, he always did a little Irish jig to let his stall pals know he'd been successful. He was washed, cooled down, fed, blanketed, and asleep within the hour. To his credit, losing was something this horse seldom took to heart. Zippy lost races but never any sleep over it.

Those two consecutive second-place finishes proved to be Zippy's most successful stretch of racing so far as a thoroughbred. The horse brought joy to his owner sparingly, and Felix cherished those special moments of relative success.

"Not everybody can be a winner," Felix would say to reporters, who were now taking an unusual interest in a horse headed for his seventy-seventh outing. When a sportswriter asked the owner if his horse, who was often described in the race footnotes as "no threat," was showing signs of melancholia, Felix was quick to put him straight: "No, he wanna run, he's always ready to go." Then, rubbing Zippy's nose and slipping him a candy, he added, "But he don't always go too good." Although Felix's message was usually upbeat, he was wearing his "Zippy Chippy" peaked cap a little lower over his eyes than normal these days.

They bumped along like that – the cocky, underachieving racehorse and his cockeyed, optimistic trainer. In their division of duties, Zippy let Felix do the worrying. Unfazed by his track performance and up to his usual shenanigans, Zippy, it seemed, loved to – no, *lived* to – torment Felix. Never having cuddled up together in the winner's circle, Felix and Zippy weren't even that comfortable with each other in the barn. "Once, I take my eye off him, and just like that . . . he got me!" said the trainer.

They were standing in front of the horse's stall when Felix turned to pick up a bucket, and Zippy turned to pick up Felix. The trainer found himself suspended in midair, yelling for help and flailing his arms around behind him, trying to get Zippy to release him. Zippy had picked him up by the collar and was holding him a foot off the ground. Felix's angry shouts at the horse to put him down were answered by the loud laughs of a few track people watching the two of them perform this shed-row slapstick act. The louder Felix screamed, the more raucous the laughter of the bystanders, many of them workers now coming over from other barns.

Eventually Zippy got tired of the gag and put his owner down. "He's a strong horse," Felix said, now that his feet were back on terra firma. "He can hold you up for a long time." Forget Man o' War and Bold Ruler; Zippy Chippy's most influential ancestors may have been Laurel and Hardy!

Strangely, despite the growing winless streak, the teacher and his petulant student had settled into a strongly bonded team over the last couple of years. Zippy would defy his jockey or misbehave on the backside, and Felix would make excuses for him. The trainer would make predictions of great success, and the horse would dash them by ten lengths. The owner would often punish his prankster by locking him in his stall and closing the shutters, but then he would check in on him frequently to make sure he was okay. As discouraged as the man might become, Felix was still reluctant to enter Zippy in "claiming" races, where his chances of winning would be much better against less talented horses, but for the price of a few thousand dollars, anybody could take possession of him after the race was over.

"I don't want some crazy person owning Zippy Chippy," said Felix. The rolled eyes of his fellow trainers indicated that might already be the case.

Given Zippy's fiery temper and irritable disposition, nobody within nipping distance was safe from the poopy-brown horse when he was in a bad mood. When his ears went straight back and his lips suddenly parted to reveal his long, yellowed teeth, you had just been warned! Zippy Chippy bit more handlers than anyone can remember and drove off every potential buyer who dared to come size him up in the barn. Any new owner coming to examine Zippy in his stall with the intent to buy him would have been wise to wear a helmet and hockey gear.

Emily "Pull No Punches" Schoeneman is friend and family to the Zipster, but not always a fan.

"I tell you, Zippy Chippy is a miserable thing who's crabby all the time, wants everything done for him when he wants it, makes faces, bites, kicks, and . . ." – and here's where the sugar-coating ended – "is not very intelligent." (On a personal note, as a man who was married once, and was occasionally accused of insensitivity, my question to Emily: "And your point is . . . ?")

"Oh yeah, he can be mean," said Felix, in a painful understatement. "Once, he pin me in the corner of the stall for almost an hour." Felix demonstrated how he had crouched and faked left while the horse blocked right. "I go this way, he go too. I go that way, he's already there."

Every head fake Felix made was met by a bigger head. Felix went down on all fours and the horse reared up on his hind legs.

"And he get his foot up in the air like this, like he's gonna kick you too!"

Finally, while still backed into the corner, Felix stopped trying to outmaneuver the monster, and Zippy dropped his striking hoof. A groom with a handful of alfalfa distracted the horse long enough for the trainer to escape the stall. Zippy Chippy's ample appetite always trumped his anger.

"He won't let nobody near him but me. Except my daughter Marisa," said Felix, his voice cracking a little.

IN THE DEPTHS OF DESPAIR,
NEVER, EVER GIVE UP!

Having been saddled up for five times as many races as the average thoroughbred, Zippy would circle the paddock before every outing, suspicious of the other horses and contemptuously eyeing his competition. He must have felt like Colonel Lewis B. Puller, surrounded and outnumbered by Chinese troops during the Korean War. With no air support and all reinforcements snowed in twenty miles away, "Chesty" Puller's two marine regiments were trapped in the Chosin Reservoir by sixty thousand Chinese troops. At twenty-five below zero, the food was frozen, the equipment was frozen, and his men were frozen. Each man was ordered to keep a bag of plasma in his underwear to keep it from freezing, until he was shot and needed it.

"There are Chinese on our right flank and Chinese on our left flank," said one of the most decorated members of the U.S. Marine Corp after a reporter covering this doomed venture into hell asked him to assess the situation. "There are Chinese in front of us for as far as you can see and there are hundreds of Chinese troops coming up behind us."

"And your prediction, sir?"

That's when the general hesitated, a bit like Zippy Chippy before he made his final decision to leave the starting gate. Said Chesty, with all the resolve of a military man worthy of his stripes and vaunted title, "Those bastards won't get away from us this time."

Zippy Chippy subscribed to this maxim of survival. In every race he ran and lost, until the word *Official* came up on the betting board results, Zippy had those sweaty buggers well within his sights and exactly where he wanted them.

SIX

*Our bravest and best lessons are not learned
through success, but through misadventure.*

Amos Bronson Alcott

A t some point, when Zippy had almost eighty losses under
his girth belt, Felix admitted that maybe his horse wasn't as
fit as his rivals. A unique labor shortage was likely to blame,
because after he bucked off nearly every exercise rider at the track,
none of them would go near him. Taking Zippy Chippy — an athlete
who preferred not to practice — out for a workout could be a career-
ending experience for an exercise boy, or, at the very least, a big pain
in the ass that required frequent attention with ice packs. So Felix
had Marisa introduce Zippy to the exercise barn . . . and the exercise
barn made a lousy first impression.

Also known as a Eurociser, the exercise track is an open-air
barn partitioned into separate sections with heavy-duty rubber
breakers. It allows several horses to jog at the same speed and at
the same time, as the overhead apparatus moves in a circle like a
midway ride. The function of the machine is to lead the horses
around automatically at a pre-set pace, thereby freeing up the
track hands to leave and do other chores.

On Zippy's first visit to the barn, he challenged the basic
design and purpose of the Eurociser. Ignoring her father's rule

that Zippy be alone in the jogging circuit, Marisa thought she'd save time by putting another one of their horses, Cowboy, in the section in front of Zippy. Once she got the machine going and the horses jogging, she went back to the barn. The system worked for five, maybe ten, minutes before she heard a great commotion and the kind of noises generally attributed to stallions in a death fight over a filly. For whatever reason, Cowboy had stopped abruptly, and the partition between him and Zippy had hit him hard in the buttocks.

"Hint, hint! Move forward! But Cowboy was one dumbass," remembered Marisa.

When the bumper swung back and slammed into him a second time, Cowboy froze in place, and the thick rubber barrier went up and over top of him. Suddenly Zippy and Cowboy were in the same section and moving forward at a good clip. Zippy couldn't believe his luck – he had found a playmate in the boring old exercise barn.

Marisa watched in horror as the two delinquents ran wild, wreaking havoc on the circulating system, getting their reins crossed, and butt-bumping each other at every turn. A couple of track hands ran to the rescue and shut the power off, and tried to get hold of the calmer of the two culprits first.

"Every time those guys got close to corralling Cowboy, Zippy would interfere and they had to start all over again. Zippy was having way too much fun," recalled Marisa.

It took twenty minutes to get control of Cowboy and another ten to harness Zippy, and when everybody left the barn it was in shambles – the power line sheared off and two bumpers smashed up.

"You could hook a hundred, a thousand, horses up to the jogging machine and this would never happen," Marisa said. Typical Zippy Chippy – whenever trouble was not following him around, he'd go looking for it.

The next time Zippy visited the exercise barn, Felix took him there himself, along with a groom and a walker. Circling the covered track in a stately fashion, Zippy appeared to enjoy it at first. Showing off for his audience of three, Zippy pranced around like he was one of those painted horseys on an antique merry-go-round. That's when Felix and the handlers felt confident enough to return to the barn.

It didn't take long for Zippy to become bored with the routine – or, worse, feel he was being ignored. So he kicked out the top board of the track's outer fence and crushed the electric box that operated the automatic apparatus. With a vengeance, Zippy proceeded to smash the jogging machine to pieces until he was unceremoniously escorted from the premises. Not willing to risk a third demolition derby, the barn manager banned Zippy from the exercise station. Mission accomplished: he would never have to train there again.

Handlers who couldn't get Zippy his food on time simply refused to bring it. They knew too well the penalty for a late delivery. Zippy had adjusted the Domino's Pizza delivery promise to suit his temperament: dinner arrives within twenty minutes or you get free first aid.

"He can be mean with people and other horses," admitted his trainer, "but he's a horse with lots of personality." Yeah, that's what prison inmates say about that special brand of criminal on death row – lots and lots of personality.

Felix's partner Emily heartily disagreed: "He's not really mean at all. He doesn't realize he's hurting you. Like that time he bit Felix in the back, he just stood there like, *What's up?*" Just goofing around is all.

Zippy's idea of fun was different from that of other horses but not unlike the eye-poking, hair-pulling, nose-twisting slapstick of the Three Stooges. If owners named horses based on performance and personality, "the Fourth Stooge" would have fit this one to a T.

After a few more consecutive last-place finishes in the late spring of 1998, Felix rested Zippy for a few months – time off for bad behavior. Mostly he would hang out in the paddock with Felix's other horses between an early breakfast and suppertime. Soon Zippy's mood improved remarkably. He didn't bite anybody for almost two weeks. He was happy being hot-walked around the barn, and he ate a lot fewer hats than normal. It was obvious this horse was quite content to enjoy the home life of a racehorse, without actually racing. It was becoming clear that Zippy Chippy saw the barn as more of a frat house than a place to rest and recover between races. He enjoyed the company of other horses, just not competitively.

Yet Zippy would get visibly excited by all the sounds that precede the trumpeter's call to post. "He hear the horn that start the race and . . . he look around . . . he stretch his neck way up to listen, like this," said his trainer. For a 130-pound Puerto Rican, Felix Monserrate does an excellent impersonation of an 1,100-pound horse.

"His head go side to side to listen for the bell, and his feet start to go . . . oh yeah, he want to run," concluded Felix, although it was never entirely clear in which direction Zippy would go once he escaped from the starter's gate.

So Felix put the racing saddle back on his friend, and the horse responded with more performances that ranged from mediocre to terrible. At this point, the tension between horse and handler was becoming heated. Whatever new idea Felix came up with, Zippy ignored. Whatever strategy the jockey tried, the horse did the opposite. Felix and Zippy were butting heads again, and their bouts were akin to playground prattle.

"Go!"

"No!"

"Will too!"

"Will not!"

"Screw you!"

Felix was putting on a brave face for the growing press corps that was constantly characterizing Zippy Chippy as – and the conspiratorial, left-leaning bias of the American media was never more evident than in their coverage of this proud horse – a loser.

"You see, one day he will be a winner," said the horse's trainer and self-appointed public defender. Desperate for a win and seeking the company of slower horses, Felix began entering Zippy Chippy in the occasional claiming race. But as everybody knew, especially the loyal band of locals who gathered to cheer the Zipster's every outing, the possibility of somebody matching the claiming price was real. A fat check from a licensed trainer would force Felix to forfeit the horse. The owner had never taken that risk before; now their relationship, such as it was, could end with the very next race.

"Zippy's like one of the family. I didn't want to lose him, but . . ." Felix's brave face was fading fast. When the tallest member of the Monserrate family posted losses approaching eighty in a row, Felix began to lose confidence in his now six-year-old boy.

"We sent him away to a farm to see how he like retirement," he recalled, with a mix of shame and sadness in his voice. Put to pasture at a nearby boarding farm, Zippy was more than put out. He wouldn't eat. He wouldn't even graze. Zippy Chippy not eating was like Lance Armstrong not doping. At that point, you just know they're losing the will to compete.

"He was always pacing in his stall. He was miserable. So we bring him home. And he was so happy . . . ," said Felix, smiling, almost tearing up.

On Saturday, May 2, 1998, the backside at Finger Lakes was still buzzing about Real Quiet winning the Kentucky Derby and earning $738,800 for two minutes and two seconds of work. Later in the month, on May 23, Zippy Chippy would run in race two at Finger Lakes for a purse of $5,100. When it came to prize money, Farmington, New York was about three planets northeast of Louisville, Kentucky.

On this clear day, on a fast track, although Thornden Park and Prince de Naskra finished ahead of Zippy, Dune Drive was eating his dust. With Benny Afanador on his back and a $7,500 claiming price hanging over his head, a rejuvenated Zippy came in third and earned $510 for his stable.

A week later, on May 30, he could only manage to finish fourth, overtaking tired rivals in the stretch. Dr. No took most of the $8,500 purse, and Zippy was stuck with loss number eighty-one. Not that Zippy's frequent failure to win a race carried criminal consequences, but in this test, Khale Police was just a few lengths off his tail.

Two weeks later, on an overcast afternoon in mid-June at Finger Lakes, Zippy crashed and burned after he and Benny Afanador got squeezed at the start and looked awkward for the remainder of the race. This too was a claiming race, but thankfully the price was a steep $15,000.

Zippy's pattern of finishes continued to go up and down like the proverbial toilet seat. One day he was nudging the butt of Toes Goes, the next he was speeding past Nixs Trick like that horse was tied to the fence post. It was there for all to see: Zippy was out of sorts and off his game, and Felix was becoming despondent.

In this loss, number eighty-two, Zippy came seventh in a race of eight maidens, finishing sixteen and three-quarters lengths behind Hilary's Kid — certainly not the longest distance he had ever put between himself and a winner, but it was a five-furlong race, which is as short as they get. On a clear and fast track, Zippy had barely managed to beat Leonard Elmer, a badly named horse who got bumped at the start and was left sputtering at the rail like an overheated car abandoned on the shoulder of the road. The men in straw hats with stopwatches were shaking their heads at Zippy's finishing time.

But Felix never paid attention to the math or the tick of a track man's watch. When he led Zippy Chippy around the paddock before a race, Felix was showing the fans not a horse but the other half of a longtime, rough, but hard-earned friendship that would someday defy the skeptics and make him proud. The fans who passed clippings of Zippy over the fence for Felix to autograph sensed some sort of history in the making.

Felix was not delusional. He did not dream of a three-race set of victories like the Triple Crown or the Breeders' Cup; he wanted just one lonely little win on any track, anywhere, with lots of witnesses present. "Once, just once," he would say to Marisa, "I want to lead Zippy to *la tierra prometida*." At Puerto Rico's racetracks, a victory circle is called "the promised land." That's all the poor man asked.

Word about the horse's adversity to winning was spreading around the world, and the columnists writing about Zippy could be cruel. He could live with the headline THE LEGEND OF INEPTITUDE; it was the line "ugly, stupid, and nasty with an international fan club" that was hard to take. Felix needed a victory to end the mockery of the media and reward Zippy's followers for their loyalty.

With no prospect of a win and running out of jockeys, Felix's record with Zippy was six second-place finishes, ten thirds, and earnings to date of $27,803, barely enough to cover his keep. While food and board bills pile up quickly, vet bills can blow the budget wide open. For the first time ever, Felix was seeing the glass as half empty – or, worse, cracked and leaking cash he did not have. Did he think of getting rid of Zippy?

When confronted with this question, Felix Monserrate nodded his head up and down slowly, then looked away and quickly changed the subject. "Backa tabacka" was just a memory, and maybe as good as it would ever get for the eccentric equine half-appropriately named Zippy Chippy. It was small consolation to his owner, but the only upsides to this horse's career were the growing legions of fans who would come to see him race at Finger Lakes and the large number of followers on simulcast programming who were betting on him from tracks all across North America. Complying with the request to pose for photographers, Felix sensed there was something curious going on here. Was it the souvenir ticket stubs the bettors were after? Proof they had the sense of humor to bet on a horse that couldn't win? Nobody, least of all Felix, knew.

A big, strong girl who worked with Emily in the same backside barn had it figured out.

"Zippy was like an 'opposite,'" recalled Krystal Nadeau. She was just thirteen years old and showing cows at the local 4-H club in the Finger Lakes when she first heard of Zippy Chippy.

"Everybody was talking about him. All my friends said, 'We gotta go and see him race.' I thought he must be a great horse like Secretariat, but" – and she giggles before she continues – "he was like the opposite."

More like opposite poles of the earth — Secretariat clinched the Triple Crown by winning the Belmont Stakes by thirty-one lengths, while occasionally Zippy's toughest opponent to the finish line was the setting sun.

Meanwhile, back at Zippy's stall number seven, Felix was staring at his horse in silence, wondering what the hell he was going to do. Getting rid of him would not involve a sale, since nobody wanted him, even as a "claimer." Getting rid of him could mean giving him up to a second career as a jumper or a show horse or an aging pet on a hobby farm. And retirement? They had already tried that, with disastrous results. Getting rid of him could also mean offering him up at an auction where horses are bought in large lots by the owners of slaughterhouses in Mexico and Canada. Although America has banned such butchery, its neighbors to the north and south have not. Sentencing a horse to death, by auction or otherwise, is such a horrid thought for caring horsemen that they can only speak of it in code: "A little girl fell in love with my horse."

Felix's mind was in panic mode as he prepared Zippy for an early morning workout and the exercise boy stuffed cotton batten in the ass of his pants. The sheer weight of their situation came crashing down on him as he saddled up his brown-eyed boy. First came the chamois grip that keeps everything on top of it from slipping off the horse's back. Should he simply and quietly hand him off to another trainer who might have better ideas and more luck? With this horse's record and appetite, even a giveaway would be a tricky deal. He might get a few thousand dollars for Zippy, but what would a new owner do with him? On went the sponge saddle pad. A new owner would definitely not race him, and Zippy loved the track. He threw the wool saddle blanket over the pad. He couldn't afford to keep Zippy as a pet on the farm — he needed those paltry $500 and $300 paydays for fourth- or fifth-place finishes to help pay for the horse's upkeep. He neatly arranged the saddlecloth across Zippy's back, the one with the number seven on the sides. Felix had received, but never answered, a call from an entertainment agent who wanted to "exploit Zippy Chippy's notoriety." Finally, on went the saddle, and he tightened the girth belt around the horse's torso. Everybody at the track had told Felix to get rid of him, but what did that even mean? Saddled up and ready to run, Zippy was just superstitious enough not to mess with their long-practiced routine, so he bit Felix gently on the arm, for old times' sake. And Felix, after making sure he didn't need stitches, seemed to appreciate the gesture. Getting rid of a horse was normally easy. Getting rid of Zippy Chippy was proving impossible.

Although the Zipster appeared keen to run and indeed went into a funk when he didn't, his owner, his trainer, and the best friend he had ever had was losing his enthusiasm to race him. When Felix Monserrate was faced with the dark dose of reality that Zippy Chippy might have to be dispatched, it was the second worst moment of his life.

ZIPPY CHIPPY AND MARV THRONEBERRY: BEAUTIFUL LOSERS, BOTH OF THEM

Bad horses — I mean really bad horses, like Ferby's Fire and Ordvou, who earned the wrong kind of fame when they were beaten by Zippy Chippy — need not hang their heads all that low. Zippy's losing ways may have left a dark stain on the track, on which these two horses may well have slipped.

Case in point: Marv Throneberry, one of the most unpredictable major-league ballplayers to ever pick up a bat and glove. Marv played first base for the 1962 New York Mets, widely regarded as the worst team in modern baseball history, with just 40 wins in a 160-game season. This team was so bad that the manager, Charles Dillon "Casey" Stengel, looked up and down the Mets dugout one day and screamed, "Can't anybody here play this game?" New York City's wonderful slice-of-life columnist Jimmy Breslin wrote a best-seller posing that question as the title.

At practice one day, weak-hitting "Marvelous Marv" was bouncing ground balls off his glove like it was made of solid steel. That's when the legendary manager, seventy-two years old at the time, relieved him at first base. Stengel hadn't played the game in more than thirty-seven years, but he was sure he could still show Throneberry a thing or two. "Stand over there, Marvin, and watch!"

Stengel barked at the catcher to hit him a ground ball, which he did. The soft roller went through Stengel's legs. (I did mention he was forty-three years older than Throneberry, right?)

"Hit it like a man!" he yelled. The catcher complied, and that one went over Stengel's shoulder.

"One more," screamed the manager, and that one hit him in the shin before he could quite bend over.

Stengel dropped Throneberry's glove and kicked it across the foul line, and as he stomped off the field he yelled back over his shoulder, "Throneberry, you have fucked up this position so badly, nobody can play it!" Practice was cancelled due to severe laughter.

Later, on Throneberry's birthday, Stengel, whose nickname was "the Old Perfessor," eased up on his favorite first baseman. "We were going to get you a cake, Marvin," said the manager, "but, well, you know, we figured you'd drop that too!"

"The Lovable Klutz" and "America's Lovable Loser" – for the sake of comic relief and memorable entertainment, some days players like these bring more value to their sports than the ones who play them well. And that's what it's all about, because if you take entertainment out of sports, all you have left are the stats.

Despite the utter futility of the 1962 Mets – you have to go back to 1899 to find a team with more season losses – the fans came out in droves. Their total attendance of 922,530 spectators was the sixth highest in the league that year. Who doesn't love an underdog?

SEVEN

A dog looks up to a man. A cat looks down on a man.
But a patient horse looks a man in the eye and sees him as an equal.

Anonymous

H is worst moment ever still brought fear into the eyes of Felix Monserrate when, years later, he remembered that dreary day in late November 1997, during one of Zippy Chippy's worst losing streaks. In the midst of one of his horse's most cantankerous spells, Felix lost sight of his darling daughter Marisa. With her chubby cheeks and dark hair, she was precious, a sparkle of kindness in his rough world of soiled stables and vocal disbelievers. A dervish in rubber boots, one second she was beside him and then she was instantly gone.

Every day before she scooted off to school, Marisa would help Felix clean the stalls and feed the twenty or so horses her father boarded and trained at the family farm near the track. Marisa was only seven years of age and in grade two at the time, but in the barn she was a fully developed groom, washing horses and shoveling shit with the best of them. Home from school in the late afternoon, she would again plunge into her chores, doing the job of a stable boy, working alongside her dad.

Even then Marisa was small for her age, a fact comically confirmed by a photo of her standing in a feed bucket in the corner of a stable, half of her below the rim, holding on to the edges.

When Marisa was ten, she mesmerized the rest of the kids at Victor Elementary School by riding Peanut, her big, black Quarter Horse, into her grade six classroom for show and tell. Every kid in the world wants a pony; Marisa had her own horse. The plan was to have Peanut appear for only an hour, but when the word got out she had to take him into every classroom in the school, and they spent the whole day on tour. Marisa wanted to bring Zippy Chippy to the event, but schools back then did not have a security routine known as "lockdown."

Marisa can't remember a time when she was not smack-dab in the center of the business of horses. As a two-year-old she would sleep in the cap of Emily's red pickup truck, parked beside Felix's barn. They would arrive at the dark hour of five in the morning, and Marisa would sleep off and on until eight. Beside her was her cousin Keri Cordero, six months older and the niece of the Hall of Fame jockey Angel Cordero. They talked about their favorite horses and played hide and seek, crawling around the truck's floor like two lumps under a bank of blankets and giggling until they cried. Once the girls were awake, Emily would bring them into her tiny tack room and give them a cereal breakfast before she was due back on the hot-walk circuit. The kids played games and watched TV in what can only be described as a glorified shed.

Sometimes Felix, Emily, and the kids would arrive at the track in the afternoon, and as the van approached the barn, Felix would jump out and scare the bejesus out of the kids by suddenly appearing at their back window, making faces and waving at them while the vehicle went downhill fast, headed for the barn. It would be years before Marisa and Keri figured out that Emily had a hand on the bottom of the steering wheel and a foot on the brake while Felix did his Charlie Chaplin routine, running beside the truck.

Almost as soon as she learned to talk, Marisa's job description included standing at the entrance to barn number twenty, pointing to the shuttered-up stall seven and explaining to anybody who wandered by, "Zippy's been bad again. He's locked in his room and can't come out." Emily had one rule for the children: they were never to leave the tack room until eleven, when all the chaotic business of prepping the horses in and around the barn was finished. Once all the horses were stabled, the barn became their very own romper room. They could roam anywhere their young and curious hearts desired. Okay, there was a second rule: never go near the problem known as Zippy Chippy.

Once, while Marisa's aunt was feeding Zippy when Felix was away, the horse had trapped the poor woman in the corner of his stall for three dark and eerie hours. It took two handlers with batches of food to distract him long enough for Nancy McCabe to safely scurry out of the cell.

Occasionally Marisa was allowed to walk Zippy, but only with her dad on the lead. Once in a while she was permitted to pet him, just as long as there was a fence or a barrier between them. But at this point in her life, Marisa was not just curious but fearless. As the young savior of stray dogs and injured cats, she was drawn to the horse that was most unlike the others. She absolutely adored Zippy Chippy.

It was early on that damp November morning in the barn when Felix lost sight of his half-pint helper. Felix's routine was to start his day by scanning the trainer's board in the main tack room to see which horses were running that day and which ones needed to be exercised on their day off. He thought his daughter was right beside him. And she was, until she noticed that the protective screen across the entrance to Zippy's stall had gone missing. No other horse on the shed row needed this extra security across the door of the stall. Somebody, probably the new groom, had mistaken Zippy Chippy for a normal horse and used only the webbing — two chains attached to his nameplate — to keep him secured in his pen. In a heartbeat, little Marisa scooted in under the webbing and ran to the far corner of the stall, looking up into the surprised eyes of the horse that seasoned handlers would feed only by delivering food at the end of a rake.

When Felix noticed that Marisa was missing, he panicked. "Anyway, I can't find her, and I look everywhere," recalled Felix. "And then the worst idea come to my mind, and I run to Zippy's stall, and there . . ." He choked up a bit and tapped a finger on the table. Felix, a man who had been around horses most of his life, froze in fear, standing motionless in front of the webbing emblazoned with ZIPPY CHIPPY.

Later, he couldn't recall how long he had stood there, quiet, motionless, staring into the dark. He thought he should call out for help, but any noise at all might spook the horse.

There, in that moment of sheer terror when the mind goes numb and the limbs go limp, Felix saw the feet of his little girl in the far corner of the dark stall, with Zippy looming over her. He started to call out for her, but no words would come. Zippy's broad backside was blocking Felix's view of his little girl, a wisp of a thing, cornered by this hulking horse. The stall was ghostly quiet, not a peep or a movement by any of them. Felix was almost relieved not to be able to see the terrified look on his daughter's face. Still he didn't do anything. Speechless, he just stood there helplessly. At one point he thought he might grab the horse by the tail and make himself the target. But if the animal wheeled around violently, he'd surely take Marisa with him.

Throw a bucket at the other wall, Felix thought to himself, *and when the horse turns in that direction, snatch Marisa from Zippy's blind side.* There was a rope on a hook on the wall, and if he could get a noose around the neck of . . .

And then Felix heard something that made him listen carefully, so he could make sure he wasn't dreaming.

Stunned, Felix heard his little girl laughing and giggling. And when Marisa walked toward her father, Zippy didn't try to block her path or, worse, raise his kicking foot to her face. Instead he pranced around her, nickering and snickering like a frisky little foal. And they waltzed around on the straw floor of the pen like that, the child laughing and hanging on the horse's mane and Zippy strutting beside her and nuzzling her in play. The source of Felix's tears switched quickly from fear to joy as he watched them play together in the stall that had always been off limits. Marisa scolding Zippy, pointing a finger at him and calling him "a very bad boy," was indeed a sight to behold. Zippy, blowing and snorting, seemed to be agreeing. They put on quite a show for Felix, one that came with uncommon relief and a great big lesson in life.

"And that," said Felix, hitting the table with the palm of his hand, "that was it. I never see that horse the same anymore."

"Yeah, everything changed that day in the stable," said Marisa. "Everything seemed better somehow."

While Zippy had always been part of the extended family, the barn people's favorite black sheep, he was now Marisa's new best friend and protector. On that fall morning before the school bus arrived to pick up Marisa, Zippy Chippy's last name officially became Monserrate. "That's when me and my mom knew that Zippy had a good forever-home with us," remembers Marisa. And Zippy, of course, was still more the black sheep than the brown horse of the Monserrate clan. He would continue to disappoint Felix, anger Emily, and confuse Marisa – so, yeah, they were definitely a family.

And the "getting rid of him" option?

"He wasn't going anywhere," recalled Marisa. "My daddy would never get rid of that horse."

"No," agreed Felix, nodding then shaking his head. "I can't do it."

Eighty-two losses or a hundred and eighty-two losses – it never mattered after the eight-year-old kid and the six-year-old pony became inseparable friends for life that day in the straw-strewn stall on a hilly spread in the rural community of Farmington, New York. After that serendipitous moment – a very close encounter that could have proved horrific but turned out to be quite magical – Felix staunchly defended his horse against all criticism.

To anyone – from an angry bettor to a skeptical track official, from a groom with a bandaged hand to a reporter broaching the subject of futility – Felix would always present his favorite analogy: "Say you have three children. One is a lawyer, doing well. The other a doctor, very, very successful. But the third one, not so smart, so he's working at McDonald's. What do you do? Ignore him?" Then Felix would pause and reach around and scratch the scar on his back and say, "That's the one you gotta help the most! That's Zippy Chippy."

Although Felix's often-repeated analogy would not win him a free coffee at McDonald's, the man was right as rain. Felix nailed the secret of the family right there! Who's the better father – the one who pays for the gifted son to get through college or the one who pays the steeper price of time and attention, struggling to see his unblessed boy through life?

With Felix and Zippy, it was not only about horse racing; it was about friends and family. An odd family, mind you – the kind where you notice in the Christmas card photo that the adopted son's head is the size of a laundry basket and his pedoinker is hanging out — but a family nonetheless.

Felix could not know it at the time, but that lightning strike of kindness and love that touched both his favorite horse and his dearest daughter sealed Marisa's fate for life. Today, the kid who once fit nicely into a food tub is a highly respected pony rider and groom at Finger Lakes Racetrack, well on her way to becoming an owner and a trainer. Marisa loves her work as much as her parents like to brag about their special daughter. With Marisa raising two small children and caring for a menagerie of pets at the same time, there's a lot to be proud of here.

Only a modicum of Zippy's goofiness has rubbed off on Marisa. Occasionally, along with another Finger Lakes pony rider, and only because it's so close to the track, she will ride her horse through the drive-thru at . . . you guessed it, McDonald's.

Much to the chagrin of wise track people, Zippy had always been Felix's pet. It just took time and a whole bunch of losses for the man to admit it. Thanks to Marisa, who first touched and then revealed the very soul of this baffling beast with a child's laugh instead of a trainer's tight lead, the horse was now firmly ensconced in his owner's household. Not literally, of course, because that crazy bugger could still kick the screen out of the television set faster than Elvis could change a channel with his .44 Magnum handgun. (Yes, Elvis actually did that, and on more than one occasion.)

Watching his little girl and his big-butted horse frolicking in the same stall where Zippy had once pinned him to the wall for sixty terrifying minutes had a dramatic effect on Felix. He saw their relationship differently after that, even changed the way he trained the horse. That single small act of affection — a little girl brushing the horse's face with a loving hand — was not lost on the track-hardened father and trainer. Once he might have given Zippy a bit of a spanking or instructed a jockey to go heavy on the whip; there would be no more of that from now on.

"Zippy, he stands up for himself. You better treat him with love or fuhgeddaboudit." And then, with a bit of a crooked smile, he added, "But he still bite me."

That didn't mean Zippy was through trying the man's patience. Indeed, the next few races would cast Felix in the role of the Puerto Rican Job, with racetrack challenges of biblical proportions. While he still dreamed of his horse winning a race, Zippy may have felt that unnecessary, what with the lineup of fawning fans snapping his picture these days and calling him their "boy." And oh, those handfuls of crunchy carrots from strangers, the fresh ones with the stems still on.

It's difficult to determine who the best prankster was back then, the horse or the kid with those big, misbehaving eyes. "It wasn't long after that that my dad caught me feeding Zippy carrots with my teeth," said Marisa. "I thought he was going to have a cow!"

I ONCE HAD
A DOG LIKE THAT

He was big and strong — half border collie, half Australian shepherd. He was every bit as handsome as a racehorse, and oh, how Jake loved to run. Fast and furious, he was, like a fox in a forest fire.

He was so fast that I introduced him to the game of flyball, a team sport for dogs in which they run a relay course against other teams of speedy canines. It's a very well-organized sport, with state, national, and international championships. Flyball is quite entertaining to watch and would be a more action-packed Olympic sport than, say, curling or golf.

At the flyball arena, Jake and I sat in the bleachers, and he couldn't take his eyes off the game unfolding in front of us. He was mesmerized by the sight of dogs of different breeds and sizes ripping down a track and over hurdles to retrieve the prize of a tennis ball at the far end of the track. At one point — and he may have been crying out for a penalty — he actually barked. Fun? Wow! Jake did everything but start the wave.

So I took him down to the practice area, where a trainer was going to put him through a few paces, and Jake ran . . . well, he ran back up to the stands and sat down. Turns out he loved to watch, not play, flyball. As far as training and practicing and securing a spot on the team — that he would leave for other dogs, dogs who had attended some Ivy League obedience school and didn't know how to enjoy a rip-roaring run at a flock of screaming geese on a beach.

I swear, if I could have run a tab for him at the dog track — good for a cold beer and a burger with everything but onion — Jake would still be there, sitting in the stands and slamming his paws together in sheer sedentary delight.

EIGHT

*Meet [trouble] as a friend, for you'll see a lot of it
and had better be on speaking terms with it.*
Oliver Wendell Holmes

Zippy's home for three years and seventy races at Finger Lakes was stall number seven in barn twenty, on the backside. Just like at every thoroughbred track in North America, the backside (or the backstretch, as it's sometimes called) at Finger Lakes serves as the stabling area and living quarters of the pony people, a small, strange, and solitary world not unlike the jerry-rigged lot of tents and trailers where circus workers live temporarily. This is the place where the callused, unseen hands of horsemen and handlers make the sport of racing horses work. Finger Lakes's backside is a timeless and shabby little village, far from the property's glittering casino. While thousands come to play the slots every day, few people attend the races, and almost nobody goes to the backside.

It's a quirky little community consisting of twenty-one long, rectangular barns, four one-story concrete residences with twenty dorm rooms each, a few circular equine playgrounds linked by roads that are usually muddy or rutted hard. A spacious canteen called Cilantro serves grilled meats and tacos as well as a lot of leafy, healthy foods so riders can keep their weight down. Here in the "kitchen," listening to salsa music, men in mismatched tracksuits shoot pool or play pinball machines, ignoring the bank of simulcast monitors broadcasting races from other tracks.

The front windows of the tiny rent-free apartments have long been filmed over by cigarette smoke, and beat-up bicycles lie on patchy lawns or stand propped up against rusted-out air conditioners. The uneven grass is trampled, not mowed. A mottled old couch and ripped-up recliner sit soaking from last night's rain under a battered umbrella. The living conditions in almost all North American racetracks are and always have been an embarrassment to the industry. Arlington Park in Chicago has been called "the Taj Mahal of racing" because of its fine track and clubhouse, but its backside, where a single bathroom once had to accommodate one hundred workers, mostly Latinos, has been described as a "ghetto." Arlington has made significant improvements to the workers' residences, but it still took the American Civil Liberties Union to win the right for four hundred children to live in the backside with their parents during the racing season.

The Finger Lakes barns, however, are spotless, with two wide aisles running the length of each barn, separating rows of stalls on each side. The bobbing heads of horses stretch over the front walls of the stalls, demanding food or water, but mostly just attention, with a variety of sounds, from a high-pitched, anxious neighing to a softer, contented nickering. And they get everything they want, almost on demand. Here, the horses are the high-priced talent. A loud complaint from one stall brings a bough of fresh hay, kicked beneath the horse's feet under the webbing that keeps him in. A stomping fit attracts a groom with a garden hose, to fill the bucket on the wall. A few horses prefer to drink from the nozzle of the hose, soaking themselves and the handler in the process. The stall floors are repeatedly mucked and replenished with fresh, golden straw.

Suddenly, shouts are heard outside: "Loose horse. Loose horse!" Workers swarm the steel-fenced exercise circle to corral a horse that has snapped his lead and is running wild inside, threatening to collide with another horse still hooked up to the circling bar.

A girl, maybe twenty, runs to the ring and shuts the machine down with the slap of a hand. She slowly walks through the gate toward the rampaging horse, talking softly but showing no-nonsense body language. Calmly, she corners the big black stallion, who surrenders to her touch. "Nice work!" yells a guy from a neighboring barn, and it's all over in less than a minute.

There are eight tack rooms in each barn, the largest being the trainer's, with harnesses and nosebands, saddles and stirrups hanging on all four walls. Drop nosebands and tongue-ties keep the horses from swallowing their unusually large tongues. On the wall for all to see is that day's worksheet, a list of which horses need to be primed for races and which need to be walked, galloped, or worked out in the exercise barn. Around every corner inside the barns are stacks of baled hay reaching nearly to the rafters.

The tiny tack rooms located near the four entrances to each barn are smaller than the stalls of the horses. There, trainers, pony riders, and grooms keep their gear. Small fridges contain snacks, sodas, and medicine for the horses. Most have cots, some have TVs, one has an air conditioner. This one belongs to Emily. "Mom" has spent every week at the track for most of her life.

There's a pleasantness around the barns in the morning as the work routines are infused with good-natured banter. "J-Rod" chides "Butch" about his favorite filly, who came in last yesterday. "Diesel Dave" and "Muscleman" jar at each other as "Mom" walks laps inside the barn, five horses every day. And yes, there's always a "Mom" in the backside, to whom others bring their troubles.

Except for the grooms and the hot-walkers, the pony riders and the trainers, people who can be identified by the crust of muck and crap on their boots, the only others to visit the backside are the vets and farriers. The track officials and stewards never come here, except in crisis. Even here at Finger Lakes jockeys have their own comfortable digs closer to the track, complete with lockers, a kitchen, TV monitors to watch themselves and the competition, a sweat box, a hot tub, a sleeping room with bunk beds, a pool table, an ice machine, and windows onto the paddock. The silks room where the jockeys' uniforms are kept is managed by the "Color Man," and the all-important weigh station is operated by the "Scales Clerk." Some jockey rooms have "spit boxes" or "vomit stalls," the second-quickest weight-loss program known to a rider. The first is a white pill that contains the egg of a tapeworm.

The backstretch workers are an odd and fascinating lot, vagabonds with seasonal jobs that move with the horses and the weather. For these grooms, hot-walkers, and foremen, the days begin at four in the morning and end around six at night, seven days a week. They are poorly paid, and holidays and sick days are unknown to them. First and foremost, there is an immense respect for animals here, a common thread that bonds together these backside workers, an endearing link between the racers and their caregivers. Secondly, come hell or high water, birth, illness, and death – the backsiders are there for each other. *They* are all they have. They intermingle and intermarry and watch each other's back. They are matter-of-fact, friendly, weary, but always polite to a visitor. Most of them have had hard lives; all of them have stories. Fights and petty crimes are common. Many are locals not afraid of hard work and accepting of low pay. Others drift from track to track, followed by the "bad paperwork" of warrants, unpaid child support, and immigration issues. On one of my visits to the Finger Lakes Racetrack, a stabbing had occurred in the backside the night before. Nobody died, but the barn people were much more upset about the cops being called in than about the assault itself.

The language of the backside is mostly Spanish, the dress code is dirty denim, and the smell is an inoffensive combination of urine and liniment, hay, and horse buns. In fact, some back-stretchers believe it brings good luck if you step in it! The round-the-clock rhythm changes from hectic between dawn and eleven in the morning to tranquil from six until dusk.

From a post time of one o'clock until the completion of the program's ninth and last race at about five-thirty, the backside is a shuttle service. With a 5:00 a.m. breakfast and a 10:00 a.m. light lunch, horses are kept hungry for the afternoon races. Horses leave for the track, excited and feisty, and return a half hour later, still pumped up and soaked in sweat. A cold shower and a big dinner await them in the barn. After dark, the only sound heard is a troublemaker trying to rouse the others; the only move-ment is the beam of the security guard's flashlight as he makes his nightly rounds, checking on the expensive inmates.

Race day is game day, and the backside looks like the back-stage of a Broadway play. That day's stars, one or two from each of the track's twenty barns, are primped and fawned over, braided and gussied up and talked to like actors about to take the stage. The afternoon matinee, with curtain-up announced by a bugler, is about to begin. Not yet saddled, that day's racers are led from the barns to the track by stable hands wearing bright oversized jer-seys, each numbered in order of the horse and its post position. It's a ten-minute walk to the track, and the horses are on edge, their muscles rippling and coats shining as they nicker and nudge their handlers with their long, gorgeous snouts. With a jerk of a harness and a harsh word, they are told to cut it out.

Once horse and handler arrive at the paddock area, the trainer saddles up his mount in an open stall and talks to the jockey about the race, now a half hour away. If the rider wants to keep working for the trainer, he listens to the instructions and follows them closely once the starting bell goes off. The horse does two turns around the circle paddock, where bettors get a chance to size him up, the first time led by a stableman, then the next with the jockey up.

A bright blaze of color from the jockeys' silks and the horses' saddlecloth moves slowly down the chute to the track, where the bugler blasts his call to post. The post parade looks like a fashion show, with bettors still judging the strutters and high-steppers as they make their way to the starting gate. Preening, posing, nodding knowingly to their riders, the horses are the stars of this festive extravaganza, and they know it. The bell rings and the pageantry of the race explodes on the track as the audience goes silent in anticipation, all eyes focused on the pack. The horses are rarin' to go. Each will perform in one colorful, breathtaking swirl around an earthen oval, winner takes top prize.

After the track's camera stops flashing at the finish line, some of these sleek and silky characters will be applauded for their efforts, a few might be booed, but most certainly one will go to the winner's circle to be photographed with the jockey, the trainer, and the owner's entourage.

On race days, Emily, who has also served as Felix's barn foreman, uses her cubbyhole tack room as a private retreat. She never goes to the frontside to watch the races, so once she's prepped the horses for the track, she escapes to her cool cubicle with its ten-inch TV, stuffed chair, and table, the top a laminated photo of her family. Emily, who loves horses more than strangers, only locks the door when media types come asking about Zippy Chippy.

"I've never been off the hill," she told me. Every day except for the track's dark days, when the horses don't run, Emily works the stalls and walks the horses of the two barns, where everyone, including her daughter, labors tirelessly from well before dawn to dusk.

Conversations on the backside might be a mix of Spanish and English, but the lingo sounds like it's from another planet. When asked how her mother and father met, Marisa said, "There was this trainer named Floyd Wright, and my mom was walking hot for him and my dad was breaking his babies."

Translation: They met at the trainer's stable, where Emily was walking horses to cool them down after races or workouts and Felix was training two-year-olds, breaking them in to become racehorses. Just so we're clear – Emily did not have the hots for Mr. Wright, and Felix is quite fond of children.

These days, instead of sleeping in the back of Emily's old red Ford, Marisa drives her own Dodge Ram. On this day Marisa has been up since 3:45 a.m. to look after her own horses on her nearby farm. She is waved through the track's stable gate, and by eight, she has taken care of her trainer's twenty horses – she's fed 'em, watered 'em, groomed 'em, and mucked out their stalls. Working the shed row with her plastic toolbox filled with grooming materials, Marisa looks like a Molly Maid, but in riding gear. At twelve-thirty, she mounts Jazz, one of her two exercise ponies, and they trot up to the track, where she will spend the afternoon as one of the track's ten pony riders, escorting that day's entries from rail to gate before each of their races. Two outriders, one in front and one behind the post parade, are there to avoid a crisis, more than likely a runaway, riderless horse. Since there is only one stable, Marisa's other pony, Gamble, is boarded at home until next month, when he and Jazz will switch places.

Mid-morning, trainers will wander in with instructions; in the meantime there are always last-minute tasks. The bandages on Mr. Hopps's knees need tightening; Isabella of Chance has an eye infection that requires a new poultice; the blinkers on Lady Lorna are not large enough for those big, beautiful eyes.

As at most tracks, the barns at Finger Lakes Racetrack brush up against the backstretch of the track, where a six-foot-wide gap in the metal railing allows horses being galloped to easily enter and exit from their stalls during training sessions. Zippy Chippy did not like to sweat on his days off. With his record of losses, it's doubtful he saw any point in workouts, so he developed a unique way of ending an exercise session.

"He'd be coming around the turn at a good clip, and as soon as he spotted the gap," remembered Marisa, "he would just stop dead and buck off his exercise jockey. Then he'd bolt through that space in the fence and trot home to his stall all by himself." There he would stand, fully saddled and in front of his pen, practically knocking on the door to get in. He did it so often it became routine, and the handler closest to his stall would simply remove his saddle and push him on in. The exercise boy would come by some time later and curse him out in Spanish.

Not long after getting comfortable in his pen, Zippy would become bored and go looking for a little adventure. Normally, the webbing of three leather straps across the door of a stall, all hooked on clips on either side of the sill, was enough to keep a horse penned. Before the full metal screen became a fixture on his stall (after, I'm sure, his handlers considered prison doors, barbed wire, armed guards, or a moat with sharks swimming in it), Zippy figured out that with a little pressure from his broad chest, he could break the snap of the top two straps and pop the third one with his knee. Then off he'd go, as the Aussies say, on a "walkabout." Exploring the backside on the trot, he would attract the attention of the horse handlers and the envy of the other horses peering out of their stalls. Yelling for help, the people in pursuit would grow to a posse that would finally end Zippy's brief escapade of freedom in some far-off, fenced-in corner of the track.

Having been summoned from his house, a very annoyed Felix would arrive and lead his horse back to the barn. Once there, he'd push him into his stall with a little more force than was necessary and slam the door in his face. And then the usual bulletin: "Zippy's been a bad boy . . . blah, blah, blah." Sometimes, when the track staff became tired of his act, they'd just ignore him until he wore himself out and found his own way home. If Zippy's handlers could have made him sit in the corner of the barn wearing a dunce hat, they would have. And then, for their personal enjoyment, he would have eaten that hat.

Marisa was sure she had seen Zippy Chippy break out of his stall in every conceivable way – under the webbing, through the webbing, out an unlatched door, through a door that latched and locked. But then one day she saw him . . . break *into* his stall. Felix and his daughter had a daily routine of turning out their stable of horses into the shed row so they could go in and clean out their pens unimpeded. They stacked a makeshift barricade of two-by-fours across the door of each stall to keep the horses out while they worked. All of the horses except for Zippy. Felix would not hear of letting Zippy loose in the barn, because although he didn't know exactly what might capture the horse's curiosity, he knew only drama or devilry would follow. Marisa, showing early signs of becoming either a union leader or a civil rights lawyer, protested that it was unfair to keep Zippy cooped up while the others got to leave their pens and play. After five days of hearing that he might be the cruelest trainer on earth, never mind the worst dad, Felix relented. Zippy was turned out to play with the other kids at recess while father and daughter mucked their stalls.

"He was fine," said Marisa. "He was running around and rearing up and having a great old time." For a while.

"I guess at some point he missed me, because we heard this crashing and banging, and . . . Zippy jumped the fence of two-by-fours and smashed his way back into the stall." With the daring of a circus horse performing the ring of fire, Zippy the inmate, finally set free, had broken back into his own pen. *Why,* he must have asked himself, *would they let me just walk out the door when they know I much prefer an old-fashioned prison break?* Once inside, he was all over Marisa – chasing her around his stable and then out to the shed row and all around the barn. Unfortunately, so was Felix. "Boy, did I get yelled at that day!" she said.

For a horse – an animal with a small brain relative to its body mass – Zippy Chippy had a well-developed sense of curiosity. Equine experts believe that a horse with a low IQ is more submissive and therefore easier to train. By that measure, the untrainable Zippy Chippy may well have been a genius.

NO, YOU NEVER GET
EVERYTHING YOU WANT

No matter how hard you try, you never get the whole package. Years ago, I wrote a baseball film called *Chasing the Dream* that chronicled the careers of three young minor leaguers trying to break into Major League Baseball with the Toronto Blue Jays.

For the documentary, I did the color stuff: interviewing ballpark eccentrics, like the amateur barber who gave free haircuts to fans at home plate during the seventh-inning stretch, and the guy who swallowed enough air to burp the national anthem. At East Field, home of the Glens Falls Redbirds Single-A franchise, I came across baseball's only season ticket–holding dog.

Dutch and Biddie Herman lived near the ballpark and loved to attend the Redbirds games, but they hated leaving Pete, their aging French poodle, home alone. I remember the couple well because Dutch referred to his wife as "the old Biddie," and every time he said that, she found it in her heart not to kick him in the balls.

So my on-camera interview was going quite well as Dutch explained how he and Biddie had sat down with Redbirds officials and worked out a deal in which they could purchase a season ticket for Pete, which would allow them to skirt the "no pets" rule. As we spoke, Pete was barking his head off behind the backstop and chasing foul balls down the lines, his season ticket secured to his collar. The fans loved the scruffy-looking mutt, the Redbirds tolerated him, and the opposing players drove him nuts by barking all the time.

Mid-interview, Dutch started wandering off topic, so I tapped the cameraman on the knee to signal that this one was a wrap.

That's when Dutch leaned over to me like he was about to spill the Fourth Secret of Fatima and whispered, "And the best is . . . when we did the deal we worked Pete's age out in human years." He looked around to make sure other ticket holders were not listening in. "Yeah. That way we got him the senior citizens' discount, too!"

I immediately got into a fight with the cameraman for shutting down the camera too soon. To no avail. I got the interview, but missed the punchline. And in the end, the director of the film scrapped the whole bit. So for Pete's sake – and Zippy's too – learn to live with the fact of life that you never get all that you want. Go for it all, settle for half, and you'll never be disappointed.

NINE

Why would I leave? I like it here.

Writer Paul Sheldon to Annie Wilkes, who has shattered
both his ankles with the flat side of an axe and has him
hobbled and hogtied to his bed, in the movie Misery

ippy Chippy's favorite people made for a very small group:
Felix and Emily, of course Marisa, an exercise rider named
Carlos Carmello, and anybody with a box of donuts. Chris
Roncone, the man with the unenviable job of caring for Zippy's
feet, never made that list.

"Zippy was a huge pain in the ass to shoe," recalled the farrier,
the memory more matter-of-fact than fond. As the Finger Lakes
shoeman, Chris would arrive at barn twenty with the names of
a couple of horses that needed to be shod that day. Most animals cooperate with the process and the farrier needs only one
"holder" to keep the horse still. Zippy often needed a team to hold
him in place, but hardly still.

"Plus, it wasn't just for this track here. Felix had Zippy running in match races and trotting events and a bunch of other damn
stuff. You need different plates for grass and different surfaces. So
it was more often than the normal thirty or forty days that I had
to work on Zippy. And man, he was a nightmare."

Bent over while taking a hoof pick to Zippy's foot with his back to the horse, the shoeman was defenseless. When the shoeing sessions turned into wrestling matches, with Chris outweighed by more than nine hundred pounds, he strongly requested that Zippy be tranquilized. Felix refused.

"Plus, Felix would baby the shit out of that horse," said Chris. "And the horse got away with murder."

Well, maybe not murder, but Zippy definitely got away with a vicious assault on an expensive, inanimate object. With no love lost between the horse and the farrier, one bright and sunny day Chris pulled up to Felix's barn in his brand-new Chevy pickup, and Felix happened by with Zippy Chippy in tow. They were out on a stroll and having a grand ol' time.

"And it didn't help that Felix had a beer in one hand, Zippy in the other. Felix is jabbering away to somebody inside the barn, not paying attention, and yeah, that's when Zippy went after my truck."

Marisa remembers the incident with the pickup truck all too well. When Zippy turned his back on the vehicle, she knew what was coming and yelled to her dad, but it was too late. "He didn't just kick it," she said. Zippy turned, lined up the side of the shiny red Chevy with his ass, and then with both back feet – recently shod by Chris, of course – he . . .

"He double-barreled that thing!" said Marisa. "*Bang.* The noise scared everybody, and nobody said anything right away." Then Felix started laughing, and the farrier, well, he became livid. Mad? Let's just say Felix was lucky that the next time he had an X-ray it didn't show a horseshoe hooked around his prostate.

Somehow, the forceful backward buck did not shatter the windows, but Zippy's hooves left two deep dents in the truck, one on the driver's-side door. The horse may not yet have won a race, but in the ongoing battle with his farrier, the final score in this match was Zippy Chippy 1, Chris Roncone 0.

Zippy wasn't the only member of the Monserrate family who gave the farrier fits. When they were based out of Emily's tack room, Marisa and her cousin Keri, the five-year-old misfits, were constantly playing tricks on the overworked shoeman.

"The worst was when Keri fixed my hand up with a clip-on two-inch nail that came out both sides, with fake blood dripping down my arm," said Marisa.

When the bleeding child approached him, crying and falling to her knees, Chris started screaming for help. The kids panicked and quickly gave up the joke, believing he might pass out from the sight of blood. While Zippy took care of the farrier's red truck, the kids helped turn the man's hair gray. In fairness, Chris never quit on the horse, and he continued to care for Zippy's feet as long as the horse ran at Finger Lakes.

Prancing and shifting from side to side, Zippy was wearing a new pair of shoes on June 23, 1998, for the third race on a fast track at Finger Lakes. It had been twenty-four days since the collision of his back feet with a new truck and his eighty-first loss, in which Last Shallbe First came in third and the last-place finisher, by the name of Saw Your Act, seemed to be taunting Zippy from behind. It had been exactly ten days since his eighty-second loss, when Bangzoomtothemoon bumped him at the start and Hilary's Kid (no, not Chelsea) beat him to the finish line by sixteen and three-quarter lengths.

The trainer, wearing his "Zippy Chippy" hat a little off kilter, looked downright jaunty. High-stepping his way onto the track, Zippy was in fine form, uncharacteristically jolly. He didn't give Felix a hard time when he put the saddle on him, he hadn't glared at anybody all morning, he didn't nip the exercise pony who

trotted beside him during the track warm up, and he even went
into the padded starting gate willingly, not rearing up in defiance
or lashing out at one of the crew whose job it was to muscle him
in there. Typically it took four men to get Zippy into the gate,
and one of them usually sought alternative employment after the
experience. But not today. There was something in the air.

On this balmy afternoon, Zippy was looking at six short furlongs to dispatch six other maidens, and if you looked closely at
the smiling trainer and his eager sprinter, the scene dripped with
surprise and possibility.

As the starting bell rang, a field of six horses verily flew onto
the track in a flourish of spraying dirt and booming hooves. They
headed for the first turn fast and stormed down the backstretch
as one. The crowd had a great view of this streaking posse hammering down the track in a riot of colorful silks, with little men
crouched on their backs.

They had almost as good a view as Zippy, the seventh horse,
who could see the race unfolding right in front of him as he stood
perfectly still in the starting gate long after the others had left.
When the RINGGGGGGGG! had gone off for all to hear, Zippy
Chippy had decided he wasn't coming out to play today. The horse,
like many a bloodied and addled heavyweight boxer, had failed
to answer the bell. He just stood there as an embarrassed jockey
whacked him on the ass with his riding crop and gestured helplessly
toward the handlers standing behind the gate.

It's fair to say that a rider who is not in motion is not so much
a jockey as a hood ornament. Benny Afanador was not amused.
He'd had bad trips on Zippy Chippy before, but not one in which
the entire field of horses was closing in on the first turn before he
could get his unpredictable mount to move. This time Zippy had
committed the cardinal sin of horse racing. He had "dwelt."

Dwelling is the term for a horse that breaks very, very slowly from the starting gate, giving himself almost no chance of winning. Zippy had added a couple of words to that definition: "slowly or not at all." Giving your rivals a thirty-length head start is a real bad idea for any horse, particularly one who is not noted for his late speed . . . or early speed . . . or, okay, speed. Generally speaking, dwelling is a terrible tactic to employ in sport. It would be like Denver Bronco Peyton Manning taking the snap from a center, then signing the ball for a charity auction before actually putting it in play. Imagine Dale Earnhardt Jr. stepping out of his National Guard Chevrolet Impala SS to personally thank the man waving the green flag at the start of the race.

Out of the gate, Zippy had delayed before, he had dawdled before, and he had even dilly-dallied before, but he had never dwelt. Racetrack officials take dwelling very seriously. They know their salaries come from the money being pushed under the betting windows, not just at Finger Lakes but at other tracks and off-track shops all over North America. When bettors get nervous about the legitimacy of the races, track stewards get the shakes and the ticket sellers start bringing paperbacks to read at work.

Oddly, Felix didn't seem all that upset at his horse's decision to sit this one out. "He don't break so good," he explained. "That's all." Perhaps he was just a little bit impressed that Zippy had found a new way to lose. Felix had never before seen his horse not going forward in a race. Even the faithful who followed this horse religiously were disappointed. Zippy could lose, of course, but not this way.

Having given away an insurmountable lead to six fellow maidens, Zippy lost the race by twenty-six lengths, and Felix had no choice but to enthusiastically follow the instruction of the track stewards: school the horse in the basics of breaking from the gate.

But that wasn't the worst of it. Now with eighty-three career losses, Zippy was just two defeats away from what was believed to be the all-time record for the most losses by an American thoroughbred. Two horses had already hit this infamous mark of eighty-five losses in a row. The smart money was betting that Zippy Chippy would make it a three-way tie at the top of that heap . . . which, when you think about it, is really the bottom of the barrel.

That "something in the air" on that day when Zippy came in last for the umpteenth time? Surprise had disappeared around the first turn with the rest of the pack, and optimism was overcome by the strong smell of horse manure. There's an awful lot of that at the track. You have to wonder if there wasn't a little shed row sabotage involved here. I mean, the farrier wasn't happy driving a brand-new dented truck, and he was the last man to work on Zippy's shoes, and we all know how that goes . . .

> *For the want of a nail the shoe was lost.*
> *For the want of a shoe the horse was lost.*
> *For the want of a horse the rider was lost.*
> *For the want of a rider the battle was lost.*
> *For the want of a battle the kingdom was lost.*
> *And all for the want of a horseshoe nail.*
>
> *Benjamin Franklin*

GEORGE CHUVALO, THE FIGHTER
WHO ALWAYS ANSWERED THE BELL

I once interviewed Canadian George Chuvalo, one of the toughest stand-up boxers in the history of the sport. Inducted into the World Boxing Hall of Fame in Los Angeles, Chuvalo fought the legends – Joe Frazier, George Foreman, Floyd Patterson, and Muhammad Ali (twice) – without ever getting knocked off his feet.

Built like a brick outhouse, bloodied but never addled, Chuvalo could take a ton of punishment before launching his own damaging blows. In front of a live audience, I opened with the following question: "Your critics have described you as more of a defensive fighter than . . ." I didn't get to finish.

"My critics should talk to those seventy-four guys I put in the hospital," replied Chuvalo rather calmly, which got an admiring laugh from the crowd. After ninety-three grueling professional fights over a twenty-year career, the man was not exaggerating.

"The night I fought Muhammad Ali in Toronto, he went to the hospital and I went dancing with my wife."

Unlike many punch-drunk boxers who slur their words, Chuvalo is not only mentally sharp, but he can also remember every detail of every one of his bouts. Not exactly the Artful Dodger, he figures he took 9,000 hits to the head in his career. I asked him how he could possibly have not received a concussion?

"No neck," he said. "I don't have a neck." Just a hunch, but he's probably right. In order to concuss, the brain needs to swing like a pendulum and bang off the walls of the cranium. Having a short neck means there is not much of a swinging motion and therefore no damage done when you get hit.

I couldn't wait to ask him about Henry Cooper. Way back in the seventies, I found myself in the Henry Cooper Pub in London, England, staring at a wall of photos of every great fighter who ever lived, including Jack Dempsey, Joe Louis, Rocky Marciano, and the original Sugar Ray, Sugar Ray Robinson.

Cooper was a small heavyweight but a quick puncher with a deadly left hook, a pugilist who outboxed and outfoxed his opponents instead of steadily pummeling them into a purple pulp, as Chuvalo did. Cooper, who once knocked down a young Muhammad Ali, was the British, European, and Commonwealth heavyweight champion. Canada being part of the Commonwealth meant that Chuvalo, the longest-reigning Canadian champion, had a legitimate chance to challenge Cooper for that coveted crown. Except Cooper knew what every fan of boxing at the time could tell you: trying to dance around George Chuvalo would have been like throwing himself in front of a big red double-decker London bus. So Cooper artfully dodged Chuvalo, wisely fighting less dangerous opponents.

One day, Chuvalo was training in a London gym when he spotted Cooper's manager, Jim Wicks. "Boom Boom," as George was known, ambled over to Wicks and, after a bit of small talk, put it to the manager bluntly.

"So when are me and your boy going to meet in the ring?" asked Chuvalo.

At this point in the telling, Chuvalo invokes a very good, very clipped English accent.

"Mr. Chuvalo," replied Cooper's manager, clearing his throat, "he doesn't even want to meet you socially!"

A high compliment, that — when one of the best in the business avoids you in order to preserve his record as well as the shape of his head. Hardly Zippy Chippy's problem, given that every horse that had a saddle wanted to race against him. And yet, both stalwarts of their sports, with all those opponents in all those battles, neither Chuvalo nor Zippy ever got knocked off his feet.

TEN

I have nothing against underdogs personally.
It's just that I wouldn't want one to bury my sister.

Anonymous

O h, sorry – that should have read "undertakers."

Two weeks later, on July 6, 1998, it was the same place, same track, same thing. The bell rang, the gates clanged open, and the pack burst forth without Zippy Chippy. With six horses in front of him enjoying a fifteen-length lead, Benny Afanador, using a lot of guts and guile, managed to move his horse up briskly into the stretch, taking him from seventh to fifth in a rush to the wire. Rallying rather well, Zippy surprisingly came in fifth by passing two exhausted horses in the stretch and finishing eleven lengths behind Bangzoomtothemoon. Although somebody swears they heard Felix turn to his horse and say, "One of these days, Alice," nothing can be confirmed.

While not last, he still finished twenty-one lengths behind the winner, Can't Stop Now, proving yet again that he, Zippy Chippy, could stop anywhere and anytime he wanted. But in the starting gate? This dwelling was a horrible habit that, if not broken, would be a certain career-crusher. The claiming price to purchase Zippy was $13,000 – which, when you think about it, should have come with a mental health background check for any prospective buyer.

"Disbelievable," said Felix. At the track steward's behest, he had worked Zippy in front of them that very morning, demonstrating how well his horse was doing getting out of the gate. Time after time, the bell went off and so did Zippy Chippy. New trick, same act. Like Lucy holding the football for Charlie Brown to kick, Zippy had promised to do it right this time, and Felix had landed flat on his ass. Apparently, the Zipster had just been messing with them.

With this, his second dwell in a row, Zippy was put on forced vacation. "For the protection of the public," read the track's official statement, "we've recommended that the horse take some time off." Not really an outright ban, but nothing you want to see on your year-end job review. "We just want him to take some time off now, and if he shows he can break, then he can run again," said a steward.

The sixty-day temporary ban went into effect immediately after his eighty-fourth loss, and the "three-strikes-and-you're-out" rule was implied but not stated. Nobody was counting on a win from this horse, but there were some expectations that he would at least run. A second or even a third once in a while would keep bettors happy and the stewards at bay. It's pretty much a given at every racetrack – if you can't get out of the starting gate, then leave the barn by the back door and don't bother coming back. Once somebody suggests attaching one of those backing-up beepers to your bum, you're in serious trouble.

Felix lamely defended his stop-and-go gelding. "He just want to see the other horses out in front of him before he run." Absolutely. At eleven lengths behind the pack at the first turn, he had a very clear picture of the task at hand.

This strategy of sizing up your opponents ahead of time often works in short-track cycling or long-distance running. But on a track, you're not likely to see Usain Bolt hanging back in the starting block after the gun goes off in order to identify which sprinter he has to run to ground in order to win the one hundred meters. Sorry, but even on *The Biggest Loser* you won't see a contestant sitting around scarfing Twinkies in order to give the others a bit of an edge.

"Then, after he wait, Zippy tries to catch up to them," added Felix, who by this point had personally trained his mount to a total of sixty-four losses, twelve in the last year alone.

Although Finger Lakes officials were not backing off their temporary suspension, they were rather impressed by Zippy's many fans and frequent bettors, who were illogically putting their money on him to win, thereby reducing what should have been very long odds. Despite having lost by a total of fifty-five lengths in his previous three races, Zippy still went off at 2–1 instead of a realistic 35–1. A storm of protest erupted in the press when Zippy was suspended, prompting one steward to suggest, "Maybe he's reached cult status."

Consequently, Zippy was placed in temporary retirement at a nearby boarding farm where the owners were quite taken by the fun-loving delinquent and especially by his spreading fame. Fans were soon knocking on the barn door for an impromptu meet 'n' greet with the Zipster.

"People like to see him run," said Felix, still not grasping the seriousness of the situation. "The old-timers who come to the track, they ask about him every day."

It wasn't just the old boys in the clubhouse who were enamored with Zippy Chippy. Families came to watch their lovable underachiever, bringing kids wearing Zippy Chippy hats who couldn't yet see over the trackside fence. The jaded backstretch workers rarely left the barns to watch a race, but they did come to the front-side to see Zippy run, curious as to what calamity he might cause.

Felix had a way of taking the sting out of a painful predic-ament with unexpected humor. When track officials and media asked him about Zippy's erratic behavior, he said, pushing his blue Zippy Chippy cap to the back of his head, "I dunno. Every time, I ask him what the problem is, but he don't answer me."

When pressed about his lopsided devotion to this particular horse when he had a stable full of racers he was training back in Clifton Springs, Felix scratched the scar on his back and reached into his bag of favorite parables, but he . . . he missed by two lengths. "Say you have three horses, and two are in university and they do well, but the other one . . ." Either that was a slip of the tongue or the entrance-level qualifications for universities in New York State have fallen lower than those of Mississippi.

If Zippy could not see the ghosts of bridesmaids past down the track, Felix surely could. Gussie Mae and Really a Tenor were taunting Zippy Chippy just around the next bend of the next race. With eighty-five straight losses each, these two hapless non-winners made up the kind of club that if they're willing to accept you as a member, you don't wanna join. With eighty-four losses, Zippy seemed to be knocking on their clubhouse door.

And his losing streak had become contagious, spreading to Felix's other twenty-seven horses. The previous year, Felix's horses had gone winless in eighty-eight starts. When asked if he was embarrassed by the poor performance of his four-footed friend, Felix became defensive: "No, no. Maidens, if they don't win, trainers dump them fast. Zippy, he's happy when he runs, and that's all I want. A horse that loses like that, you think maybe he stop eating or he lay down in his stall, but . . . but he don't do that stuff. He's a happy horse, and healthy too."

Although Zippy was attracting a wider circle of fans, jockey Benny Afanador was suddenly not one of them. The rider was furious at having been stranded in the starting gate for a second time, like he was riding a coin-operated children's pony down at the mall. With his newfound fondness for hanging out in the starting gate, this horse had managed to piss off his most faithful jockey, the one who'd been in his saddle for eleven almost consecutive rides. "This horse is making me look bad. I will never ride him again," said Afanador. One of the few jockeys at Finger Lakes willing to mount the horse was good to his word — he never rode Zippy Chippy again. While jockey Victor Espinoza likely earned ten percent, or $300,000, for American Pharoah's Triple Crown romp, Afanador, after eleven trips around the track with Zippy Chippy, was still waiting for his first winner's share of the purse.

Deeply hurt by this parting of ways (Felix and Benny had come to America together), the trainer's outward response was a shrug and then a visit to the jockeys' room.

Although he loved Benny like a brother, he knew that for the "jock mount" of $75, at this level of racing, it would not be difficult to find Zippy's next silken-clad victim.

Team Zippy may have lost its favorite rider, but never its loyal captain.

TEAM LOYALTY: US AGAINST THE WORLD
AND BARNYARD ANIMALS

That's what they all had – Felix and Zippy, Penn and Teller, Minnie and Mickey, Mickey and Billy – togetherness and team loyalty.

New York Yankees legends Mickey Mantle and Billy Martin, with twelve World Series rings between them, were best friends as well as hunting buddies. After his playing days were over, Martin did such a good job of managing the Texas Rangers that they nicknamed the team the "Turn Around Gang" and presented him with a very expensive hunting rifle, which he was dying to use. By way of explaining the devotion players had for their manager, Mantle tells his favorite story on a YouTube video by claiming that if Martin told his players to jump off a roof, they would because "they knew Billy would jump off with them." (This is also the reason that NASA scientists and neurosurgeons at Johns Hopkins Hospital in Baltimore do not fear losing their jobs to professional baseball players.)

Warning: This story may be apocryphal, which means it could have been concocted by these two gentlemen in the back seat of a hired car as they drank beer from a cooler and took turns knocking the driver's hat off. As the story goes, Mantle had a friend who owned a hunting ranch near San Antonio, Texas, and off they went. The former doctor and rancher was only too happy to see the great Mickey Mantle at his door (Martin waited in the car) and told him they could shoot all the deer they wanted, but . . . he had a favor to ask. Very reluctantly, Mickey agreed to put the doctor's twenty-year-old mule – a decrepit animal they had seen standing in the barnyard as they'd driven up to the house – out of its misery.

On the spot, Mantle decided he was going to "pull a joke on Billy." So he stomped back to the car looking angry, grabbed his rifle, and headed for the barn.

Martin was startled. "Whatsa matter?"

"We drove four hours to get down here to go deer huntin' and this guy says we can't go deer huntin'. I'm gonna shoot his mule!"

Martin tried to stop him, but Mantle ran toward the barn with his gun and . . . bang! He shot the mule right in the neck.

As the mule hit the ground, dead, Mantle heard one, two, three cracks of a rifle from behind him.

"Bam! Bam! Bam! I turned around, there's Billy with his gun! I said, 'Billy, what're you doin'?'"

Martin, loyal teammate that he was, said, "I got three of his cows."

That's what true teammates share: loyalty as blind as that doctor's dead mule.

ELEVEN

My horse was in the lead coming down
the homestretch, but the caddie fell off.
Samuel Goldwyn

While trying to ride a stalled horse, Benny Afanador was hardly the first jockey to be pricked by the pin of mockery. Because of their slight build, those in his profession are easy marks for low humor, the butt of bad racetrack jokes. One British wag defined a jockey as "an anorexic dwarf in bright colors who drives a large car with cushions on the seat and blocks on the pedals."

Truth be told, a jockey must be madly in love with horses, crave speed, and be able to dismiss fear with a shrug. Think about it: In what other profession are you followed around by an ambulance? And yet jockeys make it look as easy as a musical carousel. The bugle and bells, the clips of the whips, the pounding of hooves, the crowd that rises as one, and the applause that swells to the top of the stands – these are the sounds of music that serve as the soundtrack to the two-minute colorful chase scene of a thoroughbred horse race. Jockeys are the minstrels who bring that music to life.

Jockeys have often been viewed as second-class athletes, because they don't run or jump or throw a ball. In fact, these

men of small stature and women of slight build are the most fearless and powerful participants in professional sports. A study by
sports medicine specialist Dr. Robert Kerlan and University of
Texas researcher Jack Wilmore tested 420 athletes from all professional sports for conditioning, reflexes, coordination, and
strength. Pound for pound, the jockeys, the drivers of thoroughbred horses, rated highest of them all for strength of body and
quickness of mind.

With only bare hands and body mass, they must maneuver
a charging animal ten times their weight through a stampede of
hulking horses running hell-bent for leather at forty miles an hour,
each trying to lunge out front of the other. Sitting on a saddle that
weighs less than two pounds, protected only by a helmet and a flak
jacket, they must often push a half ton of heaving flesh through
a three-foot gap in a thick pack of thoroughbreds in order to get
to the finish line first. Wiry warriors, they work in two-minute bursts through a minefield of peril and mayhem from wire to
wire. Never mind that at age fifty-four, Willie Shoemaker gave
Ferdinand the ride of his life to win the 1986 Kentucky Derby, and
the brilliant Rosie Napravnik won the $2 million Breeders' Cup
Distaff in 2014 aboard her favorite filly, Untapable, while she
was seven weeks pregnant. That's Willie Shoemaker, who rode a
horse almost delicately, "as if he had just asked it to dance," and
the incomparable Rosie Napravnik, who softly sweet-talked her
mounts into doing everything her brave heart desired.

A horse race is a high-speed stampede of mass and chance,
with a drove of thoroughbreds barreling around every post and
turn, then hammering down the stretch to a climactic finish. At
any juncture of that trip, an innocent clip of one hoof can send
humans and horses into a mangled pile-up in the dirt. Imagine
yourself in a forty-miles-per-hour car crash, minus the car.

Danger surrounds the racetrack just like its white wooden fence. Always injured or on the mend, jockeys ride as often as seven or eight times a day; a few die every year on the track, face down in the dirt. But that is not their biggest fear.

Strong and efficient, Canadian jockey Ron Turcotte guided the splendid Secretariat to the 1973 Triple Crown, the first in twenty-five years. Turcotte's greatest fear in sixteen years of racing was not death but being crippled. On July 13, 1978, at Belmont Park, his filly, Flag of Leyte Gulf, got bumped and crumpled beneath him. When the outrider arrived at the scene of the crash, Turcotte was lying in a heap of his own limbs. He said, "My back is broken. I'm paralyzed." He was, and sadly it marked the end of his career.

The most durable jockeys ride into their forties and fifties, and there is sadness when a rider's days are done. "When a jockey retires," lamented Eddie Arcaro, "he just becomes another little man." Unless, of course, you have left a mark so deep and distinctive in the history book of racing that your legacy lives long after your saddle is hung in the Hall of Fame. Like Eddie Arcaro himself, who shares the record of five Kentucky Derby wins with Bill Hartack. Like Johnny Longden, so workmanlike they called him "the Plumber," or Laffit Pincay, who so often came out of nowhere to steal a race that they nicknamed him "Pincay the Pirate."

Of all these daredevils who have risked death daily over grass and dirt, one still stands out today, 122 years after he rode his last race. Handsome, smart, and the son of a slave, Isaac Murphy shot to the top of American thoroughbred racing in the 1800s, when almost all jockeys were African Americans. Murphy was the first rider to win the Kentucky Derby three times – in 1884, 1890, then again in 1891 – and the secret to his success was that he whispered to his horses and never used the riding crop. He won 628 of his 1,412 starts – an unprecedented 44 percent winning average and a record, like Man o' War winning twenty of twenty-one races, that will likely never be broken. Unswervingly honest, he refused to be bribed to lose the 1879 Kenner Stakes, booting Falsetto home, a winner. He attracted great crowds, people wanting to see the jockey who won races with words instead of whips.

Frank X Walker, the first African American poet laureate of Kentucky, claimed that at the height of his career, "Isaac was as famous as Jack Johnson, as fast as Jesse Owens, as dignified as Jackie Robinson, and as admired as Michael Jordan" Walker imagines him in his poem "Murphy's Secret" as a modest man who would explain his riding style this way:

> *When folks find out I'm him,*
> *they always want to know what I say to 'em. . . .*
> *. . . I rub my hands against they neck*
> *lean into they ear, pretend I'm the wind an whisper*
> *Find yo purpose. Find yo purpose and hold on.*

Isaac Murphy died of pneumonia in 1896, at age thirty-six, remembered with the words: "Famous Negro Jockey From Lexington, KY." In 1967, Murphy's remains, initially buried in an unmarked grave, were found and, in a eulogy that needed no words, reinterred beside Man o' War (1917–1947) at the entrance to the Kentucky Horse Park. The monument reads: "Honor and shame from no condition rise. Act well your part, there all the honor lies." Fellow Kentuckians, the very best in their sport of thoroughbred racing, two legends in one gravesite – sometimes the world gets it right.

TAUNTING:
THE BATTLE CRY OF THE WEAK

The practice of taunting began as a battle cry in early hand-to-hand combat, an insult meant to demoralize and anger the enemy into an erratic response. From a sarcastic remark, the taunt evolved into a clenched fist, then a cutthroat gesture, and finally a public crotch-grab.

Taunting has become so nasty, the National Football League is considering denying touchdowns to players who goad defenders by prancing into the end zone with the ball. In Europe, and particularly Italy, where soccer fans throw bananas at black players and make monkey noises, taunting has become downright vile.

"A taunt too far" happened at Cleveland Stadium in the spring of 1991, when five-time All-Star Albert Belle was taking his swings in the batting circle and a fan standing very close to him was there only to provoke. Born in Shreveport, Louisiana, Belle had been known as "Joey" since high school. The highly volatile Joey needed very little to send him off like a wobbly missile coming out of North Korea.

A solid and productive major leaguer, Belle, at 6 feet and 210 pounds (and nicknamed "Snapped" for his quick temper), was the first player to hit fifty home runs and fifty doubles in one season, a season shortened by a work stoppage. He once drove NBC reporter Hannah Storm from the Cleveland dugout with a tirade of profanities, and one Halloween night he used his truck to chase a bunch of kids who had egged his house, and actually hit one of them. Although no player said it to his face, many thought Joey was as corked as the bats he used.

In May of '91, Belle was coming off a stint in alcohol rehab, where he had changed his name from Joey back to Albert. New name, new purpose. He let everybody on the Cleveland Indians and the media covering them know that they were never again to call him Joey. Never.

First game back, Belle was warming up in the on-deck circle near the stands. That's when the fan in the front row not-so-innocently extended an invitation to the troubled slugger. As taunts go, it was a pretty good one: brief, detailed, and to the point.

"Keg party at my place, Joey."

Albert declined the offer by drilling the fan in the chest with a fastball. He was suspended for six games by the league, and the fan missed his own keg party.

TWELVE

Ask not for whom the bell tolls;
it tolls for thee, Zippy! Zippy? Wake up, Zippy!

For two months, Zippy Chippy practiced long and hard on breaking cleanly from a starting gate. He was inspired by three familiar and highly motivational words: "Run, Forrest, run!" The procedure was simple: three nervous horsemen, including Felix, would wrangle Zippy into his metal cubicle, then one would slam the bar down behind his butt and another would hit the bell. RINGGGGGGGG! Zippy broke free and clear every time. They repeated the routine until it started getting dark and everybody got tired and went home. Clearly a third dwell would not be tolerated by the track stewards at Finger Lakes. They had been embarrassed after the second fiasco in which Zippy was a non-starter; a third non-start would warrant most serious consequences.

When Felix was not working his horse, he was worrying about him. Constantly reminded by hecklers, the handlers, and the media of the looming distinction of eighty-five straight losses, Felix struggled to remain optimistic: "One of these days, he gonna snap out of it. He gonna win a race. You see."

When reminded that his horse was earning the nickname "Cellar Dweller," Felix begged to differ. The suggestion to change

Zippy's name to Bringing Up the Rear was entirely unhelpful. Felix was sticking to his story, which made Zippy look like a candidate for Mr. Congeniality. "It's not that he refuse to go," he said. "He just wants the other horses to go first, and he follow later."

Yeah, simple courtesy. Of all the things Zippy Chippy has been called – moody, stubborn, mischievous, cantankerous, skullduggerous, and three other things that require a "bleep" button – the word *courteous* has never been one of them. I mean, Zippy might bow and let another horse go ahead of him, but only so he could clip his hoof and trip him from behind.

While on his second "vacation," Zippy had a good rest, great food, and lots of attention from Marisa and the family. Mostly he would prowl the paddock with the other horses, talking mostly about the good ol' days before they were gelded. And Marisa – oh, how Zippy looked forward to her visits – would lock down the barn and play hide and seek with him. She knew the secret cubbyholes and passages. Zippy knew her scent; it was a pretty intense game, which she usually lost by a giggle.

After a few weeks, Zippy got bored. Felix would show up expecting to walk him but instead had to endure the sight of his horse going stir-crazy. Zippy would paw at the floor while neighing loudly, and then he'd haughtily thrust his nose in the air. His ears would twitch and his nostrils would flare. Zippy didn't want to walk. He wanted to race. Troubled, Zippy was snorting a lot and cocking his head, listening for the sounds of the track. Or maybe he smelled a chip wagon out on the highway or somebody eating a cupcake in the next county. Nobody knows for sure. But everybody agreed he was not happy killing time. *C'mon, let's get it started!*

"He just want to run. He want to compete again," claimed Felix.

So four days after his sixty-day ban was up, Felix and Zippy arrived early in the morning at the Finger Lakes track by truck and transport trailer. At two-thirty in the afternoon, Zippy would challenge eight other maidens over a distance of a mile and one-sixteenth on dirt. Felix took note of the race conditions: the sky was cloudy, the track was sloppy, and Zippy was unusually chippy. The distance was a bit of a long haul for a horse that hadn't raced in two months, but he appeared up to the challenge. In the barn he snapped at anybody who got near him, and in the paddock he sneered at the other horses. Those days of practicing at the starting gate had improved his break but not his tenor. The Zipster was in fighting form.

On this day, Tuesday, September 8, 1998, nervous tension suffused the atmosphere of the track, and you could feel it all the way up in the glass booth where anxious officials sat with binoculars on their desks. Zippy's new rider, Juan Rohena, must have been wondering, *Why me? Why must my name go into the record books alongside this guy?* Benny Afanador was riding Flavor o'th' Month instead of Zippy, the fans' flavor of the day. Zippy's former jockeys — Leslie Hulet, Pedro Castillo, and Jose Gutierrez — had wisely chosen other horses in this race.

Felix was confident there would be no car wreck today. He had pushed the possibility of the futility record out of his mind and instead convinced himself that this was Zippy's "must win" day. A win on this cool fall afternoon would solve an awful lot of problems. Immediately he'd get the stewards off his back. A victory meant Zippy could never have his name attached to the eighty-five-losses-in-a-row mark. And finally the horse would be the winner his true blue-capped companion always believed he could be.

"He look real good today," the trainer enthused. True enough, but nobody knew if Zippy's grumpy demeanor meant he'd challenge the others on the track for the prize of $11,200 or go after the purse of an old lady in a nearby strip mall.

Amateur bettors love sloppy tracks and long shots, and although Zippy should have been the unlikeliest shot on the board, particularly over a long and muddy mile race, as usual he went off as one of the favorites. Despite the lousy weather, Zippy's followers were out in force, but they remained strangely silent on this day. The consequence of a dwell weighed heavily on the crowd – from amateur punters to professional trainers and everybody in between. Zippy did not go easily or willingly into his number two post position, but then, he seldom did. Sister Kate was acting up as the horses entered the starting gate, but Glory a Go Go looked cool. Zippy's big butt was the last to disappear in the starting gate and – RINGGGGGGGG! – the bell went off a split second later. But when the track announcer yelled, "And they're off!", one of them clearly wasn't. The horse in the prime pole position of number two failed to leave the premises.

Despite Juan Rohena's best efforts, Zippy froze at the bell and hesitated before leaving the gate. Starting out a distant ninth, he held that final position over the long course that brought him past the grandstand twice, finally finishing last thirty-eight lengths behind the winner, Glory a Go Go. Benny Afandor and Flavor o'th' Month finished nineteen lengths ahead of him. Only the guy on the John Deere tractor who raked the track after the race hit the wire later than Zippy.

Leaving the gate last, Zippy had taken a leisurely lap around the dirt track. He had had enough time to rub his itchy nose on the near pole, stop to catch his breath at the half pole, and take a leak on the quarter pole before entering the stretch. Zippy had arrived at the finish line just as the track photographer was preparing to have his photo transferred to a milk carton.

With number one on his silks and at number one in the program, Zippy Chippy, number one in the hearts of the faithful at trackside, had come in a disappointing last by four yards more than a football field.

Zippy had dwelt at the Finger Lakes starting gate for his third and final time. Incompetence is tolerated at racetracks, which is why eight out of nine horses always manage to lose a race; failure to participate in a race in a meaningful way is not. Felix Monserrate's signature horse had hit this finish line for the final time, setting a Finger Lakes record of seventy losses without a win.

The track steward who would later ban Zippy from Finger Lakes pretty much called the race when he said, "He started way behind the field and finished way behind the field." You have to hope they don't carve those words into his headstone, but at that point in his career, it would have served as a pretty accurate epitaph.

Although the stewards had little choice but to ban a horse that refused to race, there was quite a split in the vote behind the scenes. Zippy, it seems, had become a sentimental favorite even in the hardened hearts of some track officials. Strict adherence to policy was not supposed to be deterred by sentimentality.

"It was for the public's protection," said the head steward. "If he's starting ten or fifteen lengths behind the field, that's not giving the bettors a fair shake." In the cruelest cut of all, he articulated Zippy's problem at the starting gate: "It wasn't that he was coming out slow – that's one thing. It's that he wasn't coming out at all!" As dwellers go, Zippy looked like he was trying to make a real estate offer on his starting gate cubicle in order to live there year round.

Despite his shortcomings, or more than likely because of them, the throng of people who had come out to see Zippy race that day was huge. Many in the crowd wore hats and T-shirts emblazoned with the Zippy Chippy logo. One woman wept openly when Zippy finally did amble across the finish line.

The ink was barely dry on the paperwork to officially abolish him from racing at Finger Lakes when all the big city newspapers in the Northeast waded into the fray. WAY OUT OF THE RUNNING! read the headline of the cover story in *USA Today*, with a photo of Zippy having Felix's trademark blue cap for lunch. ZIPPO FOR ZIPPY, bellowed the banner of the Syracuse *Post-Standard* over a photograph in which Felix appeared to be restraining Zippy in order to save the photographer's life. The Associated Press went with MAIDEN'S 85TH LOSS TIES MARK, while the *New York Times* topped their feature story ALL-TIME ALSO-RAN. The cutline "Horse goes for record in the futility stakes" appeared beneath a photograph of Zippy and Felix, side by side, calm, happy, and smiling. It was either a magical moment in professional sports or a world-class achievement in airbrushing.

Not only did Zippy hear the fat lady sing, but she had called him out on three straight strikes. The stewards' lifetime ban meant that Zippy would never again be allowed on the premises of Finger Lakes as a competitor.

The loss staggered Felix, forcing him to put on his bravest face ever. "I love him more because everybody puts him down," he said. Sadly, that was the best Zippy's loyal owner could muster as he got his horse settled in his stall with fresh water, a full feed bag, and a nose rub. Even the cockeyed optimist that Felix had become acknowledged that his old friend's career was probably at an end.

"He's happy. He's healthy. He will be my pet for the rest of his life," said the man who normally couldn't stop talking about his lovable, unlucky horse but on this day wandered off to a quiet corner of the barn. Zippy Chippy ended his career at Finger Lakes the same way he had started it at Belmont Park: many, many lengths behind non-winning maidens. Criticism of the horse and its owner came harsh and quick.

Said the same steward who voted to ban him: "They were throwing their money away. I'd look up at the board and there would be $20,000 bet on the horse. He was a cult figure, alright." But cult figures don't cut it in a world of rules and regulations. John Lennon and the status quo were longtime enemies. Ed Sullivan gave Elvis Presley's playful pelvis a rest. Zippy and conformity would never walk together, hoof in hand. RINGGGGGGGG! – that was their rule, not his. If he wanted to admire the crowd from the starting gate or play Simon Says with his jockey, then he would. He did. And now he had paid the ultimate price for individualism. Zippy Chippy was led out of stall seven and hustled out of barn twenty, never to return.

"That horse is just taking up space," said another steward. "You put a horse in the starting gate and he just stands there, and some-one in the stands is betting the rent, well, that's not too funny. A horse just can't waste the public's money like that."

Taking direct aim at Felix's proficiency as a trainer, Christopher Scherf of the Thoroughbred Racing Association said to a reporter, "There aren't a whole lot of horses who race past his age." He paused while the dart took flight, then continued, "The horse may be telling you something." He was right. The average racehorse retires at age five, after about fifteen starts. Zippy was now seven years old, with almost six times as many races.

Bob Matthews, a colorful syndicated columnist for Gannett newspapers, heartily disagreed with everybody and particu-larly with the decision to ban the horse. As a sportswriter with the Rochester *Democrat and Chronicle*, Bob was the scribe who started the fanfare that put thoroughbred racing's legendary dar-ling ne'er-do-well on America's radar. When Zippy went zero for sixty races, the writer with a keen eye for a great story and a blunt approach to putting it on paper made the horse known to America. Naturally, he liked Zippy Chippy; he just never bet on him. Red Smith, a colleague of Matthews' described Zippy's speed as "excellent for a mule and phenomenal for a fat man."

"They said he was a blight on bettors. Are you kidding me? He was a great help to bettors . . . all you had to do was eliminate him from the mix and your chances of winning with another horse improved immediately," claimed Matthews.

Ironically, by banning the horse who had become the track's star attraction, Finger Lakes officials were hurting themselves and cutting into their own pockets. On his final loss there, his eighty-fifth, Zippy went off at 7–2 on a tote board that should have had him at 30–1. Why? Because lots of people from all over America were betting on him, proudly showing their support for a fellow struggler. Some no doubt wanted to brag about owning a winning ticket on the biggest loser in racing history, but most bet on him because they truly hoped he would win. Through sympathy and souvenirs, Zippy Chippy had become a bona fide American celebrity and the darling of mainstream media as well.

Finger Lakes officials agreed that Zippy was certainly generating publicity for the racetrack, but in their opinion it was all bad. "The horse became a publicity item, sort of a joke," said one official. "I know Felix really likes the horse, but he should be a pet. I don't think he belongs on the racetrack."

"Not true," said Bob Matthews. "All that interest in Zippy was good. He brought a lot of people to the track in an industry that needs all the help it can get."

When one Finger Lakes official claimed that Zippy Chippy was making the track look "bush league," Bob's honesty got the best of him. "You *are* bush league!" said the sports commentator, who still hosts a talk show on Rochester's WHAM radio. "Have you looked around this place?" Had they a legal leg to stand on, it's likely the stewards would have banned Bob Matthews from their track along with Zippy Chippy.

What angered the sportswriter most about Zippy Chippy's lifetime banishment from Finger Lakes was the hypocrisy of a class-B track making such an A1 ruling. With the class thorough-breds running at Belmont, Aqueduct, and Saratoga Springs just down the New York State Thruway, Finger Lakes should have been focusing on fun. And who had more fun at a racetrack than Zippy Chippy, the "Frat House Flash"?

Now there were three infamous names at unlucky number eighty-five – Gussie Mae, Really a Tenor, and Zippy Chippy – all tied for the record for most consecutive losses in American thor-oughbred racing. The real problem was that, at about the same odds as winning Powerball, the other two longtime losers had each won their eighty-sixth race, thereby ending any possibility of stretching their dreaded streaks to eighty-six losses. For now, three shared the notorious title, but if Zippy Chippy incurred one more loss, he would have the dubious distinction of eighty-six losses in a row all to himself. The "Cellar Dweller" moniker was gathering traction.

At this unpromising moment, everybody, including family members, encouraged Felix to sell or retire the horse. At the very least, a second career was highly recommended. Turn him into a show horse, they said, or place him with a local riding stable. Really? A dancer, or a Sunday afternoon prancer? Can you imag-ine the number of pretty hats Zippy could eat at a horse show? Or the casualty list he could rack up by throwing city slickers off his back on a recreational riding trail? An even worse idea would be to convert Zippy Chippy to one of those "healing horses" that intui-tively interact with children suffering from grief or anxiety disor-ders. Just try and get your brain around that scenario: "Mommy! Mommy! Help! My head is stuck in the horsey's mouth!"

Although putting Zippy out to pasture made perfect sense to most people, Felix was not onside. "I don't care how old he is," he said. "He's trying and trying and trying, and that makes me happy. Plus, he love to run. Maybe not in every race, but still, he love to run." Felix was always on Zippy's side.

When asked if he would now sell the horse, Felix replied, "The horse is not happy with anyone else. If you go to his stall, he pins his ears back like he's going to attack you. But that's just an act. He's really just a puppy."

And Zippy? After he did a little dance around the backside of the barn to let everybody know he had run a great race, he tucked into a bag of his favorite snack, clover and alfalfa, and within thirty minutes of what his fans would call the worst — no, really, the very worst — race of his career, he was softly snoring himself into the deep sleep of an athlete who had left it all out there on the field.

And no, when you match an incredible record for consistent failure, the president of the United States does not phone you after the race. When you run that badly, you're lucky if the security guard lets you back into the barn without asking for ID.

Yet Zippy's entourage, who had lined the rail to wish him well and yell "Better luck next time," wanted to know just one thing: When could they see him run again?

YOU JUST KNOW WHEN
IT'S NOT YOUR DAY

You hear that a lot in sports — "It's not your day" — and Zippy Chippy heard it after every race for ten years, from Belmont Park to Northampton Fair and Finger Lakes in between.

Fifty years ago in baseball, the great Yankee broadcast duo of Mel Allen and Phil Rizzuto were nearly a perfect match. Considered to be one of the greatest voices to call a baseball game, Mel was calm, succinct, and dependable. Less so was Phil, or "the Scooter," talkative and famous for his unique digressions from the play-by-play. So the day Mel Allen played stand-up comedian was a real role reversal in their seven years of sharing the microphone.

During a game at Yankee Stadium, at a moment when dead air would have given radio listeners a quiet moment to reflect, Mel Allen was the one who wandered off into la-la land.

"You know, Scooter, I've been watching two teenagers exchanging kisses in the center-field bleachers."

"Really," replied Rizzuto, trying to sound enthusiastic.

"And what's interesting," said Allen, "is that he's kissing her on the strikes, and she's kissing him on the balls." To his credit — he was probably shocked into silence — Phil Rizzuto did not invoke his signature saying: "Holy cow, Mel!"

After a very long pause that allowed those who were listening at home with their kids to leave the room and laugh into pillows, Rizzuto said, "Mel, this is not your day."

On a hot day in July of 1997, Jesus Miranda was Zippy's jockey of record – and he lost. So yeah, when you lose a race with Jesus looking over your shoulder, that's how you know it ain't your day.

THIRTEEN

"Welcome to New Jersey — now go home": Often passed off as the state motto and printed on T-shirts designed for Guidos and Guidettes.

From *"New Jersey, the Attitude Capital of America"*

T he answer to the question of when and where his fans could see Zippy run again was March 22, 2000, at Garden State Park in New Jersey. In its heyday, "the Garden" was a beautiful track with a dramatic three-sectioned, iron front gate. Around the entrance loomed the gatehouse and, beyond that, the Georgian-style grandstand — both made of wood, since the 1940s war effort had commandeered America's steel.

Cold but bright, this was the first day of spring — the vernal equinox, when the sun crosses the celestial equator and hope springs eternal. Felix had moved his horse to this venerable track near Cherry Hill in January, thinking that if they were successful, this might be Zippy's home for a while. Exiled from the track at Finger Lakes, Zippy had spent the last fifteen months on the Monserrate farm, keeping fit and giving the family fits. That balance between running like a racehorse and living like a rogue had become Zippy's trademark.

Rarin' to go, he spent the morning in his stall kicking the wall for something to do and occasionally scaring the hell out of passers-by on shed row. Just getting back into the swing of things, is all.

"He been runnin' good and practicing very well," Felix shouted above the banging noise in the background. Assessing the situation, he latched and locked up Zippy's stall, hoping the horse would calm down in the dark. Now nine years old and still without reproductive hardware, Zippy was in his prime. At least, that's how his growing retinue of regular followers felt, many having traveled to New Jersey from track towns in the Northeast, including some from Finger Lakes. The thinking was that as long as Zippy was game to go, they didn't mind the drive. He wasn't just with them in spirit; they were also wearing his brand. Zippy wore leather, and his fan base wore "Zippy Chippy tacky" – colorful caps and T-shirts that carried his name and a cartoon likeness of him. One popular shirt read, You'll always be a winner with us, Zippy!

While his horse was slowly demolishing his stall, Felix was reading an oversized Hallmark card from the New Jersey contingent of Zippy Chippy's rapidly expanding fan club. His banishment had actually brought more sympathizers into his hallowed corner.

"We brought Zippy this card to try and encourage him and tell him we love him," said Judy Nason, of nearby Hamilton Township. The card was signed and inscribed by twenty members of the horse's faithful following. A woman named Elizabeth wrote, "The key to a true winner is that you keep on trying." David added, "Keep trying. God knows there are millions of us who relate to your struggles." Hearing Zippy behind him, head butting the stall door, Felix was almost brought to tears by the card.

The unswerving fortitude of a horse that keeps on going after so many disappointments had become an ongoing source of endearment for many who themselves had been smacked down in life. People responded to "the Zippy horse" with instinctive sympathy and raw emotion. It was the same feeling you get watching a border collie hopelessly trying to herd his flock of sheep as they wreak havoc on a downtown street, or a goose trying desperately to get all her goslings to cross the busy highway. Sure, they're making a mess of things, but God knows their hearts are in the right place – and above all, they're trying to do the right thing.

Zippy's disastrous record did nothing to dampen his go-get-'em spirit. The losses may have tarnished his résumé, but they could not blunt his ambition. Those three straight dwells might have cost him his career, New York–style, but nothing could curb his love of life and racing. It didn't matter where he and his owner went; a track was a track and Zippy was ready to race.

Buoyed by his loyal supporters, Zippy Chippy was stoked and all saddled up and circling the paddock at Garden State, waiting for the bugler to deliver the call to post. But the horn would not be heard on cue today, as the men in suits rushed down from their lofty lairs above the grandstand to stop the proceedings. Postponing a race is something that is seldom done. Tracks work like clockwork; the timing may seem casual to an observer, but it is exacting to the masters of the meet. The officials had stopped the show to have a serious word with Felix. They sensed a potential scandal brewing, one that tracks everywhere try very hard to avoid.

Although the trainer assured them his horse was good to go, cleared by the vet and all, the officials of this rundown track that was a year away from the wrecking ball strongly disagreed. Only minutes before Zippy was to be led out onto the red, raked oval for the colorful post parade, a telephone call had come in from Finger Lakes. Racetrack starters share information, and this was kind of a courtesy call: "You might have a problem on your hands!"

The fastidious Finger Lakes starter, noting the banned horse's name in the Garden's program, had dropped the dime on Zippy. The Garden State head steward authorized a very late scratch, and Zippy Chippy was done for the day – actually, this and every other day, as long as he was in New Jersey.

Garden State spokesman Ed Vomacka confirmed that Zippy had been disqualified because his name appeared on a list of ineligible thoroughbreds at Finger Lakes. Incredible but true – the horse had been turfed out before he hit the dirt. Zippy Chippy may have been the only thoroughbred in history to lose a race before he even got to the starting gate.

Felix was livid, incorporating a lot more Spanish and a few more expletives into his language than usual. He claimed it was a state ban, lawful only in New York. It wasn't. Zippy had been barred from racing in New York State and any other American or Canadian track that chose to honor the banishment. Almost all would. Felix could protest all he wanted, but the track officials dictated that his horse needed to get undressed and leave the Cherry Hill premises in a timely fashion. It's safe to say that Zippy Chippy did nothing in a timely fashion except eat, so his departure from the barn took longer than they would have liked. As he was led back to his stall, he was particularly peeved, because normally he liked to get a little exercise before he returned to the barn for his victory dance. Nobody was happy about Zippy being scratched, except maybe the jockey who didn't have to ride him. When Zippy was in a bad mood, riding him was like trying to stay aboard a mechanical bull during erratic electrical surges.

Felix in dirty denim had been confronted by well-dressed men his whole career – from the cheap suits of track stewards to the expensive wear of wealthy owners. Never far from his mind or beyond his bashful smile was the old English saying: "On the turf or under it, all men are equal."

While loading up for home, Felix walked past Zippy's stall with an armful of equipment, and the horse took a run at him.

A sportswriter unfamiliar with their relationship said the horse's head came over the gate with "the quickness of a cobra." Equally eye-opening to the reporter was the fact that Felix avoided the attack "with the efficiency of someone completely at ease with such defensive maneuvers."

Needing to explain the backside skirmish to an unfamiliar press, Felix said, "He's mean, but in a nice way. You know those wrestlers who talk mean but it's really nothing? I put him in that category. It's just an act."

One confused horse and one pissed-off owner boarded the Zippy Chippy tandem truck and trailer for the drive back to Farmington, New York. Once on the road, Felix was able to see the bright side of the New Jersey fiasco: Zippy's official record had not gotten any worse. Little consolation, but as they got closer to home, more and more drivers honked and waved at Felix when they passed his vehicle, spotting the Zippy Chippy logo on the driver's-side door.

One year later, Garden State Park was completely demolished, leveled to the ground, with only its iconic wrought-iron gates still standing. I know what you're thinking, but no, Zippy was not involved, although he did his best to start the process in the barn the day they wouldn't let him run.

Once a classy racetrack, today Garden State is just another North American mall with a mixed-use town center housing shops, restaurants, and condominiums. There's no pink hotel, but there are boutiques and swinging hot spots, so yeah, they paved paradise to put up a parking lot. Instead of a statue of the speedy Spend a Buck, who captured the 1985 Kentucky Derby with a courageous wire-to-wire victory . . . now they have Bed Bath & Beyond.

And the first day of spring, the vernal equinox? It is indeed the symbol of eternal hope — and also lost causes.

NOBODY LIKES TO
BE TRICKED

Walking up the ramp and into his traveling trailer for the long ride home after several months of waiting to race and then being told he couldn't, Zippy Chippy must have felt like he'd been tricked. Given the shaft, as it were, like South African golfer Bobby Cole was while playing a practice round for the 1967 Masters against the legendary Sam Snead. The seasoned veteran loved to bet as much as he loved to win, especially against the younger players on tour.

On the tee of Augusta's thirteenth hole, a dogleg left par five guarded by very tall pine trees, the fifty-five-year-old with "the sweetest swing in golf" hit the ball a couple hundred yards into the clearing where he'd have an easy second shot up the fairway toward the unseen green. "Slammin' Sam" did it just the way it's supposed to be done, including his trademark fade at the end.

The twenty-year-old Cole was pulling out a low iron to match his opponent's shot when Snead said, "You know, Bobby, when I was your age I could hit the ball right over those trees at the corner."

It was a double dogleg dare and the rookie took the bait. Bristling, the well-built young man pulled out his driver and strode to the tee, where he verily crushed the ball. Like a little white laser, his golf ball made a high arc, towering into the tops of the trees, where it knocked around a bit and then dropped into a bed of pine needles below. From there it would take at least two more shots to come even with the master's tee shot.

Cole was still eyeing Snead suspiciously as they walked off the tee and down the fairway. Then Snead smiled at him, winked, and said, "Of course, when I was your age, Bobby, those trees were only ten feet high." And Slammin' Sam, spry and sly as ever, went on to collect the ten-dollar bet.

FOURTEEN

The senator has got to understand . . . he can't have it both ways.
He can't take the high horse and then claim the low road.
President George W. Bush, admonishing Senator John McCain
while savaging the English language

With the word out that Zippy Chippy was a high-risk performer, it's likely all Massachusetts racetracks would have followed New Jersey's lead. However, Three County Fair in Northampton was not a racetrack, per se. It's . . . a county fairground. And not just any fair — America's oldest agricultural fair, shearing sheep and tossing cow patties with distinction since 1818. Besides the tractor pull and the demolition derby, beyond the tilt-a-whirl and the stuffed toy shooting gallery was Northampton Fair, a thoroughbred track that ran for ten days every year, starting Labor Day weekend and attracting quite a variety of contestants, some of whom had rarely (or never) won a race and were one step away from becoming a ride for children or from joining a police force. Some horses had been winners at bigger tracks but were now on the downside of their careers.

Beginning in the mid-1800s, fairgrounds were once a rip-roaring piece of Americana and, all over the United States, offered a crude form of horse racing for $50 purses or sides of beef or jugs of cider. Some tracks were narrow, limiting the size of the gate and, therefore, the number of horses allowed in a race. At Marshfield the horses had to run under the seats of the ferris wheel as it rotated overhead. All fairground tracks were small and referred to as "bullrings" for their tight turns. Bubba Wilson, a leading rider, recalls the routine: "Turn hard left at the French fry stand. Then hard left again where they sell funnel cakes. Takes nerve, I tell you."

In the fifties and sixties these Massachusetts fun tracks hit their peak of popularity. "Purses weren't much, but motel rooms cost $3.50 a night and beer was a dime," recalls Carlos Figueroa. As an owner and trainer, Figueroa won five races in eight days with the same horse in 1963, which warranted a visit by the SPCA. "I told them I run Shannon's Hope short distances, six and a half furlongs, no farther," he said. "This Paul Revere, he's a hero in Massachusetts but he ran his horse twenty-six miles in one night." Just the sort of marvelous, offbeat character you meet at a racetrack, Figueroa became known as "King of the Fairs."

As track ratings go – "A" for Aqueduct and "B" for Finger Lakes – the old Massachusetts fairgrounds circuit gets a "C" for chicanery. Though the racing was hugely popular back then, bettors did not much appreciate the Massachusetts circuit's lapses into unrehearsed comedy, like jockeys jumping off horses that were leading but not supposed to win the race; like a long shot bet down to even odds just minutes before a race and winning by a dozen lengths; like the track steward who read the riot act to eight jockeys that whoever was carrying a "buzzer," an illegal electric shocker, better toss it before the race started or there would be hell to pay. After the race the steward went to the starting gate area where he found not one but eight buzzers.

In the early 1970s a welcome crackdown by state police brought integrity back to the fairgrounds circuit and it flourished.

Good local horsemen took pride in presenting their best horses at Northampton, and even Kentuckian Dale Baird, the greatest trainer of all time with 9,445 wins, brought his brood to the oval in Pioneer Valley, Hampshire County.

The Great Barrington Fair track closed in 1983, leaving the Northampton half-mile oval the last fair still operating in Massachusetts. In the eighties, before the casinos opened in nearby Connecticut and the state lottery began offering scratch tickets, Northampton recorded huge handles.

In one day, Labor Day 1989, bettors laid down $893,000. Tom Creel, Racing Secretary, said, "We have fun here. We give the cheap horses a chance. Zippy Chippy deserves a chance." Not exactly a resounding endorsement by racing's head honcho, but hey, it's better than New Jersey. "Anything's better than New Jersey" became the mantra of Zippy's handlers after the Garden State Park debacle. It was easy to understand why Felix Monserrate was now referring to New Jersey as "The Bad Apple."

Competing for the crowd's interest and cash at the Three County Fair were the pigs with numbers on their backs that raced on a nearby smaller track. Pig jockeys were not allowed to be any taller than that guy on TV who used to yell: "The plane, boss! The plane!"

It was with great trepidation that Felix entered his horse in race number eighty-six at this track in western Massachusetts. At eighty-five losses and sharing the record with two other horses, at least the shame was split three ways. The odds on both Gussie Mae and Really a Tenor both winning their eighty-sixth races were phenomenal, but they did. The odds on Zippy Chippy, a horse that had lost at ten different racetracks and come dead last fourteen times, winning his eighty-sixth race were astronomical. You had a better chance at getting Betty White to pole dance on "Old Farts Night" at the American Legion, in Fredonia, New York. Not impossible odds, mind you, but long. Really long.

But did the September 5, 1999, tote board at Northampton Fair show Zippy going off at 100–1, a number that would reflect reality? No. First of all, the highest possible odds against a horse winning are 99–1, and secondly, the faithful had crossed state lines. The horse's dutiful disciples had come here to the "Baked Bean State" wearing Zippy Chippy memorabilia, taking photos, and offering him good luck charms. By race time, they had elevated him to the favorite.

Earlier in the day Felix had led his horse and his jockey onto the track where the official starter was certifying gate tickets for horses who had not raced in the last six months. It may have been standard procedure, but it wasn't until the buzzer rang and Zippy with Clemente Crispin aboard bolted clear of the machine, that Felix began to breathe again.

On this cloudy but warm fall afternoon, Zippy proved to be a "gamer." From the gate's sixth post, Zippy challenged Haylee's Halo for the lead before settling in at third place for the second half of the circuit, a position he gamely held until the wire. The footnotes told the real story: "Zippy Chippy dueled for the lead on the outside, steadied between horses on the second turn, bore out on all three turns and tired on the third turn." Zippy, it seems, always preferred the road less traveled, and the wider and longer one as well. Taking such a circuitous route may have been hereditary. Zippy's great-great-grandfather Native Dancer, easily one of the top ten thoroughbreds of the twentieth century, won almost every great race he entered (twenty-one of twenty-two), the exception being the Kentucky Derby. During that race in 1953, after being bumped twice in that Kentucky classic, jockey Eric Guerin seemed to be fleeing from danger when he led

Native Dancer on a wild chase that ended with the horse losing in a photo finish. One commenter at the time said that Guerin "took that colt everywhere on the track except the ladies' room."

Given the grand tour Zippy took, finishing third was flattering.

On his back was yet another new jockey, Clemente Crispin, the twenty-sixth rider of his career. Zippy went through jockeys the way other horses wore out their shoes. And as if the horse needed any more pressure, he had a $4,000 claiming price on him. Felix knew how badly Zippy needed a win to end the cursed streak, and the claiming race offered easier competition.

Zippy managed to end up in the money, and, most importantly, after the race the stewards did not have to go looking for him in the starting gate. He won $250, enough to cover the gas money for the return trip home to Farmington. They say it's lonely at the top, but the bottom can't be much of a prize when you're nothing for eighty-six. Once the results were posted, all three horses who finished behind him committed suicide.

Felix was discouraged but stuck by Zippy with the same blind faith and innate stubbornness for which the horse himself was famous. After Zippy lost his eighty-sixth race and became the sole holder of the most fruitless record in racehorse history, you could hardly expect Felix to be effusive in praise of his enigmatic gelding. I mean, this is the horse that would spin out on the turns or bite another horse near the finish line or go over and visit some diminutive relatives at the Pony Rides or try to snag a hot dog from a dozy kid on the merry-go-round, and what did Felix have to say? "If this horse wanna run, he run. He give you the best he got. But he don't wanna run all the time." And really, who does? It's tiring and it can get you down, especially if you're looking at nothing but big, sweaty butts all the time.

Confidentially, Felix was flat-out relieved. His horse had finally broken from the gate and had had a good trip around the track — and, above all, he had not been claimed. For the marked-down price of $4,000, somebody, anybody, could have bought the now quite popular Zippy Chippy on a whim or a bar bet or just for a laugh. Having dodged that bullet, Felix vowed never to enter Zippy in a claiming race again.

Now that Zippy Chippy alone held the record for consecutive losses, Felix had little to lose by continuing to race him. Any thoughts Felix had about hanging up Zippy's halter were trumped by a gush of glory from the unlikely source of *People* magazine. In the May 8, 2000, issue featuring Julia Roberts's smile on the cover, Zippy was profiled in an appropriate section slugged "also-ran." The magazine described Zippy's pedigree as "bluegrass blue blood." Felix, who had been broadsided by Zippy that morning, characterized his horse as "meaner than an outhouse rat," while Zippy just wished with all his heart that magazines were printed on pancakes instead of paper. A year later, at the same Northampton Fair fall meet, Zippy was back for what proved to be his best race ever, in front of an overflowing crowd that was almost exclusively there to watch him. September 1, 2000, was a brand-new day for Zippy Chippy.

Covering the event for the *Daily Hampshire Gazette*, Scott Cacciola was impressed by how Zippy "paced serenely around the stable . . . hardly [giving] a glance of recognition to the dozens of media types that had gathered around his stall." As the horses lined up behind the starting gate for this five-furlong maiden match, Zippy could hardly ignore the presence of his fans. "The name Zippy Chippy seemed to emanate from the grandstand like a mantra," wrote Cacciola.

Oh, how Zippy loved an audience. Watching him in the barn, Andy Walter, also of the *Gazette*, observed: "He had dancing feet, and he would sometimes swing a wider arc to impel human bystanders to move out of the way." Following the horse outside, Walter added: "The show really began when Zippy cantered out onto the track. With jockey Juan Rohena onboard, he walked the length of the homestretch, then turned around when he reached the end of the stands. Zippy began kicking his hind legs out and to the right, higher and higher, as the laughter of the crowd grew. Zippy, it seems, has a sense of humor, or a Type A personality."

Out of the gate lickety-split, Zippy took the lead and never looked back. He dispatched no less than three horses – Carousing, Riches Rocket, and Black Rifle – to take the all-out lead. Out front by six lengths, Zippy was not so much running on a dirt track as swimming in unchartered waters. At the far pole he had Black Rifle by a head, and with great resolve and confident strides he held that two-foot lead all the way into the stretch. That's where things got rough.

Into the stretch Black Rifle's bumping became so bad that Rohena held Zippy back a bit. The Zipster strained hard on the reins and recovered enough ground to keep pace with his brawling adversary. As the two drew up head and head in front of the grandstand, Zippy was fighting off a belligerent Black Rifle, who was getting way too close and ramming him as they sped toward the wire.

The crowd went wild. A loud roar erupted from beyond the fence, the punters screamed and whistled, and the faithful waved their winning tickets as Zippy Chippy now led a field of seven horses down the dusty chute. Normally, leading a race, Zippy would be nodding to his closest rival that it was safe to pass on the right. Not today. Today Zippy was in the zone. Today Black Rifle would need the greatest race of his dismal career to beat him. So far, in six outings, Black Rifle had never finished better than sixth.

Calling this classic duel, the track announcer could barely believe his own words: "And here they come . . . Zippy Chippy and Black Rifle, it's Black Rifle and Zippy Chippy . . . it's Zippy Chippy and Black Rifle . . . and at the wire it's Black Rifle by a neck!" After the initial sounds of anguish, the track went silent. It quickly became clear to all in attendance, including Felix Monserrate, that Zippy Chippy had very nearly won a race. It was so quiet, as the Texas playwright Horton Foote would say, that you could hear an ant piss on a pillow.

Juan Rohena and Zippy Chippy had been banged around by Black Rifle's wiry and wily Frank Amonte Sr., who even at the age of sixty-three still liked to ride rough. Furious, Rohena immediately lodged a claim of foul with the Northampton stewards, alleging interference in the stretch. Chaos erupted on the track. Rohena was standing in the saddle, screaming at the officials up in the booth, while Felix was grabbing the jockey by the leg, yelling, "No, no, no – I don't want him to win like that. Not on a protest!" Ten very tense minutes passed while the inquiry sign flashed on the board and the stewards screened the tape. Badly needed comic relief was provided by Carousing, who had thrown his rider, Bubba Wilson, and was now enjoying being chased around the track by the outrider. Zippy Chippy and Black Rifle circled in front of the grandstand while their riders eyed each other contemptuously, with Rohena still jabbering at a silent Amonte.

Both jockey and trainer knew Zippy had won the race, fair and square. What would Felix do if the stewards allowed the complaint to stand, dropping Black Rifle to second and elevating Zippy Chippy to first place? Not wanting to win on a technicality, would Felix then protest the protest?

None of it mattered in the end as the stewards dismissed the official complaint, as they most often do. The track record's footnote read simply, "Just missed." The results, the controversy, the dubious record might best be described by the name of the horse that finished third: Judge Not.

Oh why, oh why couldn't the race have been four and a half furlongs instead of five? Why couldn't Zippy have leaned in a little at the finish line? Why didn't Rohena give his horse a sharp clip with the crop coming up to the wire? Why couldn't Black Rifle have arrived at the track constipated that day? So close, and yet . . . Zippy Chippy was once again best man to yet another groom, Black Rifle, who today stood tall at the altar. With this, the first victory of his career, which would end sixteen days later at the same track when he was retired after no one claimed him, Black Rifle became the third thoroughbred to win only one race in his lifetime, and it happened to be against Zippy Chippy. The Zipster's losing was a curse that bordered on a conspiracy.

"Next time lucky," his followers repeated as they lined the fence and surrounded the paddock to congratulate him. "He's got heart," said fan Marie Klebart, who had driven up from South Windsor, Connecticut, to see her favorite horse. Amazing many onlookers, Zippy had pulled a "Mitt" – as in Romney. With no business being in the race, he actually made it exciting and oh-so-close. Zippy had lost, but only by that big, hard, mule-like head. In doing so, he earned $510, which would cover not only the gas but the snacks and tolls on the trip along the New York State Thruway.

A loser by a neck, Zippy Chippy had run a bold and gritty race, his closest brush with victory ever and, sadly, his eighty-seventh consecutive loss. Meanwhile, the horse's exploits were being heralded internationally as no less than twenty-five million copies of *Guinness World Records* hit the bookstores, announcing, tersely and factually, "The most consecutive losses by a racehorse is 87, by Zippy Chippy . . ."

One person not lining up to buy a copy was the tireless trainer who loved the sport and the excitement it brought to his otherwise quiet existence. Having guided Carrie's Turn to eight victories in a short period of time, including the Finger Lakes Stakes, Felix had been to the winner's circle, even if Zippy had not. Yet when the yelling stopped and things calmed down, it was clear that Felix had more fun losing with Zippy Chippy than he had ever had winning with Carrie's Turn.

Naturally, Felix was impressed and inspired by Zippy's valiant performance. "I'm proud that he gave me a good race today. Second is good," he said, beaming. It still wasn't champagne, but those first cold beers tasted especially good to the two of them that day.

It was becoming increasingly clear that as a trainer, Felix Monserrate's level of excellence was definitely not that of a New York Yankees manager or even the assistant manager of a Jiffy Lube, but he and Zippy were in the thick of it again, and the world of horse racing was watching. Scrappers both, they had gone to war many times — sixty-seven times as a team — and they had come out the other end, alive and ready to re-enlist. After the Black Rifle brawl, the dream of winning had been reignited in the mind of the owner and in the hearts of tens of thousands of the horse's fans. Knock, knock, knockin' on the door of victory were horse and owner together.

Nipped at the wire and with a third-place finish before that, Zippy was on a roll again. After his best effort ever, he had this blissful faraway look in his eyes, a kind of dazed gaze of disbelief. Excited but confused, he seemed to be asking those around him in Barn M, *Where am I and what just happened?* Zippy had that once-in-a-lifetime look – the "Bronko Look."

ZIPPY'S
BRONKO LOOK

There were bad days, when the starting bell freaked him out or the watering truck nearly backed over him or a Latino hot-walker called him "Zippy Nova," which sounds like the name of a shooting star but actually means "Zippy Doesn't Go!" There was a long list of things that pissed this horse off, and he must have been constantly thinking, *What the hell's going on here, anyway? I try and I try but the world just won't cooperate!* Emily Schoeneman later recalled the times when Zippy got "the look": "He'd be standing quietly in his stall, and his eyes would glaze over and look skyward. His head would be tilted up and to one side in a pondering pose, and it seemed he was looking at something nobody else could see."

A facial expression set somewhere between sudden curiosity and an altered state of amazement, the "Bronko Look" comes not from a bucking bronco but from a football player.

Bronko Nagurski, the toughest payer in the NFL in the thirties was a great fullback and lineman for the Chicago Bears. Head down and running like a freight train, he once carried the ball through an entire team, stopping only when he hit a concrete wall. Legend has it that when he got to his feet he told a teammate: "That last guy hit me awful hard." Tenacious and fearless, born in Rainy River, Ontario, to Ukrainian parents, Bronko played hard and partied harder. After a big win at a Bears victory celebration, Bronko had a tad too much to drink and fell out of a window at the bar where the team was celebrating, landing one story down and out cold on the sidewalk.

When he finally came to, there was a cop standing over him.

"What the hell happened here?" asked the cop.

With that look of calm and utter bewilderment, Bronko replied, "I dunno. I just got here myself."

Zippy would often get that look that Bronko Nagurski perfected. At night, deer staring down cars on highways also have that look.

FIFTEEN

If a man does not keep pace with his companions,
perhaps it is because he hears a different drummer.
Let him step to the music which he hears . . .

Henry David Thoreau

On September 16, 2000, one year after Black Rifle ruined everybody's day, Zippy Chippy went off at the Northampton Fair as the 2–1 favorite. His longtime fans were now pinching themselves and thinking, *Good lord, this horse just might win a race!* Having seen it all before, Juan Rohena was not so quick to jump on that bandwagon.

From the number eight post, farthest from the rail, Zippy broke best and shot to the lead. He led the six-and-a-half-furlong race at the three-quarter pole by a head over Sadler's Critic. At the half pole he surrendered to Sadler's Critic by two lengths but roared back strong as the two leaders entered the stretch. Neck and neck, stride for stride, they battled for home. As Zippy moved up to recover the lead, Sadler's Critic made a bold move to go inside, allowing Miner's Claim to come up suddenly and fast on the outside of both of them. Sadler's Critic pulled slightly ahead as Samjackie confronted Zippy for second place. Zippy typically chose to go wide where there was less traffic, but of course this meant more ground to cover. Tired, he faded as his two challengers drove hard to hit the finish line, coming in third behind them. Zippy had again been beaten by two horses who themselves had never known victory.

Yet a second-place finish followed by a third was nothing short of a vast improvement for a horse that used to mistake the starting gate for a Comfort Inn. The Zipster was making people forget all about those record-setting losers Gussie Mae and Really a Tenor. Zero for eighty-eight starts, he alone was daring to go new distances, while others had fallen by the wayside.

There was a weird kind of upside-down, favorable rating index happening here. Although Zippy was still losing, finishing two for two in the money was quite remarkable, as attested by the large crowds and increased press coverage. It was like when Toronto mayor Rob Ford admitted smoking crack and binge drinking: after his confession, his popularity rating shot up six points in the polls. If your support base is enamored by you and also somewhat loony, then anything is possible.

Doing a victory jig for his adoring followers, Zippy was on a holy tear, which brought a proud smile to Felix's face and prompted him to pay his big four-footed friend the highest of compliments: "He been losin' real close lately."

With his fate sealed at eighty-eight starts and his record losing streak confirmed by *Guinness World Records*, Zippy had earned a nice and comfortable retirement, and now was probably the time. With winter approaching and Zippy coming up to his tenth birthday in the spring, Felix shut him down.

After all, he wasn't the losingest horse in the whole world. An English steeplechaser by the name of Quixall Crossett had, at this point, lost 98 races in a row and would go on to lose 103 races in an eleven-year career. And here's the kicker: Quixall Crossett was a jump horse. On most jump courses, horses have to clear twenty low, hedged fences. Neither Deep Blue, once the world's most powerful computer, nor the fanciful mind of Felix Monserrate could ever imagine Zippy Chippy racing on a track where hedges are used as hurdles. In no time at all, Zippy's jockeys would be known as "hedge hogs." That would be just cruel. Quixall Crossett once lost a three-and-one-eighth-mile race by an astonishing one hundred lengths, something Zippy Chippy could never manage . . . mainly because American tracks are so much shorter.

At fifty-seven years of age and battered by setbacks, Felix was getting tired. He and his horse were starting to feel their ages. Yeah, he should probably put his buddy out to pasture at the farm. Still, there were all those adoring fans, thousands and thousands of them.

Then, at the end of 2000, just as Felix was warming up to the idea of retirement, *People* magazine did a follow-up article on Zippy, reporting that his "perfect track record remains unblemished." Zippy didn't quite make it onto that issue's list of the twenty-five most intriguing people of the year, which included Michael J. Fox, Hillary Clinton, George W. Bush, Tiger Woods, and The Rock, he of the overarching eyebrow. Fittingly, Zippy came well back in the field of celebrities, a place where he was quite comfortable.

Having just signed a contract with the Texas Rangers that would assure him $25 million a year for ten years, Alex Rodriguez was a featured celebrity that year. Home from the 2000 Summer Olympics in Sydney, Australia, with five gold medals around her neck, Marion Jones was covered in the same issue. Am I the only one who sees the inquiry sign flashing with great urgency here? Imagine a celebrity match in which both "A-Rod" and Jones, subsequently disgraced for using performance-enhancing drugs, fade in the stretch as Zippy Chippy, the honest warrior, rushes up between the two cheaters to win the Trustworthy Stakes and the top spot on the cover of *People* magazine. Ah, life: so unfair and yet . . . yeah, so unfair.

The magazine people showed up at the family farm with a huge tortoise for the highly hokey photo shoot. "That thing was huge," Marisa said later. "You could almost ride it!" Under a photo of Zippy nudging the terrified turtle, the caption read, "On his home turf, Zippy Chippy noses out the competition." In the photo, the turtle looks like he's about to abandon his shell and make a run for it. Zippy looks like he's been tricked. *How can I eat this thing with all that armor?*

The article made reference to a previous edition of *People* that had tagged Zippy as "the losingest horse in racing history." Felix shrugged it off. "Every time he runs, he comes back happy. I don't get disappointed, no matter what." Emily, who loves horses more than humans, locked herself in the house for the afternoon of the shoot. Forced to pose next to a stupid, land-dwelling reptile, Zippy wished he was with her. And yet, for the growing legions of people who related to Zippy on a very basic level – you lose, we lose, life is tough, and you do not suffer alone in this world – the magazine had nailed it. One fascinating personality was he, the Zipster.

He had been singled out by *People* magazine for his one undeniable gift: consistency. From paddock to gate, gate to wire, and finish line to backside, Zippy's behavior was solid. Before every race he would fidget nervously and bob his head vigorously in the paddock as Felix gave him instructions for the impending test. He would neigh and nod as if he knew exactly what was expected of him. And he did know, because despite all their squabbles and disappointments, these two guys understood each other. *I get it, Felix. Start strong, keep pace, drive hard for home.* Then the bugle would sound, but Zippy wouldn't hear it because from another area of the barn, from another part of the brain, he would hear Frank Sinatra singing, "I did it my way."

So it wasn't Zippy's fault, it was Frank Sinatra's fault. No, it was Henry David Thoreau's fault for telling everybody they should listen to some far-off drummer instead of the manager, and that it was okay for everybody to pass you by like they were on a subway train and you were taking a leak up against a building, which they used to do in New York City before the Big Cleanup. Thoreau encouraged everybody to go sit quietly by a pond for hours at a time and gaze at their navels, which is really, really difficult to do if you're a horse.

By the time Zippy reached the track, all his brain power had been reduced to a really shrill Steven Tyler scream, and he was trying to remember whether Felix had locked the barn door before or after he got out, and . . . then he'd say to himself, *Just stop. Right now. Focus.* And then that goddamn bell would go off, and Zippy would stay calm by staying put in order to assess the situation, which cost him a lot of time and earned him a lifetime ban from most American racetracks. So, you see, this horse just could not win for trying.

It was not easy for Marisa to watch her father throwing his hands up at the finish line, cursing under his breath and watching the pride of his stable galloping down the dirt track, struggling to find another way to lose.

Felix had spent too many afternoons watching the horse he loved like family not keeping pace with his companions, time after time after time. But Felix could always find goodness in a failed performance by Zippy, and after he had bandaged his routine bite marks, he would tell the horse that everything was okay, that there was always next year, that eighty-nine would be the charm, even though everybody knows eighty-nine is a number just itching to turn ninety.

And that was their life – a numbers game played by Zippy the independent and Felix the codependent. It was an odd and awkward relationship – Zippy and Felix, Felix and Oscar, Oscar the Grouch and Elmo. Slowly but surely they had adapted to each other, and now it was love on another level – okay, a lower level, but love all the same.

They were less like an old married couple, the kind you see sitting in restaurants not talking to each other, and more like a couple of army buddies who had fought in the trenches of a war that was not over. Yet losing the battles did not stifle their spirits, and they celebrated small victories together: a second here, a third there, a couple of cold beers each in the quiet of the shed row at the end of a long day. They had accepted each other and their predicament. They mellowed. Their constant bickering turned to laughter, because really, what else can you do but laugh at the ridiculous? And from there on, life was easier for both of them. Now, way too late to separate, Felix and Zippy were staying together for the family and the memories and the records, such as they were. The horse was still an athlete, the man was still a trainer; both were still players in the only game they knew and loved – horse racing.

So with few prospects and less hope than an airline pilot attempting a safe landing after a Canadian goose strike over the Hudson River, Zippy and Felix plodded on together, and life got better for them both. Stubbornness and perseverance have their rewards. The trick was to harmonize these two strong traits against the competition, not use them against each other. One day Zippy and Felix would take a day off and go to the ballpark together, and there would be fun in their lives once again.

HORSES JUST
WANNA HAVE FUN

I was fifteen years old in the fall of 1961, and although I had only a vague notion of a racetrack being located at nearby Fort Erie, Ontario, I certainly had heard of Puss n Boots. He was the horse famous for going for a swim in the middle of a thoroughbred race.

Trained by the great horseman Frank Merrill, Puss n Boots was brought to Fort Erie from Gulfstream Park in Florida, where he had earned the reputation of a promising sprinter but a bit of a nutter. During one outing a piece of paper flying around the Florida track had sent him into a tailspin, and he almost jumped the rail to get away from it. Brown, hard-nosed, and nondescript, Puss n Boots looked a lot like Zippy Chippy.

It was a hot September afternoon at Fort Erie, a beautiful track naturally appointed with shimmering infield lakes, well-trimmed shrubs, and flowers in full bloom. Puss n Boots was leading by five lengths at the top of the stretch on the mile-and-one-sixteenth turf course when the jockey's right-handed whip to his bum set him off. Apparently he was fine with a slap on his left cheek, but never the right one. Either Merrill hadn't told the jockey about this particular quirk, or the rider just forgot.

Whacked and wanting to flee the track, the horse spotted a narrow opening in the hedge, which was used mainly by the groundskeepers to enter and tend to the infield gardens. At full speed and carrying a very startled Ronnie Behrens on his back, Puss n Boots shot the gap. The quick left turn sent the jockey sailing over the horse's head and onto the ground, sprawled out. Approaching the infield lake at full speed, the horse suddenly hit the brakes, and a disbelieving crowd of 14,106 people got to see Puss n Boots slide slowly into the water, ass-first.

Trust me, when a bettor puts a wad of money on a rising star like Puss n Boots, expecting him to win the race, the last thing he wants to hear from the horse is the sound of a really big splash.

Immediately, Behrens jumped into the lake to save his horse . . . until he remembered he could not swim. Immediately, trainer Frank Merrill went thrashing into the lake to save his jockey . . . until he remembered he too could not swim. With one horse and two men now flailing away in deep water, the entire starting gate crew kicked off their shoes, stripped down to their skivvies, and then plunged into the lake like a team of very pale lifeguards. A big horse, a small skiff, three guys mostly naked, and nobody said, "You're gonna need a bigger boat"?

Although the gate guys hauled the jockey and trainer out of the drink, that horse just wanted to have fun. Leisurely, he swam in circles in the middle of the lake like it was his private backyard pool. It took a man in a rowboat and the starting crew forty-five minutes to get a hold of Puss n Boots and lead him to land. They all got a standing ovation.

This amazing moment in horse racing history is commemorated annually with Fort Erie's $30,000 Puss n Boots Cup, after which the winners – jockey, trainer, and owners, but no, not the horse – jump into that same infield lake.

I can only imagine if Zippy Chippy and Puss n Boots had been stablemates in Florida. Top of the six o'clock news: "This afternoon, at Cypress Gardens near Winter Haven, Florida, two stray racehorses tried to ride Nemo the Killer Whale, and in the process accidentally crushed to death Twiggy the Waterskiing Squirrel. The horses were last seen headed for Disney World on the shoulder of State Road 400." Yeah, Zippy and Puss – a two-horse, one-week, Jimmy Buffett–style spring break.

SIXTEEN

*I just don't want to see you give up on your dreams 'cause
you're holding onto the one thing that's letting you go.*
From the movie Small Town Saturday Night

The only way Felix Monserrate would ever get one of his
horses into the Kentucky Derby would be to arrive at
Churchill Downs late at night and bribe a security guard to
let them both in the side door. Felix did, however, have a keen eye
for the obvious, as well as a flair for fairground theatrics.

One day – and this usually meant trouble, if not outright disas-
ter – Felix came up with an idea. This was not the result of a sit-
down family meeting with Emily and Marisa to create a new plan
for Zippy Chippy, since the old one (horse racing) had not been
working out so well. Over time, in nearly forty years of teaching horses how to race, Felix had noticed two things that were
both related and irrefutable. First, horses run faster than humans.
This idea may have come to Felix as he was picking himself up
off the ground after being head-butted by Zippy from behind.
Horses were definitely faster on their feet than people, which is
why you would never see the 130-pound Felix Monserrate in a
race around a dirt oval track with the 1,100-pound Zippy Chippy
splayed across his shoulders, although I understand men do that in
Finland with their wives. Honest – it's called *eukonkanto*.

The second thing Felix knew to be true was that humans loved to watch horses run, especially his own little impulsive imp. Bingo! Humans watching horses race against humans. Bottom line: have fun for a change, because all this losin's gettin' real old.

Luis Rivera, a former jockey and president of Rochester's Puerto Rican Festival, championed the idea of just such a celebrity match race, because Zippy Chippy was badly missed by his local fan base since he had been given the heave-ho from Finger Lakes. Dan Mason loved the idea because outrageous stunts were part of his job as general manager of the Rochester Red Wings.

The event was billed as the "2000 Red Wings Derby" and scheduled for an early summer's evening at Frontier Field, home of baseball's Triple-A International League Red Wings. Zippy Chippy, with a career record in losing to horses, would race against Jose Herrera, the Red Wings' speedy center fielder with an impressive 155 career stolen bases. "Man against Beast" flashed on the scoreboard. The posters read "Horse against Human." Zippy's followers lapped it all up. If any horse in the world needed a win, any kind of a win – against a human, a tractor, a senior citizen on one of those electric scooters – it was Zippy Chippy!

The mood was light and breezy at Frontier Field as approximately nine thousand spectators showed up to party with the Zipster and watch the race, which was staged before a night game that pitted the hometown Red Wings against the Scranton/Wilkes-Barre Red Barons. Although there was no betting, money still changed hands ("I'll take the exactor – horse to win, human to come second"), with lots of laughter and family fun. At the concession booths, the ballpark's traditional white hot dogs crackled and the Scotch ale spilled into large plastic cups, leaving a beige head of froth at the top. Hootin' and hollerin', the faithful brought gifts of food for Zippy and newspaper and magazine clippings for Felix to sign. Felix might have looked skyward and given a grateful thumbs-up to circus impresario P.T. Barnum. This sideshow was coming together nicely.

A confident Pedro Castillo sat comfortably in the saddle, which was belted over a green and white blanket emblazoned with Zippy Chippy's name. Pedro wore white silk pants, a Red Wings tunic over a black long-sleeved shirt, and a great big grin. With a white braid running the length of his neck, white leather reins and bridle to match, and four white leggings wrapped from ankles to knees, Zippy looked absolutely angelic. Trotting onto the dirt warning track, he kept nodding and looking up at his fans, who were packed onto the walkway above.

Wearing tight white pants, a black T-shirt, a gold chain, and his Rochester Red Wings hat sideways, Jose Herrera looked like he meant business. This was not a new or unusual situation for the speedy ballplayer. He told the press the story of how he used to race against horses on a farm in his native Dominican Republic, which makes you wonder what the game of baseball looks like in that country. No naïve rookie, Herrera had already spent two seasons in the big leagues with the Oakland A's.

Up in the grandstand, nobody dared to go to the bathroom, and everybody had an opinion. Finger Lakes Racetrack handicapper Dave Mattice said the odds favored Herrera because the distance was too short. "If Herrera had to carry a jockey," Mattice joked, "it would be a lot more fair."

The racecourse had been meticulously mapped out in the outfield with double lanes of white lime that would keep the competitors a healthy distance from each other. Zippy had never bitten a ballplayer before, so there was that temptation Felix had to worry about.

Approaching the start, a groom steadied Zippy on one side while Felix and a beaming teenage Marisa held him on the other. Manager Dan Mason beckoned the racers to the starting line, where he held a black and white checkered flag high above his head. Dan raised his free hand to engage the crowd, and immediately they began the countdown in unison.

"Ten!"

"Nine!"

The players on the sidelines razzed Herrera unmercifully.

"Eight!"

"Seven!"

Herrera and Castillo exchanged words in Spanish and then laughed like hell.

"Six!"

"Five!"

Zippy's fans punched the air with their fists, keeping time with the chant.

"Four!"

"Three!"

The happy mob waved their ball caps high over their heads, and their cheers could be heard out on the street.

"Two!"

A cameraman on the sidelines, jockeying for a better angle, crashed into his sound technician.

"ONE!"

The flag came down, a roar went up from the crowd, and the starter yelled, "Go!"

The race unfolded like one of those TV dream-scene ripples: a horse nods knowingly toward the stands, bowing to his retinue of admirers, while a skinny guy in red and black runs for his life. The same horse starts to graze the outfield grass, thinking,

Man, this is a lot better than that scraggly stuff at the track. Suddenly the crowd is yelling, pointing at the sprinter. The jockey slaps the horse on the rump. From the sting of the crop the horse bolts, the base stealer hits top gear, and the Red Wings Derby is on.

The noise was deafening, the runners covered the distance quickly, and the whole thing was over in less than seven seconds. Given that Zippy's distant relative Man o' War had a full stride of 28 feet and Usain Bolt, the world's fastest human, legs it out at 9.35 feet, the result of the race was a logical and foregone conclusion. Keeping in mind the biological precept that horses are naturally faster than humans, the race wasn't even close.

Zippy Chippy lost by three lengths. Yeah, horse lengths. A human beat a horse in a footrace! Even though one of their own species had won the race, the humans in the stands were stunned and disappointed.

There's no doubt that Zippy was eating grass when the flag came down, but it's entirely possible that when Dan Mason yelled "Go!", Zippy took that as a term of encouragement and started eating faster. Herrera definitely broke from the starting line early, but no inquiry was called and no umpire was present. One fan claimed that when the ballplayer took off, Zippy gave one last long look at the guy in the stands hawking soft pretzels. *Yum. Sweet mustard.*

Years later, I tracked down Pedro Castillo in Philadelphia, where he was struggling to make a comeback as a jockey. Dividing forty yards by two disparate strides, my question to Pedro was one of basic mathematics.

"Pedro, WTF happened there?"

"All I can say," said the jockey, an affable man with a gleaming white smile, "that horse, he be very unfocused. Very unfocused."

Castillo, who had seen many of Zippy's failed starting-gate strategies, said, "Just as the checkered flag came down, Zippy got hungry." Off to a terrible start, Zippy did, however, have Herrera running for dear life at the finish line, but the distance of forty yards of outfield turf was not enough for the horse to overtake the ballplayer.

"We close pretty strong," said Castillo. "But we run out of real estate."

New rule governing contests of speed between two distinctly different species: *Most*, I repeat, *most* racehorses, but not all racehorses, are faster than human beings.

The speedy center fielder was carried off the field in triumph on the shoulders of his teammates high-fiving everyone in sight. Zippy got back in his transport trailer and went home to have supper. *Good lord*, he must have thought as he looked out the window of the trailer, *now I'm probably banned from ballparks too!*

Highlights of the race were shown during that night's news hour on all three major American networks. Later, clips would appear on the *Today Show*, *Good Morning America*, and ESPN's *SportsCenter*. Newspapers from around the country ran humorous features on the human-versus-horse race, including *USA Today* and the *New York Times*. Fortunately for Zippy, there are dozens of TV monitors at racetracks but none in the barns.

Jose Herrera got more press running away from a food-obsessed horse than he ever did stealing bases. At year's end, *Baseball America* heralded the race as their top minor-league promotion of the year, and Dan Mason was the toast of the town. How typical, Zippy running his little heart out in order to make some other guy look good.

"He let Jose win to make him feel good," said Felix. Yes, the curse of courtesy had crept back into Zippy's sense of fair play. Although it rocked his own personal theory about the velocity of two-legged versus four-legged animals, Felix took the loss rather well. "Forty yards is not enough for him to get warm," said the trainer. The scribbling reporters could only laugh.

Ever the stubborn trainer, Felix still believed his horse could outrun a human being. The racing strategy did not change: stay the course and soon, very soon, they would celebrate victory together. The solution was simple – all they needed to do was find a slower ballplayer. Yeah, they were having fun again.

THE GREATEST WORST
OLYMPIAN EVER

Does the name Michael Edwards ring a bell? How about "Eddie the Eagle"? Failing to make the British national team as an alpine skier, Eddie took up ski jumping since few others would dare. Eddie was just marginally better than most of the spectators who came to watch his event. When he got word that he had qualified for the 1988 Calgary Olympics, he was working as a plasterer in a mental institution in Finland.

The Brits had never had a ski jumper and did not possess a ski jump anywhere in the country. An oddity, Eddie became a world-famous ski jumper in the same way that four guys from a country without snow became the legendary Jamaican bobsled team: he applied for a job that didn't exist in his country. Eddie offered to throw himself off the end of two ramps that stood 230 feet and 295 feet above the ground, respectively. "Brilliant," cried the Brits. "What's the worst that can happen?"

So there was Michael Edwards at the Calgary games, an Olympian mainly because he wasn't afraid of heights, wearing six pairs of socks to fill ski boots that were three sizes too big and a loose nylon jacket over three layers of jerseys. He was twenty pounds heavier than his closest competitor and extremely farsighted, which explained the big round glasses with lenses the thickness of Coke bottles. Once his ski goggles went on over his glasses, fog covered the lenses so that he was partially blinded as he barreled down the jump track. As one cruel description of him read, "A fat, blind tub of lard hurtling though the air on a pair of skis was England's greatest hope in jumping." Because he always had a goofy smile behind the huge glasses, the press dubbed him "Mr. Magoo."

Despite the fact that Eddie looked more like a welder than an Olympian, his keenness to participate in a strange and dangerous sport and his unflinching drive to go head-to-head with the best endeared him to sports fans and television viewers around the world. Although British TV referred to Eddie as "the world's worst ski jumper" and described his style as "flying through the air like a stone," they always added, "but we love him."

Like a true anti-champion, the more Eddie struggled and lost, the more he short-jumped to a last-place finish, the more wildly popular he became. Finishing dead last in both jumping events, he drew bigger crowds than any other athlete, becoming the runaway sensation of the Calgary games.

Flying through the air with the greatest of awkwardness, almost overnight Michael Edwards became Eddie the Eagle. He had accomplished his wild and lifelong dream: he was an Olympic athlete. If entertainment value and courage count for anything in sports, then he was the best of the lot.

At the closing ceremonies, Calgary Olympics chairman Frank King etched Eddie's legacy in stone: "At these games, some competitors have won gold, some have broken records, and some of you have even soared like an eagle." The crowd went berserk, chanting, "Eddie! Eddie!" until they became hoarse.

Just as with Zippy Chippy, the power of the media and the faith of his following had made Michael Edwards the world's best-known athlete, with his earnings jumping from £6,000 a year to £10,000 an hour. He had willed himself into a superstar with the talents of an ordinary bloke.

Similar in style and identical in record, Eddie the Eagle and Zippy Chippy were kindred spirits. Both underdogs, they had nothing to lose, which made them free: free of pressure, free of pretentiousness, free of losing. Free. If these two guys had ever met, there's no doubt in my mind that Zippy still would have bitten that crazy Brit in the ass and eaten his plastic goggles.

We humans have always rooted for the underdog, with the same innate decency that forbids us to kick a man when he's down. Not only is it the right thing to do to encourage and trumpet the efforts of the less blessed, like Zippy Chippy, Eddie the Eagle, Daniel "Rudy" Ruettiger, Job, and the '62 Mets. But also, there but for the grace of the gods and lucky charms go we. Help the guy who's drowning, lest someday you fall into the drink yourself.

SEVENTEEN

You're better off betting on a horse than betting on a man.
A horse may not be able to hold you tight, but he
doesn't wanna wander from the stable at night.
Betty Grable

At Rochester's Frontier Field the following August, they found him — the slower ballplayer, that is. In "Man against Beast II," prior to a Wednesday evening game pitting the hometown Red Wings against the Ottawa Lynx, Zippy Chippy lined up next to center fielder Darnell McDonald in another "four hooves versus two feet" match race. This time Red Wings general manager Dan Mason had insisted on a fifty-yard dash, ten yards longer than the last one, "in order to give the horse a chance." Felix, who either ignored the slam or didn't get it, had agreed.

Aside from the fact that the human wore sunglasses and the horse wore blinkers, and that the ballplayer was single by choice and the thoroughbred was a bachelor by surgery, the two were pretty well matched. McDonald wore his team's black and white colors, while Zippy wore Jorge Hiraldo, dressed in red, white, and blue silks. With just fourteen wins in 213 starts that season, Hiraldo needed a victory almost as much as Zippy did. Pedro Castillo, Zippy's former jockey, was not available for this sequel. After losing to a human being, Pedro changed his name to Wedgie White and moved to a U.S. nuclear testing site in the Pacific.

The twenty-two-year-old McDonald, who had been a phenomenal high school football player, tried to badmouth his opponent: "We all know who's gonna win. This horse knows too. I will come out victorious."

"You better," said his teammates, knowing that if he didn't, he would never live it down.

But everyone — as William Shakespeare demonstrated so well — has a fatal flaw, even a two-hundred-pound speedster drafted number one by the Baltimore Orioles. McDonald's Achilles' heel, as they say in sports, was that he did not spend enough time watching television reruns. If he had, before he started with all that trash talk in Zippy's face, he would have known that "a horse is a horse, of course, of course, and no one can talk to a horse, of course, that is, of course, unless the horse is the famous Mr. Ed."

The hype was high, the crowd was huge, and redemption was on the minds of Zippy Chippy's ragtag band. Many thought McDonald cheated, taking off at the start before the flag came all the way down. Felix didn't notice, because he was still jabbering away at his jockey, standing on the starting line. Zippy didn't notice either, because . . . *What the hell's that up there? A buttered popcorn wagon? What did they do, switch the warm pretzel thingamajig with . . .*

Ouch! Zippy took one to the tush. "And they're off!" Sprinting all out, it was obvious that Darnell McDonald was not just racing Zippy Chippy; he was running against the precedent set by last summer's winner, Jose Herrera. A loss would mean a season fraught with horse jokes from teammates and a lot of neighing from the opposing dugout.

The ballplayer held his early lead until the forty-yard mark. Jorge Hiraldo stretched his horse out, and Zippy's full stride overtook McDonald's short, pumping progress. It was those last ten yards that put Zippy between the ballplayer and the finish line, as he blew by McDonald at the wire by one length. It was close but a win is a win, and a win by Zippy Chippy causes people to make the sign of the cross all the way from Rochester to the Vatican.

"I might have got him at forty yards, but that extra ten yards put him over the hump," said McDonald. "From behind I heard this *dah-doomp, dah-doomp, dah-doomp*. At this point I knew it was over. Zippy had an extra gear today."

Jorge Hiraldo was over the moon: "Zippy was ready today. Last year he was a little nervous." The jockey was also relieved. Returning home to the backside to explain how you and your horse got beat by a guy wearing his ball cap backwards is never an easy thing to do. Jorge was particularly pleased to still be aboard Zippy Chippy at the end of the race. No rider of horses likes to be bounced over the outfield fence like a ground rule double.

The thousands of Zippy fans — salt of the earth and compassionate to a fault — who had come to the ballpark early to be photographed with the record-breaking racehorse went wild. Zippy's reward was not a purse of first-prize money but a twenty-five-pound bag of carrots, which he demolished as soon as he returned to his trailer. Surrounded by smirking media types, Darnell McDonald was eating crow.

Even the family was impressed with Zippy's first-ever win over anybody or anything. "He may not have won against other racehorses, but he won today," said a beaming Marisa, Zippy's good luck charm. For Marisa and two of her girlfriends, accepting the great big trophy (which Zippy tried to eat) to the applause of the crowd was the thrill of a lifetime. Proud as a father watching his kid get his first hit or score his first goal, Felix must have looked at Zippy and then over at the Ottawa dugout and thought, *I wonder how fast one of them Lynx can run?*

Darnell McDonald had never lost a race to a human before, let alone a horse. He, of course, blamed his manager: "They should never have added those extra ten yards." The loss ended his career as a professional ballplayer. Disheartened and demonized, he spent the rest of his life traveling the country by bus and later hitch-hiking, trying to win races against other horses, then donkeys, then ponies, first the sad ones that come to town with the carnival and finally miniature ponies that can fit inside a dog's traveling cage. Eventually, homeless in Florida, he was arrested for trying to break into the Pensacola Greyhound Track. Darnell once raced a chicken across the road and then just sat there wondering why.

Okay, the truth is, Darnell McDonald had a pretty good career in Major League Baseball, playing for five teams, including the New York Yankees, over eight years. But he would never race a horse again. He had that written into his contract.

Zippy, however, was enjoying hanging out with his new two-footed rivals, probably because they didn't fart and snort as much as those who were – okay, born in a barn. Enthusiastically, he took on one more ballplayer the following summer, easily beating outfielder Larry Bigbie by four lengths over the forty-five-yard course. The media coverage of Zippy was so intense that Bigbie, who went 0–4 at bat that day, was still a highlight on ESPN's *SportsCenter* that evening.

The unsung hero of these races was longtime Frontier Field groundskeeper Mike Osborne, who followed Zippy's every move . . . with a shovel. "I volunteered," he said, "because I love horses and I love baseball." A lesser man, when told he ought to have loftier goals in life, might have replied, "What! And quit show business?"

At the ballpark with thousands of people cheering for him, Zippy had left his bad attitude back at the track. He was easy to handle and a pleasure to ride. Carefully considering his new and improved record of two wins and one loss to humans, Felix sounded almost cocky: "He ran to win. He doesn't want to lose anymore."

Inspired by beating a person, Zippy Chippy would go on to triumph over fellow horses – but, sadly, not thoroughbreds. On St. Patrick's Day at Freehold Raceway in New Jersey, he beat Paddy's Laddy, a Standardbred horse. Paddy's Laddy was a pacer rigged in such a way as to prevent him from running free and at full stride. Heavily harnessed, a pacer does a kind of fast and rhythmical goose step around the track. With no such restrictions, Zippy nipped the fancy dancer at the wire.

Similarly, at Batavia Downs, a harness track near Buffalo, New York, Zippy went up against a trotter named Miss Batavia, who was also trained and tied in such a way as to not actually run. Zippy won yet again against a horse that was handicapped by a harness. Oh, and by the way, Standardbred horses? They also have to drag carts behind them. And the people sitting in those carts are an awful lot larger than jockeys.

"They just love that horse," said John Clifford, the publicity director of Batavia Downs. "Everybody, even people who knew nothing about racing, knew who Zippy Chippy was."

The attendance at Batavia Downs doubled for Zippy's appearance, and his legion of relentless followers showed up to fawn over him and take photos. The first one thousand fans through the door received a Zippy Chippy T-shirt. Along with the $7.50 chicken BBQ special, you could get a free photo taken with Zippy Chippy, but you had to hire an off-duty cop to protect your plate of food.

"People were crazy about him," remembered Clifford. "Everybody knew him. Everybody knows his name. Ask anybody who won last year's Kentucky Derby and they'll hem and haw. But mention the name Zippy Chippy and they say, 'That's that horse that never wins!'"

Zippy's diehard fans brought bags of carrots, small homemade gifts, and copies of *People* magazine for Felix to autograph. Although Zippy embodied the track's motto, "You will always be a winner at Batavia Downs," neither win against the Standardbred horses improved his official record. They did, however, show that all things being unequal, he could be a champion.

Enjoying the banquet circuit more than his racetrack schedule, Zippy was also feted at a Christmas cocktail party at the Moose Lodge in Canandaigua, just down the road from Felix's barn. Hors d'oeuvres were served on a plate, not in a bag, and the music was provided by Mixed Emotions. All proceeds went to the local charity Happiness House, where a plaque now sits, honoring the horse's fundraising fight against cerebral palsy. Zippy's hooves are imprinted in cement, bringing to mind more bad jokes than I have space for in this book.

However, the life of a celebrity and one of America's most fascinating personalities is not as glamorous as you would think. At his second charity appearance, also at Moose Lodge, Zippy got third billing behind the guest speaker, a guy named Jarod who told his signature story about how he once encountered a wolf cub. A few Rochester Rhinos soccer players also made an appearance. To add insult to injury, Zippy was featured last on the program, behind a classic car show, a raffle, and — have these people no sensitivity whatsoever? — a tortoise-and-hare race. Man, this horse might as well have been owned by Rodney Dangerfield and named Itellyalgetnorespect.

All well and good, but Zippy's social calendar was cutting into his racing program. With four straight wins on his chart — two against guys who don't run too well while they're laughing and two against horses shackled at the shoulders and legs – it was time to get the Zipster back on the track and doing what he did best: watching the world and other horses go by.

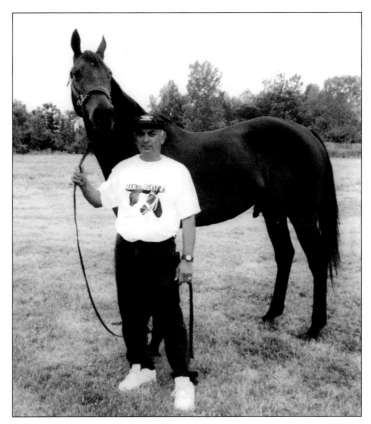

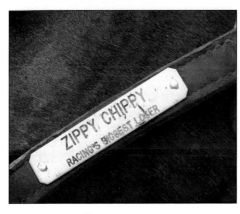

Top:
Team Monserrate.
Ten years of tears, beers,
and unrehearsed comedy.
In the business of racing,
they warn you to "never
love a horse," but . . .

Bottom:
To Zippy's halter plate,
they could have added
"And Crazy-Ass Horse of
the Century."

Hungry, Zippy tries to eat exercise rider Milton Delvalle, starting with his hoodie. Bored, Felix makes a note to bump up the feed bucket.

Later, Zippy goes after a pair of pants to match the sweater he ribbed off of Milton.

Top:
*The Great
Zippy Chippy, like
Secretariat, only
opposite. There will
never be another
like him.*

The Zipster, with Pedro Castillo in the saddle, is about to disappoint 9,000 of his fans by losing to speedy center fielder Jose Herrera. Man — 1, Beast — 0.

Felix and Zippy Chippy were possibly the two most stubborn players in thoroughbred racing. "We may be down, but we ain't done."

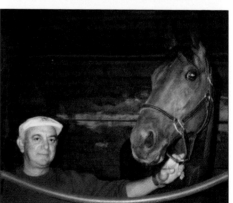

Top:
At Rochester's Frontier Field, Zippy Chippy and Jorge Hiraldo are being led into the history book where they redeemed themselves by finally winning a race. Man — 1, Beast — 1.

Bottom:
Zippy loved racing at Northampton Fair in Massachusetts. He felt so close to his fans and the candy floss.

Michael Blowen, owner of Old Friends at Cabin Creek, bet $5,000 that Zippy Chippy would earn more as "The Charmer of Cabin Creek" than he ever did racing. They both cashed in, big time.

*Bottom:
Old Friends at Cabin Creek near Saratoga, New York is a retirement farm for former racehorses; a peaceful refuge for them to spend their autumn years.*

Clockwise from left:

The precise moment that Zippy Chippy and Red Down South met. Since then, they have been inseparable stablemates.

Zippy Chippy picks the pocket of William Thomas at Cabin Creek. Admits the author: "I am scared shitless of that horse!"

After fifteen years of professional racing, which includes 132 trips around the track, now it's time for Zippy Chippy and Red to just hang out and think about what might have been . . . and carrots.

Marisa at three in a feed bucket. Fortunately, Zippy wasn't hungry that day.

Bottom right: *Marisa, five, celebrates her father's 41st birthday.*

Bottom left: *Marisa Monserrate today — out of the feed bucket and into the serious business of training horses and pony riding at Finger Lakes.*

IF ZIPPY CHIPPY WERE A CITY,
HE'D BE BUFFALO, NEW YORK

Unlike those folks who slag the "Queen City" for its snow, Super Bowl record, and contribution to fine dining – chicken wings – I quite like the place. (I still hold Frank and Teresa of the Anchor Bar personally responsible for my high cholesterol.)

Buffalo has great bars and restaurants, "talking proud" citizens, the quaint and colorful Broadway Market, and the Albright-Knox Art Gallery, one of America's finest. Having reclaimed their waterfront and rediscovered their Frank Lloyd Wright architecture, Buffalo right now is enjoying an amazing makeover. With its skating rinks in the winter and paddling on the Erie Canal in the summer, Canalside is an outdoor wonderland attracting tens of thousands of visitors. From 1972 to 1979, the Buffalo Sabres boasted "the French Connection," the most exciting line in hockey history.

As a university student in 1970 I was certain I was going to win the contest to name Buffalo's new NHL team with the Buffalo Badgers. As an expansion team with a rocky road ahead, I thought the badger was perfectly emblematic – a nasty and aggressive little weasel who will not only come into your campsite and gorge himself, he will also urinate on what's left over so nobody else can have it! Our slogan was going to be: "Oh sure, you might come into our rink and beat us but when you get dressed to go home, you're not going to smell so good!" Instead they went with the Buffalo Sabres.

Yet Buffalo has, in the past, suffered from Zippy Chippy Syndrome – you take one great stride forward, and somebody bumps you two lengths back. Thirty years ago, the symbol of the city's cultural renaissance was a work of art called *Green Lightning*, commissioned by the city and created by sculptor Billie Lawless. Everybody supported the project, but nobody really understood what it was. It just looked like an unlit jumble of neon tubes on a silkscreened background.

But when they plugged it in on the night of the grand unveiling, oh yeah, they knew what they were looking at! When the neon lights lit up the sculpture in the sky, mayor Jimmy Griffin's head almost exploded. His guests, dignitaries including governor Mario Cuomo, either stared at their feet in embarrassment or put their hands over their mouths to stifle laughter.

Billie Lawless's neon-and-wire masterpiece, meant to spearhead the rebirth of Buffalo's entertainment scene, was a vivid depiction of — wait for it — two penises dressed like the Planters peanut character, doing a snappy little dance number and wearing top hats, white gloves, and tails. Yeah, *Green Lightning* — shuckin' and jivin' with well-dressed junk. For cartoon characters, they sure had heart, these two dicks dancing like crazy.

Going ballistic, Griffin pulled the plug immediately and then tried to have the artwork destroyed after dark, for which he was later found guilty in court of violating Mr. Lawless's civil rights. Apparently there is nothing in the United States Constitution about the "right to bear schlongs." Oddly, *Green Lightning* was displayed in Chicago for the next ten years without a whisper of protest.

I'm thinking it was just a matter of a bad title. *Green Lightning* was abstract and meaningless, and just confused everybody. I've always been a believer that the title of a piece of art should state exactly what the beholder is looking at. My first choice for a title would have been *It's Just One F—king Thing after Another*. And, talking titles, "Billie Lawless" may have been a better name for the Zipster than "Zippy Chippy."

Buffalo and Zippy Chippy – hard not to love them, even if they're an acquired taste. Like suicide wings, beef on weck, and Flutie Flakes.

EIGHTEEN

*If you have raced with men on foot and they have worn
you out, how can you compete with horses?*
Jeremiah 12:5

W ow! Jeremiah, the double threat — a bullfrog and a prophet!
For Zippy's eighty-ninth career race, in mid-February
2001, Felix moved him to Penn National Race Course in
Grantville, Pennsylvania, just outside the state capital of Harrisburg.
Despite dwindling attendance, Penn National still offers thoroughbred racing almost fifty-two weeks a year, four days a week. It's survival was assured when it was twinned with Hollywood Casino,
which boasts six restaurants, including the Celebrity Grill and
Glitterati's. Really? Grantville, population 3,650, has "glitterati"?

Though Felix was pleased that so many fans showed up in
Pennsylvania to watch Zippy race, his gut must have been churn-
ing. With all of those consecutive losses, it was always hard to get
excited about the next race, and almost impossible to build upon
something positive from the last. Plus, Zippy's eighty-seventh
loss, his greatest race ever, in which he was repeatedly bumped
and eventually nosed out at the wire by Black Rifle — that one still
hurt. And yet here was his horse, staring at a much younger field,
sashaying onto the track like a champ. Zippy Chippy at ten years
of age was not only sound, he was irrepressible.

On this day, the dank, cold air chilled the bones of horses and helpers alike. The $10,000 purse attracted a higher brand of horses than Zippy was accustomed to running against, and it showed. Zippy's six-furlong trip around the dirt track was as unremarkable as the ride given him by his jockey, Pedro Carrasquel. The goofy gelding was outclassed by a bunch of four-year-olds – he finished last and nearly thirty-three lengths behind the winner, Bidakeno.

It was not the loss that boggled the minds of track officials but the 4–1 odds Zippy carried from the gate to the finish line. "The odds were a lot lower than they should have been," said one track steward. "A lot of people bet with their heart and not their head."

Race number eighty-nine had not been Zippy Chippy's lucky number. At least, not as lucky as it was for the late Anna Nicole Smith when she married a guy that age, thereby inheriting $475 million when he suddenly died a year later of – and here's where it gets interesting – old age!

As he trotted happily back to the barn, it was clear that nobody had more fun losing – and this was his eighty-ninth loss in a row – than Zippy. Except maybe a feisty but somewhat untalented ballplayer just up the road from Harrisburg. There, in the city of Williamsport, Pennsylvania, lived Zippy's human double.

Asked to name the greatest catchers in baseball, a fan might suggest Yogi Berra or Johnny Bench. Maybe Carlton Fisk or "Pudge" Rodriguez. Now, add Dave Bresnahan to the list. Three decades ago, Dave Bresnahan was a twenty-five-year-old second-stringer with the Class AA Williamsport Bills. Both the catcher and his team were headed nowhere. In a meaningless late-season home game against the Reading Phillies, Dave remembered why he'd gotten into the game of baseball in the first place: fun! Sports, games, balls, and bats were designed to create fun.

You were supposed to feel a sense of joy tear-assing around the bases and making diving catches just so you could get grass stains on your pants and drive your mother crazy. But with the Bills mathematically eliminated from the playoffs, nobody was having much fun on this hot day in August of 1987.

So instead of throwing the ball back to the pitcher, Dave pulled a potato out of his pocket and fired it over the head of the runner on third base. Earlier that day, he had taken care to sculpt the potato into the shape of a baseball. In fact, he had gone through an entire bag of potatoes until he found one that was just the right shape and size. Nobody could believe what they saw: a catcher wildly throwing the ball over the third baseman's head into the left field. Certainly not Rick Lundblade, the runner at third who trotted home on the overthrown pass ball to score what he thought was the easiest run of his young career.

Before Lundblade touched home plate, however, Dave pulled the game ball out of his catcher's mitt and tagged him out. Bedlam ensued. Spectators exchanged strange looks; this was followed by nervous applause, a few boos, and finally lots and lots of laughter. The umpire who finally figured out what the hell had happened confiscated the potato and awarded Lundblade a scored run on the play. Even the guys in the Phillies' dugout were cracking up. One teammate took Lundblade aside to give him the bad news – he'd been traded for a potato to be named later! Everybody was having fun again.

The Bills' parent club, the Cleveland Indians, saw little humor in the practical joke, first fining Dave Bresnahan, then firing him from the organization. "Jeopardizing the integrity of the game" is how they put it. As if Barry Bonds, Mark McGwire, and Sammy Sosa had enhanced the integrity of baseball by using performance-enhancing drugs to put up record-breaking numbers.

Plus, the Cleveland Indians were hardly the New York Yankees. Back in the Tribe's bad old days, as they toiled on the natural grass field of futility, nobody could understand why a capacity crowd of 74,438 would come out each spring on opening day, especially to the rundown concrete mausoleum of Cleveland Stadium, nicknamed "the Mistake by the Lake." Erie, it really was. The puzzling part was that attendance dropped to a meager few thousand diehard fans for the next game and all of those that followed. The explanation came from a long-suffering Indians supporter, who said, "Every baseball fan in Cleveland comes out on opening day because it's the last chance to see the Tribe play before they're mathematically eliminated from the playoffs!"

So it was with a high degree of hypocrisy that the Cleveland Indians gave Dave Bresnahan his walking papers. The catcher left the game quietly, like the soft sound of a spud landing on outfield grass. Suddenly unemployed, the ex-catcher said he might run for governor of Idaho . . . on the potato ticket.

But soon others also remembered that baseball was originally a playful pastime and not the nasty business it had become with false records, ridiculous contracts, corked bats, spitballs, and grown men peeing in bottles. The *Chicago Tribune* named the ex-catcher the "1987 Sports Person of the Year." Jumping on the Bresnahan bandwagon, the Williamsport Bills started hosting charity Potato Nights – "Bring a potato and get in for a dollar." In 1988, they held "Dave Bresnahan Day" and retired his number fifty-nine uniform. More than four thousand fans showed up to pay tribute to the world's most famous "tater tosser," hearing the former catcher deliver the best deadpan sports quote of the decade: "Lou Gehrig had to play in 2,130 consecutive games and hit .340 for his number to be retired. All I had to do was hit .140 and throw a potato."

When you're not having fun, sometimes you have to invent some. Today the potato sits preserved in a jar in a baseball museum in Southern California, and "Spuds" Bresnahan, as famous as Zippy Chippy and for all the right reasons, is still having fun. Sometime later, U.S. vice president Dan Quayle claimed it was the best *potatoe* trick he'd ever *scene*.

ZIPPY CHIPPY MAY HAVE LOST,
BUT HE NEVER CHEATED TO WIN

At Delta Downs in Vinton, Louisiana, on January 18, 1990, a very mediocre horse by the name of Landing Officer miraculously upset the nine-horse field and won the race by a convincing twenty lengths. A stunning feat, it was a full thirty-two lengths better than his last outing. Nobody could believe it. Actually, nobody could see it! Just before the starting bell rang, a dense fog had descended upon the track, and the announcer had to stop calling the race because he could no longer see the horses.

Sprinting through this "pea souper," it seemed that Landing Officer was so fast, the jockeys who believed their horses had come in first and second had not even seen the winner hit the wire.

But then a steward higher up in the booth counted only eight of the nine horses as they sped past the grandstand the first time. Taking a page from the infamous Rosie Ruiz's racing strategy – "how to win a marathon without actually running" – Landing Officer and his jockey had hidden in the wet, white mist at the top of the stretch, sitting out the first lap of the race. When they heard the field coming around the far turn, they sprinted to the finish line by those twenty lengths that were suddenly not so convincing. Just as Rosie was photographed at the finish line of the Boston Marathon wearing fresh makeup, Landing Officer was barely breathing hard.

Taking a shortcut is frowned upon by racetrack officials. Jockey Sylvester Carmouche was charged with fraud and subsequently suspended. (Yes, of course it had to be his idea; horses aren't smart enough to fix a race!) And say what you like about Zippy Chippy's less-than-stellar record. He obeyed the rules and covered all of the required distance in order to lose.

"Winners never cheat, and cheaters never . . ." Well, Zippy never did either one of those things.

NINETEEN

Perfection is attained by slow degrees;
it requires the hand of time.
Voltaire

An athlete on a hot streak catches everybody's attention. Joe DiMaggio's record fifty-six-game hitting streak brought America to a breathtaking halt in those summer afternoons of 1941. Cal Ripken's 2,632 consecutive games played astounded baseball fans and team doctors everywhere. From 1915 to 1940, the Edmonton Grads women's basketball team put up 502 wins, 78 of them in a row. Pakistan's professional squash ace Jahangir Khan won 555 straight matches between 1981 and 1986. However, for the believers, apparently it doesn't matter if the record is going the wrong way, accumulating losses instead of wins. Records are records, and Zippy was setting a new one every time they wrangled him into the starting gate . . . hoping like hell he would find his way out.

The year 2001 marked the one hundred and eighty-third consecutive year of the Three County Fair and the seventy-first year of operation for its racetrack. At ten years old, Zippy had just gone through a long, cold winter in the snowbelt of the Finger Lakes, and with retirement still a possibility, there was some doubt as to whether or not he would be back for the start of the race season.

Over the past six months, he had received more fan mail, appearance requests, and media interviews than ever before. Concerned about the absence of the track's biggest draw, a reporter from the *Daily Hampshire Gazette* called Felix at home.

"You better believe we be there," said the trainer. "If I die, fuhgeddaboudit. But if I don't die, we be there." Track officials at Northampton took that as a yes. No doubt about it, Felix and Zippy shared some admirable traits – like enthusiasm that could not be dampened by a hailstorm, and the work ethic of a Canadian beaver.

On Sunday, September 9, the first day of the fall meet, the midway smells of popping corn, frying onions, and accidents at the pig races wafted around the track. As he strode out onto the reddish dirt for the ninetieth race of his career, Zippy Chippy looked like the embodiment of confidence. And why wouldn't he answer this call to post with an ounce of bravado and a strut in his step? He was coming off what for him was a winning streak. In a relatively short span, he had trounced two baseball players and two non-thoroughbred racehorses that were trussed up and lugging vehicles behind them.

It was apparent from the outset that the little fairground track in Northampton was not prepared for the media hype celebrating Zippy Chippy's blind perseverance and dogged willpower to continue to run professionally. Racing against a field of maidens with a combined 0-for-132 loss record, Zippy attracted a feature writer from *USA Today*, the *CBS Sunday Morning* television crew, and staff writers for all the major newspapers from Boston to Albany. Looking past the hordes of cameras and microphones at the other horses, who were not surrounded by reporters, Zippy knew only too well that he was the star of this show. A nip here, a hat grabbed there – his unpredictable antics kept the media both on edge and keenly interested. If he could have read his own press clippings, there's no doubt that at this point in his career he would have been communicating with Felix through his agent.

When the bell rang, Zippy, with Juan Rohena aboard, broke clean and chased a couple of young pacesetters during the early stages of the race. From the fifth position out of the chute, he wound up fifth at the finish. His performance was described tersely as "through early," which is great if it's Friday and you're trying to beat the traffic home. Not so good if you finished sixteen and a half lengths behind the winner, Love Flight. The only horse he beat was Steel Surfing, who failed to finish after "buck jumping" and "high kicking" his way out of the gate. Perhaps he was just mocking Zippy's running style. Who knows?

In his next start at Northampton six days later, again with a modest purse prize of $3,100, the chart described Zippy's performance as follows: "dueled, steadied second turn, bore out all three turns, tired." Well, at least he dueled instead of dwelt. However, floating wide on the turns cost him his stamina, and loss number ninety-one was in the books. Oddly, Limited Speed came in first and Timing Perfect came dead last.

One disgruntled bettor loudly voiced the opinion that Zippy Chippy was so slow that his jockey had to call home from the halfway mark to tell his wife he'd be late for dinner. True enough: Zippy Chippy, more than any other professional racehorse, did not like to be rushed. He was never ahead at the wire, but he was certainly ahead of his time and well out in front of today's "slow movement."

Speed boils our blood these days, while deadlines dominate our brains. Soon we will have "virtual assistants" to read our books and give us thumbnail summaries. After Toyota got rid of the "andon cord," which every employee could pull to stop the assembly in order to address a fault immediately, production increased dramatically. So did the problems the company was postponing fixing. Today Toyota is the world's largest manufacturer of cars and the world's largest recaller of cars, thirty-one million and counting.

One-Minute Bedtime Stories is a popular collection of fables parents can read to their children in sixty seconds or less. They're a little different, in that Snow White is a neurotic chain smoker and two of the dwarfs are named Speedy and Gonzales. These nano narratives accelerate those quality moments with the kids so you can spend more time lying in bed not sleeping, worrying about all the things you have to get done tomorrow, most of which you didn't have time to get done today.

Our planet no longer rotates on an axis; it spins on an axle and leaves behind the sounds of screeching tires and the smell of burning rubber. The world itself deserves a whole lot more from its residents than merely making it go faster. Ironically, speed in this digital age is killing the sport of horse racing; the young cannot comprehend the beauty of a gloriously slow afternoon at the track.

We seriously need to slow down, relax, and abide by a new "It takes as long as it takes" mantra. I say *new*, but that's only in relation to us. Zippy Chippy always followed the slow and easy path, both in life and on the track. Was Zippy's first loss any different from his ninety-first? Not really. Did the pressure of rushing, running, pushing, and passing others in order to get ahead of them cause Zippy to get stressed out? Hardly. He was ten years old and playing tag with four-year-olds around a half-mile dirt pile. It was fun.

Despite his age, Zippy Chippy's routine remained the same: get up, eat, go out, take a whiz, walk to warm up, drop a load, toss the exercise rider, lose a race, walk to cool down, shower, kick Felix in the ass if he was around and just before bedtime, and yell "Fire!"

to keep the other horses in the barn on their toes. *Repeat same regimen tomorrow, unless they lock me in my stall again for no apparent reason.*

He didn't just respond to the beat of a different drummer; he slow danced through life, the way Ray Stout and Cathy Billyard did at my high school prom. We were certain that if we watched them long enough and closely enough, we would see their feet move eventually.

Slow is good and calm is nourishing, and if we are to save ourselves from ourselves in this time-sensitive, 24/7 workplace we call life, we need to look no further than the pace of Zippy and the patience of Felix. Sometime soon, when we all get back to a measured and manageable quality of life, it will be important to remember who led us all the way down the stretch to this conclusion – Zippy Chippy and the man who loved him like a son. The slow movement has to prevail; healthcare systems cannot possibly keep pace with chronic stress, which, according to the Human Sustainability Institute, is now directly linked to the leading causes of death: heart and lung disease, cirrhosis of the liver, suicides, and accidents. Remember, Zippy was breaking records for serenity long before slow became cool. And Zippy's records did not come with the cumbersome baggage of – what do you call those shiny things with the engravings? – oh yeah, trophies. In the race toward tranquility for a saner, better world, Zippy Chippy set the bar for leadership.

And his fans – appreciating the boldness of this horse that dared to take them in a different direction, to buck the odds, to forgo speed in favor of amusing misdeeds – came out in record numbers to watch this endearing scamp perform. Zippy's career had been guided by the hand of time, not the stopwatch of the track.

EDDY
"THE BOOK"

In the summer of '68, I was painting Eddy's house and occasionally covering his illegal betting business whenever his day job got in the way. There were no less than four bookies working out of four different hotels in Welland, Ontario, and Eddy was the worst of them. While a good bookie wrote his bets down on flash paper that would burst into flames at the touch of a match, Eddy recorded his on the sports page or the electric bill, or on the back of his hand if he was in a hurry. Most bookies had limits, but Eddy would take any bet at any time and dare you double or nothing if you won. Eddy was the original "Be kind to animals" guy; he gave all his money to the horses. On the days when he did make money, he'd go to Garden City Raceway the same evening and lose his winnings on the Standardbreds. He was a very bad bookie and a hopeless gambler, which is like a pimp with an addiction to sex.

One day Eddy filled his station wagon up with kids, his own along with some of their friends, and took them all to Marineland in Niagara Falls for the afternoon. Upon returning home, he realized that with all the ticket stubs and food wrappers flying around at Marineland, he had accidentally thrown away the previous day's betting log, which he had written on a napkin. Quickly he put all the kids back into the car, drove to Marineland, and, despite the attendant telling him that the park would close in thirty minutes, again doled out the cash for ten tickets. He spread the kids out in different directions and had them go through trash cans looking for "Daddy's grocery list." They never found it. That evening he had to call every person who wagered with him and ask them what they had bet on the previous day's races.

On a good day Eddy might take in a few hundred dollars before he managed to gamble it away. On that day he lost $1,200.

"How can that be?" I asked.

Eddy laughed at my naïveté. "Look, kid," he said, "if I asked you what horse you bet with me yesterday and you already knew the results, you wouldn't give me a loser, would you?" Some guy who had not won a bet all year had the daily double twice.

The first time Eddy got caught taking book, a judge threw the case out of court for lack of evidence. He was trying to swallow his bets, which were written on a page from a telephone book, when the cop who was choking him around the neck suddenly let go because Eddie was turning blue. GULP! Evidence disposed of.

Second time not-so-lucky, but fortunately Eddy served his time at a low-security prison not too far from Waterloo Lutheran University where I was studying, so I could visit him. The man is long gone, but oh, what a pair they would have made, Eddy and Zippy Chippy. The world's worst bookie covering the odds on the world's worst racehorse.

TWENTY

Life is one race I never want to win.
I'd rather stroll around enjoying the scenery.
Aditya Chandra

B y 2002, with only three racetracks in the Northeast allowing Zippy Chippy to participate in their programs – Northampton Fair in Massachusetts, Penn National in Pennsylvania, and ThistleDown in Ohio – Zippy's travel schedule was grueling.

Four months past his last race and now eleven years old, Zippy's best shot to win came on January 31 at Penn National on a cold, clear day, with a considerable purse of $10,100. He started in the fourth pole position, where he broke cleanly from the gate only to fall back to sixth in the seven-horse field. He struggled to catch up to the pack, breezing along at a pace less hectic than the one set by the other horses, horses that had thoughts of winning. As the footnote read, he "shuffled" back to last place, where he remained for the rest of the race. Zippy wound up thirty-three lengths behind the winner, Judge Me Ladies. Dancing to his own beat, Zippy couldn't even manage a little jig with Dig That Jazz.

As he trotted down the track toward the barn with the tote board behind showing his favorite 7–2 odds, Zippy was nodding his head in approval. As the fans crowded the apron's fence to get close to him, everybody, including the horse himself, was aware that with this ninety-second loss in a row they were making history. Fans at small, tattered tracks like this one and bettors at simulcast screens and off-track windows all over North America were wagering on this darling ne'er-do-well.

Before Felix and Zippy had left on this road trip, a researcher at Syracuse University Press had contacted Felix asking for biographical material on his infamous gelding. The university published the prestigious *Encyclopedia of New York State*, and Zippy Chippy's story was being included in their next edition. When he and Zippy arrived at the Northampton track, Felix was shadowed by a Los Angeles screenwriter who recorded his every move. "He's the neighbor of the guy who made the movie about the other horse," said Felix, referring to *Seabiscuit* producer/director Gary Ross. "He thinks my horse is a better story."

Owner and horse may have been getting a little full of themselves. A cartoon by Pierre Bellocq referencing Laura Hillenbrand's fabulous book *Seabiscuit* was still making the rounds. In it, Zippy is lounging inelegantly in his stall, book in hand and phone to ear when he says: "Great book Laura! Now, what about the other modern day American legend?"

Zippy's racing career was transcending speed and records to resonate with real-lifers, those who lived in that hard place called everyday reality. From the standpoint of the spectators as well as the guy who counts the track money, he'd certainly done his job. Using the dirt ovals as his stage, Zippy the bad actor always gave a great performance. Whether he dwelt or drifted wide, challenged the leader or dueled with the nag that was running dead last, he always found a way to deliver high-value entertainment. Each outing was colored by unpredictability and chock-full of suspense. Be it zany humor or socking drama, Zippy delivered like a champion. Ever the optimist, more than ever surrounded and outnumbered by naysayers, Felix's comment was "They'll have to catch him next time!" Lord knows, after some amusing track theatrics, they usually did.

On the long drive back to Farmington from Penn National, Felix gripped the wheel hard trying to think of a new strategy for Zippy's next race. But behind him, riding in his mobile trailer, Zippy wasn't worried at all. He was taking in the countryside and having fun scaring people who walked by his van at rest stops. Zippy took his mission – making people smile – seriously.

However, some sportswriters didn't understand Zippy's role as a consummate equine entertainer. One columnist referred to the horse as a "low-stakes mistake." Really? Today, more than a half century after its debut and spectacular failure, a mint-condition 1958 Edsel Citation convertible purchased for under $4,000 sells for $100,000. In 2010, the Liberty Head nickel, an American five-cent piece mistakenly "struck" with the year 1913 instead of 1912, sold for $3.7 million. A mistake is only an error, unless it's a massive, unique, mind-boggling mistake. Then it becomes a highly valued folly, a one-of-a-kind rarity, a thing of exclusive beauty, and a piece of unusual history. I'm referring, of course, to the dashing cad, not the poorly designed car.

Back at Penn National a month later, Zippy racked up loss number ninety-three. Three to Tango won that race, and even Patient Pete came in thirteen lengths ahead of Zippy, who for some reason put the brakes on coming into the stretch. By dwelling on the track and not in the starting gate, Zippy had come up with a new way to not win. At least this time he beat somebody – Ferby's Fire, by half a length.

Equibase, the online record of thoroughbred racing, will forever show that Ferby's Fire was beaten by Zippy Chippy! That's like when former U.S. attorney general John Ashcroft, at the time a senator from Missouri, lost reelection (we're talking incumbent here) to a dead guy! You don't live down losses like that in just one lifetime. Ferby's Fire would run one more race, then pack it in. Once you're beaten by Zippy Chippy, pulling a Dickie Dee Ice Cream wagon down Elm Street becomes a more appealing profession.

Changing the subject as he undressed Zippy in the backside barn, Felix quoted his hero, the late President John F. Kennedy. Felix would regularly remind his handlers at the track, mostly Puerto Ricans, of the patriotic tether that tied them to their new homeland, America, and the president who embraced believers of the American dream.

"My fellow Americans," he said, hoisting a can of beer as Zippy tilted his head, trying to grasp the words, "ask not what you can do for your country, but what your country can do for you."

Yes, "disbelievable" but Felix always got the words ass-backwards, and his training techniques were lost on his horse, and . . . the man had a good heart and he meant well, okay?

BAD BLACK JACK:
ZIPPY CHIPPY'S REAL FATHER

Officially, Zippy Chippy was born on April 20, 1991, at Capritaur Farm in upstate New York, and sired by a stallion named Compliance. However, while watching the coverage of the fiftieth anniversary of the assassination of President John F. Kennedy, I think I spotted Zippy's biological father. With his large head and dark coat, Black Jack, the well-built, riderless horse in JFK's funeral procession, looked an awful lot like Zippy Chippy, complete with a small white star on his forehead.

Black Jack had become a funeral horse in the same way Zippy Chippy had become a thoroughbred. "He was not suitable for riding, he wouldn't pull anything, he threw all his riders, and he refused to go on parade." That from the man who recruited him. Sound familiar? Sixteen years old at the time of JFK's funeral, Black Jack was not qualified for anything except strutting proudly down the street as the caparisoned horse in military funeral processions.

Despite his ornery attitude, Black Jack was much admired for his spirit and great physique when he joined the army at Fort Myer, Virginia, on November 22, 1952, to be all that he could be. He served in the Third U.S. Infantry Regiment, known as the Old Guard, performing the duties of the riderless horse in more than one thousand Armed Forces full-honors funerals.

America's grief on that cold and somber Monday in late November 1963 was mirrored in the sight of Black Jack clomping down the eerily quiet streets of Washington, D.C. All along the parade route, mourners wept amid the muffled rumble of military drums. Carrying a saber and an ebony English riding saddle with black boots reversed in the stirrups, Black Jack was led by nineteen-year-old Pfc. Arthur Carlson, who must have done horrible things in his previous life to draw this particular assignment. The riderless walk began with the horse stepping on Carlson's foot and ripping his boot off.

"I thought he broke a couple toes on my right foot, but he didn't," said Carlson later.

On what was supposed to be a stately walk along Pennsylvania Avenue from the Capitol to the White House and on to St. Matthew's Cathedral, Black Jack kept throwing his head back and dancing around his handler. He pounded the pavement loudly when he was supposed to be standing still, frequently fidgeting whenever the procession slowed or stopped. At one point the video shows him high-stepping down the street with his head and tail bobbing like he's auditioning for the Royal Canadian Mounted Police's Musical Ride. By protocol, poor Carlson was forbidden to scold his steed or even speak to him as Black Jack dragged him sideways and then forward, finally pushing away the man's hand with his nose. At the White House, instead of standing at attention, he kept resisting his handler in the same way Zippy always fought the crew that tried to cram him into the starting gate.

After witnessing Black Jack taking Carlson for a wild walk from a position directly behind the horse-drawn caisson carrying the coffin of the slain president, a writer from the *New York Times* kindly described him as "spirited and difficult to handle."

Normally serene and dignified, the caparisoned horse is supposed to be the sacred symbol of a fallen soldier who is never to ride again. At no time, however, did Black Jack bring the expected pomp and circumstance to the event being watched by a TV audience of 175 million.

On that fateful day in Washington, Black Jack looked like Zippy Chippy on the loose and raising hell on the backside. Surprisingly, the Kennedys were not at all upset, believing that Black Jack had personified the spirit and individualism of the other Jack. Their beloved Jack.

The similarities between the two hell-raisers is uncanny, and I for one believe that crazy-ass Black Jack was Zippy's long-lost biological father. Make no mistake about it: in addition to all his other antics, Zippy Chippy was perfectly capable of f—king up a funeral . . . in his spare time, of course. He was still mostly a racehorse.

TWENTY-ONE

If you win you will be happy.
If you lose you will be wise.
Anonymous

elix would wait the rest of that winter and the following summer before he entered Zippy in another race. As races go, the one at Northampton Fair on August 31, 2002 – and I'm not saying Zippy was the sole source of racetrack humor – was a laugher.

Sir Jouncewell, a horse that had never won before and had seldom been out in front of anything except his own exercise pony, went wire to wire. Never relinquishing the lead and paying $63.20 on a two-dollar bet, Sir Jouncewell showed what can happen when a career maiden finally breaks his cherry at long odds. A horse named Mecke Mouse hauled his big, flopping ears to the finish line twelve lengths ahead of Zippy Chippy. The only horse Zippy beat was King's Marquee, whose jockey eased him up at the third turn so that he failed to even finish. But the real kicker was that Zippy lost by twenty-four lengths to a horse named Mr. Peanut. That had to hurt. Somebody should have called foul on the name alone and ordered an allergy alert. No stranger to the bad name game, Mr. Peanut once came in eleventh in a race that included D'Gonne Gonne and Dinky Doo.

To those who bet the horses logically – the same type of people who failed to see the reincarnated baseball stars in the movie *Field of Dreams* – it looked like just another loss for the horse who had never won a race. What they didn't see was Zippy before the race, snorting and shaking and rearing his head like he was ready to go to war. What they didn't see was the same horse that had beaten only one competitor that day come back to the barn and do a little Buffalo shuffle for all his handlers and groupies. His demeanor said it loud and clear: *King's Marquee, my ass! I sure showed that guy!* Of course, he was referring to that one poor bastard who, seeing how far he still had to go to the finish line, faked a coughing fit and quit.

It took so little to make Zippy Chippy happy. Why? Low expectations. With nobody filing his retirement papers, Zippy had the world in the bottom of his banged-up water bucket. The track Zippy followed in life was always fast and firm, even if the race results were a little muddy. The aspirations of his owner and trainer were equally unexceptional. "He break good today," said Felix of the horse's ninety-fourth loss. "But today is not his day."

It would take science twelve years to catch up with Zippy and Felix's secret recipe for wellness. A recent study on mood disorders by researchers at England's University College London revealed that people with low expectations are much happier than those disappointed by not reaching lofty goals. The researchers didn't go so far as to claim that ignorance is bliss, but they did show that underachievers are measurably more satisfied with their lives than all those Type A personalities and *Forbes*-listed people who are only too happy to blab about all their winning strategies in their books, usually titled something along the lines of *The Seven Simple Secrets to Success.*

If your goal is to get home from work as quickly as possible while collecting curses and middle fingers from the drivers you offend, then you probably wouldn't be the type of person to bet on Zippy Chippy. But if your goal is to get home safely to enjoy the family around a fire or the supper table, arriving a little late because you stopped along the way to help somebody with car trouble or to rescue a stray dog, then yeah, you would probably drop a bill on the endearing Zippy, knowing that the chances of him winning were remote but that it was possible nonetheless. It was those two-dollar, well-wishing bettors who enabled the horse to have a career as a professional thoroughbred. These people see that, more than a single result or a big score, life is about the race, the journey, the getting there. A slow hand, an even keel, sights set on a big beach ball of a target, can bring lasting fulfillment in life.

I have heard older, successful couples refer to their "salad days," those early years of beginning a life together, building businesses or careers. Depending on which folklore you favor, those good ol' days refer to the greenness of judgment or the innocence of youth or more literally that period of struggle and sacrifice that came with meals that were more lettuce than meat. But the wistful sigh and knowing smile that come with the memory say that those days, the thin times, were the best times of their lives. Rewards come later, but the real joy in life comes from just being able to stay in the game. Although Zippy's big nose was never photographed hitting the wire first, he did savor every moment of a match.

On September 8, over the same fast Northampton track, Zippy went off at 9–1 and finished fourth by fifteen lengths in a seven-horse field. When the three leading horses began bumping each other in the backstretch, according to the race footnotes, "Zippy Chippy raced wide and never threatened." Hey, it's a beautiful day at the track – who needs that nonsense? Zippy gladly took his longevity record and $185 back to the barn. On that day Mr. Peanut didn't just beat Zippy by fifteen lengths – he beat everybody! Yes, in a weird kind of bar-snack mix-up, Mr. Peanut lost his cherry. Adding salt to the wound, jockey Willie Belmonte took Mr. Peanut to the wire ten lengths ahead of the field. Finishing dead last, Timing Perfect's timing was fatally flawed.

Now bested in succession by Mr. Peanut, Unblessed, and Takin' Up Space, Zippy Chippy was losing to some of the saddest names in horse racing. If there was ever a horse named Dead Last that finished dead last in an eight-horse race, Zippy Chippy would have created some sort of calamity in which he managed to come ninth. Nonetheless, arrogantly strutting back to his stall, Zippy always won the postgame performance by two or three lengths.

Track media wondered aloud why Felix was still running what they referred to as his "hapless horse." They strongly suggested that Zippy was long overdue for retirement. In fairness, although Zippy now had ninety-five consecutive losses, in 2002 the Chicago Cubs hadn't won the World Series in ninety-four years, and nobody was calling for that franchise to be dismantled. The Cubs to this day have a strong and loyal fan base, because, like no other professional baseball team in existence, *they are the Cubs*. *Allegiance*: a strong word, a good word, that gets so little play these days.

"He keeps going because he doesn't like to stand in his stall all day," said the trainer, looking at the reporters like they were probably the sort of underachievers who did. *But he can't win*, chorused the critics. Zippo! Like the Lighter: Flaming Out Again, mocked one sports headline. Beaten but Alive: Loss #95, bellowed another. But Felix Monserrate, who obliged when asked to autograph those same clippings, paid no attention to the headlines.

"If you keep trying, you maybe will make it," he said. And with that, the man who always stood shoulder to shoulder with his horse even though he could probably walk right under him without knocking off his trademark blue "Zippy Chippy" cap began to prepare his pony for career race number ninety-six.

Success is in the trying just as surely as the proof is in the pudding, whatever that actually means. Failure can be as fleeting as fame, unless you have the courage to carry on. You can bury a lot of bad stuff behind you when you're completely focused on the next big contest. That's where Zippy's strength came from: the hope of the next test, the anticipation of another race.

Felix could understand and accept Zippy Chippy's losses, but he could never abandon the prospect of success and the pride in saddling up his horse one more time, chasing that elusive win that nobody but he and Zippy's fans believed he would ever achieve. They were going the distance together, hell or high odds.

So seven days later, over a fast track and under a cloudy sky, in a short race with a small purse, Zippy Chippy boldly went out and put on a very unspectacular performance for his ever-expanding club of fans. With the noise of the fairground's midway drifting over the track, Zippy ended any suspense the contest might have generated early on. Fifth into the stretch, he simply drifted off across the track in a dream world of his own. He finished six lengths behind a thoroughbred who was actually his own age, an eleven-year-old maiden named Quincy Kid. Lots of Power throttled back at the wire, coming in second by a neck. The newspapers enjoyed their usual headline humor: No Fix: ZIPPY CHIPPY HITS 96.

Mike Moran, a longtime sportswriter for the local *Daily Hampshire Gazette*, still remembers the sadness that lingered that day long after the press had packed up and gone home. It was raining softly when he finally found Zippy in a stall way back of the fairgrounds. "He was so alone," said Moran. "There were no horses near him, nobody around. There was just Zippy Chippy and two empty cans of Coors Light on the edge of his stall."

Thinking a change of scenery might mean a change of luck, seven months later Felix wrangled Zippy into his transport trailer for the five-hour trip to North Randall, Ohio. The nearly ninety-year-old ThistleDown racetrack, now merged and renamed ThistleDown Racino, is a one-mile dirt oval close enough to Cleveland that you can still smell the smoke from the massive bonfire that Cleveland Cavaliers fans built in the summer of 2010, using LeBron James jerseys as kindling.

At the new ThistleDown, now owned by Caesars Entertainment, the slots that never stop have revived the track that now offers one hundred racing days each year. Although the glittering casino outshines the one-mile dirt oval, still, they come – the handlers of horses, the jockeys, the walkers, the grooms, the trainers leading their mounts from backside to trackside – mostly for love and what little money they can manage to squeeze from the long hours in this unusual trade that many of them have been born into.

Running in the first race of Wednesday's card on April 16, 2003, the ThistleDown adventure produced a particularly poor performance, with Zippy finishing last by nearly thirty-two lengths. This meant that the winner, Mr. Chris Gibbs, hit the wire, got his photo taken in the winner's circle, and was cooled down, brushed up, and sitting in the corner of his stall reading the *Daily Racing Form* by the time Zippy crossed the finish line. As the trackside wiseass always says, any horse that loses by thirty-two lengths should be clocked with a sundial instead of a stopwatch.

Newcomer Benjamin Cacha Padilla had a nice ride around the track aboard Zippy, and at that clip he was able to take in some of the sights. All that scenery, all that greenery – why not take the long way home? At twelve years old, Zippy now held a record of twelve thirds and seven seconds. By comparison, Mr. Z ran a tad faster in last year's running of the Ohio Derby on the same track and took home a winner's share that was $270,000 more than the Zipster's career earnings of $29,952 to date. The Ohio Derby is ThistleDown's signature stakes race with a total purse of $500,000. Horses of Zippy's caliber have to pay to watch this derby from the sidelines.

Ten hours in the back of a truck for an eighth-place finish, eighty-two dollars, a new record of ninety-seven consecutive losses – who thought this trip was a good idea? Having seen Zippy lose by sixteen lengths to a horse named Dude Anonymous, Felix must have wanted to buy up all the official results sheets and burn them behind the barn. But then, Zippy would have likely enjoyed that, his very own bonfire of the vanities. You just couldn't win with this guy. Headed for home, Zippy Chippy was just four days short of his real day of birth, April 20. Oh, if Mom could only see him now, she'd . . . she'd probably give up breeding.

Even by Zippy's racing standards, the horse was now officially underachieving, and Felix sensed it might be all over for his boy. Zippy could almost smell the scent of oat bran and mothballs coming from the Old Friends farm near Saratoga Springs, where over-the-hill horses like him went to carpet bowl and guess how many jelly beans were in the bell jar. And yes, he did love jelly beans. However, after almost five months of mulling things over, Felix decided against retirement and brought Zippy Chippy back to what was now his favorite track, Northampton Fair, the site of some of his best near wins. "He had," said the trainer, "some really close calls here."

The handicapper who had witnessed Zippy's running of seventy races at Finger Lakes did not believe that Felix was enjoying the fun the press were having at Zippy's expense. Said Dave Mattice, "I think between races, Felix enjoyed the notoriety of Zippy's losing streak, but when he got him saddled up in the paddock, Felix's aim was to win. He was all business once the game was on."

Trotting out onto the track for the first race on this balmy Saturday afternoon on the sixth day of September, Zippy looked like he was going to kick some serious ass. His head was high and his gait was assertive as he loped down the track toward the start. Even his companion pony seemed impressed that he wouldn't have to do any Zippy Chippy herding today. Yet many at the track that day believed this would be Zippy's last race. One more last-place finish – or, worse, failure to finish at all – and even the fun-loving Northampton stewards would not be amused.

"He feel good here," said Felix, "close to his people." With its triangular track surrounded by a Ferris wheel and fast food booths, it was hard not to be close to people at Northampton Fair, especially the ones with sticky fingers and pink cotton candy stuck in their hair.

Felix wondered which horse would show up today: the one who would focus on the start of the five-furlong course and give himself a chance to win, or the one who played the part of a prison lifer, not caring to leave his cell even when the door burst open? Felix never wanted to relive the nightmare of Zippy's banishment from Finger Lakes; it was a permanent stain on his training record.

Dwelling may have been a dark thought rattling around in the back of Felix's mind, but no such thoughts were troubling Zippy. Today Zippy Chippy proved to be a gamer, all business from bell to wire, or as Felix liked to say, "from posta da posta."

Breaking clean and fast from his eighth hole position, Zippy looked like the racehorse Felix always knew he could be. Head down, rider up, Zippy flew from the gate, lean and mean with a mission in mind. Aboard Zippy Chippy for the first time, jockey Howard Lanci just let him go, no direction, no whip necessary.

Zippy passed the rest of the field early and, believe it or not, easily. At the near pole, he was about six lengths ahead of the pack of seven maidens. Zippy did not try to trash talk the other horses or bite them or slow down to let them catch up. He took the lead and held it, still six lengths out front at the second pole. Even when he was challenged by Short Notice and tailgated from behind by Unblessed, Zippy kept out in front coming into the homestretch, although his six-length lead had shrunk to a half a length. The crowd cheered wildly, and Felix and Zippy's handlers yelled themselves hoarse. (Sorry.) Heading home, the horse found himself in a place he'd seldom been before – first. He was lunging now to stay ahead of Short Notice, while Unblessed dogged them both from behind. Racing to the wire, Zippy was clinging to the lead, holding on by only his toenails.

He battled Short Notice right to the very end in front of a roaring grandstand crowd, head to head, shoulder to shoulder, with riding crops slapping a whole bunch of asses as the pack scrambled toward the finish line. The two horses hit the tape in almost a dead heat, except Short Notice was leaning in. A winner by one lousy neck. Spent but still spunky, Zippy Chippy finished second by two feet. The heart was strong, the legs a little less so, and for one brief, dazzling moment, it had looked as if the Zipster's fortune and fate would come down to lucky number ninety-eight.

But wait! A yellow inquiry sign began flashing on the board. A foul had been claimed! Zippy's former (weren't they all?) jockey Willie Belmonte, who today was aboard Unblessed, lodged a formal complaint claiming that Short Notice had interfered with his mount in the first turn. It was obvious to the crowd that Belmonte and Unblessed had been bumped by Edgar Paucar's winning mount, but was it intentional, and did it affect the outcome of the race? With the most to gain from the inquiry, Howard Lanci stayed away from the fray, taking Zippy for a jog far down the track.

Silence dampened the mood of the track as bettors took their eyes off the inquiry sign only long enough to check their tickets. If Belmonte's claim of foul was upheld, then his horse, who had come in third, would be moved up to second and Short Notice would be disqualified. The second-place horse would be moved up to first place, thereby making Zippy Chippy the race winner. Oddly enough, once again the Zipster's future was in the hands of the men with binoculars strapped to their foreheads and video monitors on their desks.

For some of the longest minutes of Felix Monserrate's life, the track steward pored over the tapes of the race from every angle, trying to analyze the alleged foul. The officials saw the clash, they agreed there was bumping, but was the hit deliberate and therefore a foul?

"He ran a good race," said Felix nervously, nodding toward his horse, who was still out on the track wondering why he wasn't being led back to the barn as usual. That bucket of cold water hanging from the wall in his stall wasn't going to drink itself.

As the four horses involved in the inquiry cooled down and mingled in front of the grandstand, the winner's circle remained vacant. Zippy looked at it, somewhat confused. *Gee, I've never been in that place before. Is it new?*

And then . . . a collective sigh came up from the crowd as the ominous INQUIRY on the sign was replaced with the decisive word OFFICIAL. Foul play had been ruled out. Willie Belmonte's claim had been denied. Having lost the race and then the appeal, Zippy Chippy had been beaten both at the wire and up in the booth. This was the closest Zippy had come to winning in nine years of trying, including the mesmerizing match against Black Rifle that had taken place exactly three years before.

"He was in front by six lengths," said Felix, the excitement in his voice betraying the fact that he'd never before witnessed his horse with such a commanding lead. "They had to run to catch him today. He was on top today." They nodded in unison, the trainer and his fidgeting horse.

For five fast furlongs over soft and hallowed soil, Zippy Chippy had been on fire. Full-striding down that beaten path, he looked downright Jack Londonish: *I would rather that my spark should burn out in a brilliant blaze . . .* Today Zippy knew where the finish line was and how to get there in a timely fashion. In less than two divine minutes, it seemed that Zippy Chippy had had his bum patted by the gods of thoroughbred racing.

If Felix was stunned by the loss, Zippy's fans were devastated. The horse himself was so upset that he shaved a full ten seconds off his backside victory dance. Back in his stall, he polished off his dinner like it might be his last meal ever. Racetrack officials could be fickle, but feed bags were forever. Many believed this would have been an excellent place to hang up Zippy's halter, while he was almost on top for once. However, Felix, seeing the glass as half full and then topping it up with a can of Coors, took the near win as a sign that things were finally turning around.

Yeah, in the trainer's eyes, Zippy's losing streak was ripe for the breaking.

"You watch, next week. We gonna win," boasted Felix, talking to anybody and everybody at once. "This much he lose by," he said, as if he were telling a fisherman's tale about a trout he'd hooked and lost.

And Zippy may very well have won the next time out. He was fit, he was primed, he was due. But torrential rain that week washed out most of western Massachusetts and the race card along with it. From horses to humans to Mother Nature, there were many obstacles to winning a race, and Zippy Chippy had come up against them all. His racing season was done. A sad bit of irony here is that Short Notice only ran three races in his career, using this one to crush the Zipster.

The squeaker with Short Notice made all the sports headlines. LOSS NUMBER 98: AT LEAST ZIPPY GOT OUT OF THE GATE! Nobody knew it at the time, but this valiant duel with Short Notice would be Zippy's last great hurrah.

Zippy Chippy's future as a racehorse may have been in serious doubt, but according to Felix, the rest of his life never was: "Even if I die, my daughter is never going to let him go out of the family. He been like family for all of us." Felix Monserrate, president and CEO of the American Foundation of Underdogs.

THOSE CURSED AND BLESSED CHICAGO CUBS

Plagued by a 106-year championship drought, the Chicago Cubs had the dubious distinction of being the worst team in Major League Baseball and professional sports in general. Incredibly, the NFL, the NBA, and the NHL hadn't even been created back in 1908 when the Cubs' sad streak began.

Known as the "Lovable Losers," the Cubs haven't even appeared in the World Series since 1945, when the Curse of the Billy Goat came down on their superstitious heads. All was going well for the Cubs that year; they were up two games to one against the Detroit Tigers. Billy Sianis, owner of a popular pub called the Billy Goat Tavern, was in the stands cheering on his hometown heroes. Murphy, his goat, was right beside him, drinking beer and eating everything the fans threw his way. But there's always one party pooper, and this one happened to be P.K. Wrigley, the owner of the field and the franchise. He ordered that Sianis and Murphy be removed from the ballpark because they were "stinking up the joint."

Outraged, Billy left Wrigley Field with his goat in tow, but not before he uttered those fateful words: "The Cubs, they ain't gonna win no more." The hometown team lost that game, as well as the series, to the Tigers. With the Cubs out of the playoffs yet again, the tavern owner sent a telegram to Wrigley that read, "Who stinks now?" The Cubs did not win a National League pennant until 2015, seventy years after "goatgate."

And yet the team was still wildly popular with American sports fans, fiercely defended and much loved by their diehard following. In the summer of 2013, the Cubs finished in last place, but they were second in attendance. When true fans swear allegiance to their team, the game itself makes the trophy look tiny. A ballpark for the ages, a sunny day, the Cubs, a chili dog, and a beer — what's not to love about America's pastime? Believers in the Windy City may moan and groan, but they could never get mad at their Cubs.

Before the fall of 2015, the closest the Cubs ever came to breaking the curse and the losing streak was at Wrigley Field on October 14, 2003, when they were about to defeat the Florida Marlins in game six of the National League Championship Series. They were up 3–0 in the game and 3–2 in the series. Moises Alou jumped high from the warning track to haul in a long fly ball from the bat of the Marlins' second baseman, Luis Castillo. But a guy in the stands beat him to it. Cubs fan Steve Bartman interfered with Alou by reaching down and grabbing the ball that was about to enter his glove. Rattled and believing the Curse of the Billy Goat was back, the Cubs quickly gave up eight consecutive runs and were eliminated from the playoffs the next day. The ball thief was escorted from Wrigley Field by police for his own protection in what is now known as the "Steve Bartman Incident."

Great spoilers in sports history: Billy Sianis, Steve Bartman, Black Rifle, and Short Notice. I hope you're all quite proud of yourselves.

TWENTY-TWO

Every day may not be good, but there's
something good in every day.
Anonymous

hould he, would he, ever race Zippy Chippy again? That
was the question Felix Monserrate was asked every time he
faced the media as well as his family and fellow tracksters.
Although his answer was yes one day and no the next, he knew
one thing for sure. When people – and yes, Zippy qualified as a
person; after all, he had been covered in *People* magazine – stop
doing what they love, they die from the inside out.

"People say, 'Put him inside the fence, he will be happy.' He
will not be happy. Not Zippy," said Felix, the homestretch philosopher. "It's like when someone is working for thirty years and
he loves his job and you retire him, send him home, he get sick.
People die from doing nothing." Standing next to Felix, Zippy
swished his tail back and forth liked he was agreeing with his
trainer . . . or simply swatting flies.

Felix was bang on. Anything with a soul, be it humans or
horses, shrivels up and retreats into a shell when separated from
the love of life. Far too many people fail to make a healthy transition to retirement and die slowly, longing for a return to their
life's work, which is all they ever knew.

So, hand to harness and over uncertain ground, Felix and Zippy continued to walk the rocky path of racetrack life together. Both wanted to finish as winners in their careers, but the synergy and the alignment of the stars had so far never been quite right. Whether it be in the sweet stillness of dawn, or the end of a long day sharing a beer, there was always more hope in their stable than hay. Although second place was as close as Zippy had ever come to winning, number ninety-nine had a real ring to it. Plus, Zippy loved the Three County fairgrounds; you could smell the hot dogs browning on a midway grill all the way from the starting gate. People standing around with food in their hands, distracted by the sounds of the rides, were easy targets for the Zipster.

Saturday, September 4, 2004 was a nice day in western Massachusetts, perfect for a long race of six and a half furlongs in order to win a slice of a $3,100 pie. Thousands of fans showed up to see Zippy Chippy make his ninety-ninth career appearance, and his tenth at this now rickety yet rich-in-history track. They came in throngs adorned with clothes bearing his name; they bet in big numbers, knowing the tickets would probably never get cashed. They celebrated the mere sight of him. Here at Northampton Fair, Zippy was not just another horse. Here, he was listed as the fairground's top attraction, followed by the Russian American Kids Circus, an all-day blues festival, and Megatron, "the world's largest mobile roller coaster." And, given the steel shoes he was wearing, don't think that he couldn't have kicked the crap out of that machine too!

It was also exactly one year since Zippy had missed the first win of his career by a neck, followed by an inquiry denied. Now thirteen years old, Zippy charged around Northampton's paddock, preparing for yet one more race against seven other members of racing's Never-Won-One Club. A cherry would be broken today; the only question was whose.

The Zippy Chippy story was resonating with audiences everywhere. The media, both local and national, stood five deep around Zippy's stall, peppering Felix with questions he had answered so many times before. They were harder on Felix than usual, claiming that ninety-eight losses in a row was plenty for this horse's career, calling yet again for his retirement. Other trainers, jealous of all the attention Zippy was getting, were also highly critical of Felix. They dropped lines to the press like "mockery of the sport" and "sick of hearing about such a great loser."

Three County Fair, very pleased with the commotion he created and the money he generated, sided with Zippy Chippy and not his critics. Said steward Russell Derderian, "Fans realize that betting on Zippy Chippy is probably a hopeless pursuit, but that doesn't stop them."

Zippy, on the other hand – who made it a point never to read his own press clippings or listen to trainers, particularly his own – was bristling to get the bridle on. Hell, he'd almost won his last time out! He had beaten his former jockey Willie Belmonte by two feet at the wire. He had won $500. He had embarrassed Streak Face and Stoker Bill by eleven lengths. Zippy Chippy was on one of his best losing streaks ever!

The real odds of him winning this race were almost incalculably long, but on the scale of sentimentality, a horse all hopped up and ready to roll at two losses shy of a hundred carries a lot of weight. A klutz maybe, but this horse had guts. Zippy's resolve in the face of overwhelming odds and near-certain defeat made for a story that only common folk could relate to. While the handicappers and horsemen laughed at the horse that had never won a race, lines of little people, real people with hard jobs and soft hearts, gathered on the apron of the track. *Been there too, big guy,* they were saying with thumbs up and fists pumping above their Zippy Chippy hats. They nodded in empathy, they clapped their hands in commiseration, and they shared the unspoken dream of winning someday too. Maybe today?

Think about it. You're a vacuum cleaner salesman who has just had ninety-eight doors in a row slammed in your face. How eager are you to make the walk up the steps to house number ninety-nine and force yourself to knock on that door? They called him hopeless and they described his efforts as lame, but they were wrong. This horse had game. The press could print all the silly headlines they wanted – 98 AND LATE AGAIN – but this was a horse who walked the walk, ran the race, and finished them all. Say what you want about his record; a decade after being gelded, Zippy Chippy still had balls.

Shining from a slight sweat and pulling his handlers along the paddock walk, Zippy neighed and nickered his approval to the gathering of groupies. Taking the lead from Woody Allen, Zippy had come to believe that with this bunch, half the job was just showing up.

As the colorful medley of maidens and their riders gamboled toward the starting gate, a rumble of thunder rolled over the race-track, spooking some of the horses. But not Zippy. A triple threat today – number one in the program, number one at the pole, and number one in the hearts of the crowd – Zippy was unfazed by the lightning flashing in the distance. Breaking cleanly from the start with an easy gait, Zippy took a good lead, but his early sprint was checked by jockey Joe Riston, who pulled him to the rail at the first turn and steadied him into the middle of the pack. After that, Riston "sat chilly" on the horse, doing nothing but going for a ride. Perhaps he was saving some of the speed Zippy had shown in his last race for the late stages of this one.

By the first pole, Summer Deposit had assumed the lead, with Zippy in a comfortable third. By the half pole the leader was ahead of the pack by five lengths, and Zippy had dropped back to fifth place. Into the stretch, Summer Deposit held strong to the lead while Zippy slipped back to seventh, fighting his rider all the way down the stretch. Frankly – and he'd had these heated discussions with Felix before – why did he even need a jockey? They were always pushing and shoving him around, holding him back when he was ready to fly, slapping his ass with that whip when it was obvious he was tired or wanted to slow down and maybe have a quick visit with his fans in the grandstand. Plus, he'd be a helluva lot faster without 112 pounds of aggressiveness on his back. Jockeys! They were worse than mothers-in-law and backseat drivers.

It was clear that Zippy's enthusiasm had been curbed. He never recovered his pace. Summer Deposit rolled to an easy victory, and Slim Cat, Father Dooley, and yet again Takin' Up Space all hit the wire ahead of Zippy, who finished thirty-two lengths behind the winner. Officially, Zippy came in last, because Ordvou pulled up lame. One smart-ass in the backside said that by the time Zippy got back to the barn, he tiptoed in so as not to wake the other horses.

As Zippy snorted and kicked, Riston tried to cool him down. He looked like he was mad as hell, like he'd been wronged. Later, in the tack room, the jockey put it all on the horse. "He seems like one of those attitude horses," said Riston. "It just seems like he couldn't ever settle down and couldn't relax."

Obviously totally unfamiliar with his mount, the rider could not have been more wrong. He was not an attitude horse. Zippy Chippy was Attitude Horse of the Century.

Felix was uncharacteristically furious, and not above throwing the blame across the room. "The jockey wouldn't let him run," he said. He railed into the microphones, using the harshest words he had ever uttered to one of his riders.

Felix took one last look at Summer Deposit having his picture taken in the winner's circle and being petted by a clutch of well-dressed family members. He was taking this loss bitterly. It wasn't often that he criticized one of his jockeys — mainly because they were usually so mad they didn't hang around long enough for him to talk to them. But the frustration was showing on the man's face when he gave his take on Zippy's performance: "There wasn't any speed in the race, so I told the jockey to go for the lead and stay there as long as he could. But he don't do that for me."

As if he needed another problem beyond the ones that came naturally to him, Zippy had been shortchanged. Objects in the barn seemed louder than usual today as they collided with Zippy's shoes. "The people love him because he always tries," said Felix. Still, the sadness lingered in his voice and eyes as he finished, "Zippy has the right to be mad."

All things considered, this should have been Zippy's best shot at a win. He had been eager, the field had been slow, and a win had been in the rarified air of the impending storm that had started in the sky and spread to the expectant fairgrounds crowd. Today of all days, Zippy needed a bad ride like Dr. Phil needs a haircut. Riston had ruined the race, but Zippy took the rap — ninety-nine losses in a row. To err is human; to go zero for ninety-nine straight is . . . horse. To mark Felix's words, Riston had ridden this horse for the last time.

Zippy should have gone off at Ordvou's odds of 84–1, but fan loyalty had put him on the board at 5–1, the favorite of the day. All you gotta do is believe.

Those who watched the race but declined to bet rated their chances of cashing a winning ticket on Zippy Chippy as about the same as seeing a man go to the moon in a lawn chair propelled by a bunch of helium balloons. Hey, it could happen, but . . .

As his people gathered in the barn after the race, rubbing his nose and spoiling him with treats, the press cornered Felix with one question in mind: Would he finally stop the bleeding at ninety-nine losses, or would he go for one hundred even?

"We're just taking everything a day at a time," he replied. Smart thinking, because if you don't think every day is important in its own right, try missing one once in a while. But as he walked away, clutching Zippy cautiously by his leather lead, Felix shook his head and smiled to himself. *The media*, he thought, *they never ask the right questions*. The correct question was, *What do we have to lose?*

WHAT EXACTLY ARE THE ODDS OF A MAN GOING TO THE MOON IN A LAWN CHAIR?

A lot better now that Larry Walters of North Hollywood, California, has pushed that envelope up into the jet stream.

Time magazine's Man of the Year for 1982 was the computer, "Machine of the Year." Bad choice. Me, I picked Larry Walters, who went where no man had dared to go before, at least not in a lawn chair. Larry accepted the challenge of the human spirit and showed amazing resourcefulness, and although (as any woman could have predicted) he did screw up big time, he also did not die. Far too many men perish after uttering the words "Watch this!"

Larry had experienced a Peter Pan–style dream in which he hooked himself to a bundle of balloons and floated high past the sprawling Los Angeles metropolis and into the desert beyond. This, I think, is the dream of every man who wears a cap with a red feather on the side and a leotard that is way too tight. So Larry built his dream ship, which consisted of a fold-up aluminum lawn chair attached to forty-five helium-filled weather balloons and a bunch of milk jugs full of water for ballast. Simple by design, Larry's home-made dirigible had going-up power, coming-down weight, and a lawn chair where a cockpit would normally be. His on-board equipment consisted of a two-way radio, an altimeter, a wristwatch, a Coke, a sandwich, and a pellet pistol. Because he lacked a pilot's locker, Larry's aviation tools were selected for their ability to fit in the front pockets of his pants.

I know what you're asking yourself: Why the wristwatch? Well, that was so Larry could make it home in time for supper after his inaugural flight. The purpose of the pellet gun was to shoot out the weather balloons in the event he had to make an emergency landing.

On the morning of July 2, 1982, Larry strapped himself into his helium-charged contraption, christened *Inspiration 1*, intending to follow his flight plan, which went over Long Beach and then headed three hundred miles east, over the Mojave Desert. Southwest Airlines was a little peeved, because normally that's their route.

Larry was tethered to earth by three ropes tied to his Jeep; his girlfriend cut the first one and the other two snapped unexpectedly, and – WHOAAAAA! – "Lawn Chair Larry" launched prematurely.

Rising faster than a speeding basket, he reached an altitude of fifteen thousand feet in a matter of minutes. Witnesses agreed that anything that leaves the ground that fast is usually taking supplies to the space station. Not one but two commercial airline pilots, from Delta and TWA, reported the sighting of a man in a lawn chair flying through the primary approach corridor of the Long Beach Airport. Drug testing being what it is in the airline industry, it took great courage for the pilots to report Larry to the control tower.

Still rising and getting dizzy in the cold, thin air, Larry began his descent by shooting out the weather balloons, until he accidentally dropped the gun overboard. Lawn Chair Larry came down out of the sky faster than . . . well, faster than a guy strapped into a lawn chair and attached to really heavy milk jugs. As he headed for a crash landing on a golf course, the balloons's cables somehow wrapped themselves around a power line. Dangling from the wire like a tangled-up puppet, Larry miraculously failed to die. Eventually he was rescued by some golfers, who were given a Breathalyzer test by police after they reported what they'd seen.

Larry subsequently appeared in magazine ads for Timex, the maker of the wristwatch he was wearing during his flight.

Larry's Timex took a licking and kept on ticking, but for years his face twitched every time he spotted a lawn chair.

Larry was paid $1,000 for the Timex ad and fined $1,500 by the United States Federal Aviation Administration for entering international airspace without an airplane.

Free-falling from three miles out of the sky in a lawn chair — guys like Larry and horses like Zippy Chippy do not fold, no matter what the odds.

TWENTY-THREE

When the world says, "Give up,"
Hope whispers, "Try it one more time."
Anonymous

On a gorgeous late summer afternoon in Northampton, Massachusetts — September 10, 2004 — the trainer and his horse-for-life went through their early pre-race routine. Zippy was fed and watered, washed and dried. The track vet had been by earlier to check his legs, jogging him up and down the shed row to make sure he was sound. No swelling and no limping meant no late scratch necessary. Zippy was fit as a fiddle. Okay, an old fiddle, in that he was being prepped for race number one hundred while the total number of races of the seven other horses was eighty-two.

Felix gave him the game plan: break clean, keep pace with the pack, and sprint for the wire mid-stretch. The horse nodded in agreement, and when Felix turned to grab his harness, Zippy knocked the trainer's hat off with his nose.

"Zippy is healthy and happy," said Felix. "He wants to run. We get a terrible ride Saturday, but with a shorter race and another jockey, I think Zippy can win his one hundredth race and then probably retire."

There they were, striding side by side, headed for Zippy Chippy's historic one hundredth post parade. Together still, despite so many things that could have derailed their relationship along the way. During that extraordinary number of races, Zippy could have suffered a career-ending injury. Similarly, Felix could have suffered a career-ending injury, delivered by Zippy's large teeth or back feet. Zippy's record of ninety-nine consecutive losses didn't seem to bother either the man or the mount — at least until some smart-ass hot-walker strolled by their stall singing, "Ninety-nine bottles of beer on the wall, ninety-nine bottles of beer . . ."

Zippy Chippy seemed to attract wise guys like flies to an unkempt pen. Back home in Rochester, the hot topic of the day was the naming of the new commuter ferry that would link that city to Toronto. *The Breeze* seemed to be a clear winner, until a letter from Mike Mumford of nearby Greece, New York, appeared in the *Democrat and Chronicle*. "Good name but bad bet," it read. "In honor of the legendary racehorse Zippy Chippy, I suggest the ferry be renamed *Zippy Shippy*." Zippy had always been the butt of jokes by America's most high-profile comedians. Now the amateurs were weighing in.

Calm and all saddled up, Zippy heard the paddock judge yell for one last time, "Riders up!" With a push from Felix, Willie Belmonte vaulted up and aboard the horse. Jockey and mount were comfortable with each other. Zippy had shown the rider the respect of never having tossed him down the track like a human bowling ball. Many of the horse's exercise riders wished they could make that claim.

It was twenty minutes to post time, and the odds were tumbling fast in Zippy's favor. The jockeys took one turn around the paddock's walking ring, feeling the quiet power of the beasts beneath them and getting a sense of their dispositions on this day. Today the paddock was a free-for-all, with fans three deep at the fence and parents holding children on their shoulders. Willie Belmonte had to smile at the irony of the horse with the worst record in the race getting all the attention of a Derby winner.

A steady crowd still poured through the fairgrounds gate, half of them climbing the steps into the covered grandstand, the rest staking out prime positions with lawn chairs down on the tarmac. With Zippy running in the second race, many of them had arrived late. It was a brief five furlongs with a low purse of $3,100, but none of that really mattered, because this was not your usual racetrack crowd. These people were common, mostly rural folk, here to watch their lovable aging gelding close out his career. They were loud with laughter and effusive with their affection for this unpredictable half ton of trouble who, when he twitched those ears and bared those teeth, could easily be mistaken for a jackass.

The real racetrack aficionados could be identified by the forms in their hands and the pencils behind their ears. Most stood in front of a row of eight television monitors that were simulcasting races from other tracks. Others sat quietly handicapping races in "The Clubhouse," which here at the tri-county track was really a multi-vehicle garage set up with long tables and folding chairs. A few people with programs in their back pockets lined up at the Steak on a Stick stand. Northampton was no "Big A" like Aqueduct; its dining area was more coffee-truck concession than four-star establishment.

At 1:45 p.m., everyone, even the track staff and vendors, gathered to watch the horse of the hour prance out onto the dirt oval for his one hundredth appearance as a professional thoroughbred racehorse. When the bugler called for the parade to post, there was a smattering of applause for the first six horses that emerged from the paddock and sauntered onto the track.

But when horse number seven came into view, the party at the fair was on. Women screamed, men whistled, and the cameras clicked like never before, because this was Zippy Chippy's century entry, most certainly his last race. This was small-town history anointed with national importance. This would become the kind of firsthand folklore reminiscing that seniors pass on to their bored grandchildren.

With his bright-orange silks nicely matched to his dark-brown mount, Willie Belmonte waved for the cameras and winked at the crowd gathered at the rail, close enough to touch. With eleven wins in five days of racing, he was the leading jockey at this meet. "He's pretty photogenic, huh?" he said, as Zippy took it all in stride, bobbing and nodding and teasing his flock.

Once out onto the track that had so many tight turns it was nicknamed the "bull ring," perhaps sensing that his rider was stealing the spotlight, Zippy threw a hissy fit. He reared up and kicked backwards until Felix and a handler ran onto the track to calm him down. Belmonte quickly dismounted before he got tossed and added his weight to this tug-of-war. First the crowd laughed, and then they applauded; they had already gotten their money's worth, and Zippy hadn't made it to the starting gate yet. Subsequently, the *Baltimore Sun* ran a photo on the front page of its sports section showing the horse up in the air, ass-first, with three men struggling to bring him back to earth. The headline read, AT RACE 100, HARD TO BLAME "ZIPPY" FOR BEING CHIPPY.

Not optimistic about the outcome of the race, Belmonte remounted his number seven horse and joked that it would be better if Zippy got his photos taken "at the other end of the race." He meant, of course, the winner's circle, a place Zippy had avoided all his life like it was the showcase for buyers from a French canned food company called Viande de Cheval.

The punters of this short race ignored Zippy Chippy, considering him a non-factor. At the other extreme, fans of Zippy Chippy, both here at Northampton and at tracks all across North America, pushed enough money through the betting windows to make him the 2–1 favorite. That is, one chance in two of winning for a horse that had lost ninety-nine races in a row. With this, his eleventh career appearance at Northampton Fair, the management could have divided the wagering windows into two categories, with one marked "Bet with Your Head" and the other "Bet with Your Heart."

This fall fairgrounds classic pitted Zippy Chippy, the veteran who had pounded it out at ten racetracks, two Standardbred ovals, and one baseball outfield against a bunch of snot-nosed (really, when they get all excited and sweaty, the stuff is flying everywhere) three-year-olds who would never know the feeling of losing ninety-nine times in a row. The total age of any four horses in this race was twelve. Zippy was thirteen. Ageless, Zippy Chippy was losing races when some of these young bucks were ponies being rented out for birthday parties.

Judy Peck, a fifty-eight-year-old mother of six from nearby Springfield, Massachusetts, wearing a Zippy Chippy T-shirt and a Zippy Chippy hat and carrying her Zippy Chippy scrapbook under her arm, spoke for the entire faithful flock when she said, "I guess I'm always cheering for the underdog. We're hoping one hundred will be the charm." A Boston Red Sox fan as well, Judy had a large framed photograph of Zippy on her kitchen wall at home.

The odds on her hero had risen to 7–2, making him the second favorite in the race by the time the bell sounded to open the starting gate and the field of horses rushed to the rail. All except Zippy, who turned to the crowd and reared up slightly, doing what appeared to be a poor imitation of Mel Gibson's stallion in *Braveheart*.

"It was really something to see," remembered Judy. "All of us — and there was a lot of us — were yelling and screaming Zippy's name, and as soon as he left the gate he stopped to look to see who was calling him. He knew his name, and he kinda turned to the crowd to acknowledge the applause."

Taking a bit of a bow on his two hind legs was an entirely new maneuver for Zippy, as far as anybody could recall. Leaving the gate like a walking circus horse was almost as unique as not leaving the starting gate at all. I mean, really . . . a curtain call! Who saw that one coming? Willie Belmonte, who had somehow managed not to get thrown off during this spectacle, hustled his mount back up into the pack, but the late start and extra speed needed to catch the others cost them dearly. The leaders forced Zippy to the outside, and Belmonte took him five wide around the first turn. Zippy definitely did not need the extra distance added to his trip round the tri-county oval.

Coming into the homestretch, Zippy was closing in on the third horse, Trick Me Not, who was only four lengths behind Big Shoulders, the leader. His head was bowed, his legs wobbled a bit, but in closing, he never wavered. Even his following beyond the fence found it quite amazing that the Zipster, after his bow-to-the-crowd start, was challenging the front-runners all the way down the backstretch.

And then he faded, gradually at first, and then badly. Seven steeds in front of him rushed past the grandstand as one. As Biggs surged to a two-length win at the wire, it wasn't hard to spot Zippy Chippy — alone, lagging, flagging, and last.

While Biggs and his jockey, Jesse Hall, were being photographed for posterity in the winner's circle, Zippy was having his riding saddle unceremoniously removed from his back. While Biggs had a floral wreath hung around his neck, Zippy was walking back to the barn in his sweaty and somewhat wrinkled birthday suit. While Biggs's record would list just this one win in a short and shabby career of eleven races, Zippy could only dream of a victory in nine times that many trips around the track. Plus one. This one. But whereas Biggs heard only the clicking of a camera, Zippy Chippy listened to the applause of an adoring entourage who had gotten exactly what they came for.

"Broke in the air from the gate" is how one sportswriter described Zippy's start. "And the beat, or better yet, the beatings, go on for Zippy Chippy" is how he summarized the final scene.

Felix seemed to dive headfirst into a deep pit of denial. "Zippy got a bad break today, but what are you going to do?" he said. "You have to take what they give us." Desperation even brought a religious bent to his way of thinking: "We said we were going to win, but God said no. Zippy had bad luck this week and bad luck last week, and I hope to God he gets better luck next week." This was strange stuff indeed. Normally after a big loss, Felix would console himself with a couple of cold beers and a President Kennedy misquote.

"I want to keep him running until he tells me he doesn't want to run anymore," said Felix. "The curves here are just too sharp."

Scraping the bottom of the barrel of blame with this landmark one hundredth loss, Felix first put it on God, then on lady luck, and finally on the track. Fortunately Zippy's greatest fan, Judy Peck, wasn't standing nearby, or he would have blamed her too.

"We were pretty sad," said Judy, "but Zippy really tried his best. He nearly caught up to the rest." After the horse was toweled down, cooled off, and blanketed down, Felix treated Zippy to a cold beer, which the cocky horse mistook for champagne.

In his less-than-illustrious career of running in one hundred races and even more training sessions with approximately seven or more horses in front of him each time, or galloping in those early time trials behind the round rumps of a rotating roster of young thoroughbreds, not to mention the one hundred parades to the post following the backsides of all those additional exercise ponies, Zippy Chippy had looked out at the bulging haunches and writhing buttocks of thousands of . . . okay, to put this in better perspective, in his lifetime Zippy Chippy had to look at more horses' asses than President Barack Obama did the last time he addressed a joint session of Congress. Not a pretty sight for man nor beast.

You hear it a lot in sports: "There's always next year." But not for this guy, at least not on a racetrack. There wouldn't be one more race, or another season. They say that when the going gets tough, the tough get going. When the going got impossible . . . well, that was the beat that the Zipster covered. Zippy Chippy had lost 'em all and won none, and yet who looked like the champ by the time he got to the backside? The Zipster did a little winning spin, preening for the cameras and inhaling sugar cubes from the sticky fingers of those who had stuck by him all these long years.

Then, standing along the wall of his stall, lost in his thoughts, Zippy seemed to let it all sink in – one hundred saddlings, one hundred bugle calls, one hundred bells, one hundred trips around a circular track with the crowd rooting almost exclusively for him. At this monumental moment, Zippy was likely talking silently to his life partner. *Felix, I have to say, you were there for me when I was very nearly sent to the meat factory. You were there in my corner when I lost eighty of my one hundred fights. You were there when I almost won but got nipped at the wire by a nose and then a neck. And you were there when I lost a race to a man in short pants. Felix, as the old joke goes, you're a f—king jinx!*

"I'll remember that day forever," said Judy Peck. Yes, it had been a memorable day, a milestone day, a beautiful day. It just wasn't Zippy Chippy's day.

Anxiety, remorse, worry – these were all emotions unknown to this horse. Sometimes victory is not flashy or splashy, like those racecar winners who continue the moronic tradition of dousing each other with perfectly good champagne. Sometimes victory is as simple as a quiet voice that says, *I really tried my best, I did, and . . . well, I'll bet that bastard who won was using performance-enhancing drugs.*

A reporter at the scene described the final curtain call of this distinguished actor who had had a record-setting run in the theater of thoroughbred racing: "He didn't kick. He didn't pin his ears back. He didn't move. His big, brown eyes turned glassy and he blinked. His head dropped a little and he drifted off to sleep."

Sweet dreams, unconquering hero. Hail the horse that used his less-than-illustrious career to fight against overachieving, winning at all costs, and, of course, unnecessary perspiration.

OLD GUYS DOING LAPS
AROUND THE TRACK

Zippy Chippy and jockey Frank Amonte Sr. serve as inspirational examples to all of us who are aging faster than Big Pharma can increase the price of the pills that are supposed to keep that from happening. (I love it how so many of us now refer to ourselves as "middle-aged." Accurate in my case only if I make it to 138.)

In his last start, the one hundredth of his career, Zippy ran against seven horses, all ten years younger than himself, and despite a "buck" and a "bore" he came back for more and caught up to the youngsters in the stretch. A year later, on that very same Northampton Fair track, Frank Amonte Sr. became the oldest jockey to win a thoroughbred race when he booted home Cuff the Quote, cleverly threading his mount through the pack until they were three lengths ahead of the rest at the wire. Those who put two dollars on him got back a princely sum of $22.60. "Father Time," as the other riders called him, was just one day short of his seventieth birthday.

Born in 1935, Frank starting riding in New Orleans, and since then, he's ridden in every place with a pari-mutuel window, including Cuba back in the days when they were still chasing Castro around the mountains.

In July of 2001 at Brockton Fairgrounds, the sixty-five-year-old Amonte got banged up in a three-horse collision, suffering three broken toes, a chipped ankle, and a concussion. Three days later he rode Flight Path to the wire and then the winner's circle. "You can't devote much time to recuperating at a place like this," he said.

The father of nine children, Frank was still riding at seventy-six when officials at his home track of Suffolk Downs forced him to quit. They labeled him an "insurance risk." Fit, vegetarian, and holding a doctor's certificate of good health, Frank fought forced retirement all the way to court.

Although Frank was well liked, many jockeys filed complaints against the aged jockey because quite often when he was coming down the stretch, weaving in and out of traffic, he would forget to turn his blinker off.

Can you imagine if they ever teamed together? The Zipster, with one hundred outings, and Senior Frank, with 1,734 career mounts, using their longevity and experience to outsmart and outlast the entire field to win Saratoga's Stool Softener Stakes? (In that winner's circle, they inhale oxygen instead of champagne.)

The remarkable African American baseball pitcher Satchel Paige was right after all: "Age is a case of mind over matter. If you don't mind, it don't matter."

TWENTY-FOUR

Every story has an end. But in life,
every ending is just a new beginning.
From the movie Uptown Girls

There are bad ideas, there are horrible ideas, and then there was the choice of Zippy Chippy's second career. It was a good but onerous decision for Felix to retire his horse from active racing, after ten years and ten times that many trips around the track.

"The racing officials at Northampton wanted Zippy to run again, but we stay home," he said. "We had bad luck the last couple races. Zippy, he's tired."

Of course they wanted Zippy, and especially his entourage, back. Squeezed by casinos and a burgeoning state lottery, the racetrack was now desperate for spectators. Sadly, exactly one year and one day after Zippy's last race on September 10, 2004, the track closed down for good. It's a shame they didn't invite Zippy back for the closing day; he would have loved to have taken the barn down all by himself. The nearly two-hundred-year-old Three County Fair continues to operate to this day, but sadly, another American horse track is now a vacant lot. Today only California offers horseracing at fairgrounds.

In December 2004, three months after his final race, thirteen-year-old Zippy Chippy began a new career as an everyday exercise pony at Finger Lakes Racetrack, minutes down the road from Felix's home stable. The owner was not his usual over-the-moon, optimistic self when it came to Zippy's occupational transition: "I'm not sure he'll like it, but I'm going to give it a try." *Not sure?* As a father, Felix never handed his teenagers hard liquor along with the car keys and then hoped for the best, but somehow he thought this might be a good idea?

In his new position as a track pony, Zippy would be a kind of paid escort. With a handler riding him instead of a jockey, he would tag along with horses as they limbered up before eventually arriving at the start. He would accompany thoroughbreds before and sometimes after races, offering companionship and helping to keep them calm.

Once the champion of also-rans, Zippy was now a red carpet date, a rental horse being paid to prop up real racehorses, just like he was not so very long ago. Suddenly he had been reduced to a stable pony after being the headliner in many of his one hundred races, during which he had become one of the most photographed racehorses in America. What could possibly go wrong with this plan? Ironically, Zippy's job was to help other racehorses at the same track that had banned him for life for dwelling – that is, not racing. So yeah, there was still some bitterness there.

Apparently, Felix had not fully explained the job description of an exercise pony to Zippy, but that was not unusual. According to Marisa, her father did not possess . . . how can I put this . . . keen communication skills. Marisa's love for her father hardly stops her from teasing him. "My dad's very funny," she said. "He just doesn't realize it." Between keeping Zippy out of trouble and keeping his ears from becoming snacks, Felix was not always calm and focused.

"He would be all excited and he'd say, 'You gotta go right now and get Flying Free from the exercise barn!'" said Marisa. "And I'm like, what the hell? And then he gets even louder, and his hands are going and he's yelling at me. 'You know, Freedom Fighter. You gotta go and get him right now.' And I'd say, 'Do you mean Floating Alone? That's his name. Floating Alone!' And he would say, 'Yeah, that's the one. Go get him!'"

Marisa's fondest memory of growing up working with her father was another one of his misspeaks. Instead of saying "Marisa, you're so beautiful, to me," he would say "Marisa, you're so beautiful, like me." "I mean, I know what he meant," she recalls, "but it still cracked me up."

Not well schooled in his new duties, Zippy assumed he was supposed to race against the horses he was being paid to accompany. He kept challenging the horses to a run, and the fact that neither one of them had to get into the starting gate pleased him even more. When that didn't work, Zippy dug deep into his bag of skills, honed during a decade of racetrack chicanery, and . . . he began biting the other horses. He also bumped the other horses, which had the opposite effect of calming them down. Then he bucked off his exercise rider. Then he raced up the stairs of the grandstand, broke into the track official's office, and kicked the crap out of the stewards who had banned him from racing at this very track. Okay, that one I made up.

After only a few trips onto the track accompanying other horses, it became abundantly clear that Zippy was having the same soothing effect on the other horses that cocaine had on Charlie Sheen. In short, Zippy Chippy did everything a track pony was not supposed to do, and his escort career ended just like his racing career: with great relief all around. And why wouldn't it? He had gained national fame and a following of millions doing pretty much the opposite of what a racehorse is expected to do. You don't rack up one hundred losses by toeing the line, listening to the manager, or just going along to get along. Zippy Chippy had used his ten-year professional career to become a superb and internationally recognized shit disturber. And now they wanted him to be My Friend Flicka?

It was rugged individualism that made his first career such a success, and it would be this same singular spirit that would cost him his second. Sorry, but he didn't need a playmate while he was in the serious business of losing a record number of thoroughbred races, and he wouldn't pretend to be a chaperone now that he no longer answered the call to post. If Zippy had been allowed to procreate, I am absolutely certain he would have fathered the first foal in history to be born with a middle finger. The best that can be said is that no animals were seriously harmed in the implementation of this experiment, thank God.

As a result, Finger Lakes Racetrack established a new rule that all horses applying for the job of exercise pony must first put up a damage deposit. Okay, I made that one up too, but seriously, what the hell was Felix thinking? What next, Pete Rose for commissioner of baseball? Richard Nixon's mug up on Mount Rushmore? Rob Ford for mayor of Toronto? Hey, wait a minute, that car wreck actually happened!

AS THEY SAY IN THE BARN,
LOVE IS A MANY-SPLINTERED THING

Felix loved Zippy Chippy in much the same way that Roy Rogers loved his golden palomino, Trigger.

Referrring to a woman in his songs as "gold diggers" and "tight-waisted, winky-eyed flirts," it became clear that the King of the Cowboys was spending way, way too much time alone on the range.

Apparently, Dale Evans, the love of Roy's life, his co-star, and his wife for fifty-one years, was not much of a feminist. I mean, she heard those lyrics and she carried a gun, yet she let Roy live to the age of eighty-six.

Zippy's one hundred races were matched by almost one hundred films that Roy and Trigger starred in together. Friends, pets, and business partners – Felix and Roy adored their horses.

Trigger and the "Singing Cowboy" danced together as he sang about that four-legged friend who would never let you down in the end.

I too have loved and lost three wonderful four-legged friends. My tabby Wedgie, I buried by the creek where he liked to torture frogs. Malcolm, my buck-toothed cat, was cremated, as was Jake, the best and most handsome dog in the world. (Was too! Was too!)

Call me unadventurous, but it never once crossed my mind to have any of them stuffed. In a feat of taxidermal engineering, Roy Rogers had Trigger stuffed in a rearing-up-on-his-hind-legs position and displayed him proudly in the foyer of his California home. As soon as you opened Roy and Dale's front door, there he was, this muscular beast, all golden coat with a flaxen mane, in his attack mode, just waiting to kick the gun out of your hand.

Although I still have trouble believing anyone would want to stuff a pet, I do remember hearing Dale Evans on a radio talk show promoting her autobiography, *Rainbow on a Hard Trail*. The host of the show finally got around to asking her the question I'd have led with: "Why in the world would Roy have Trigger stuffed?"

"Because," replied Dale with great enthusiasm, "Roy just loved him so much."

Since then, every time I touch the urn of one of my pets, I have a kind thought for Dale Evans. I can't tell you how relieved I was that Roy died before Dale did, because I know . . . he just loved her so much.

TWENTY-FIVE

Oh, my friend, it is not what they take away from you that counts.
It's what you do with what you have left.
Hubert Humphrey

"**D**omestic terrorism orange alert! Warning to all American retirement institutions that accept horses as residents: Zippy Chippy is looking for a home!" For the owner of a boarding farm, receiving a request to permanently room and board Zippy Chippy was akin to learning that Mike Tyson was booking a long stay at your quaint little B&B.

Six years of semi-retirement had passed uneventfully for Zippy Chippy since he last raced in 2004 for his one hundredth consecutive loss. Reflecting on his victories — two against baseball players and two against horses in leg restraints — it seemed that thoroughbred racehorses had been Zippy's more persistent problem. Unofficial retirement for Zippy included training sessions during the season with Felix's other clients at the Clifton Springs stable and wintering at Whispering Winds Farm in nearby Penfield, NY.

Approaching twenty years of age, Zippy looked good, his health was fine, and he remained unusually agile, suffering no long-term effects from the pounding punishment he had endured in a decade chasing faster horses around some of racing's most unforgiving tracks. Zippy was in good shape. Except for the scars and bruises in the shape of a horse's hoof, Felix was in pretty good shape too. Emotionally, though, Zippy's trainer, owner, and father figure wavered back and forth about the horse's future. "I've got him for a long time," he said. "Then somebody take him from me? I don't think so. Even if he retires, he will always be in my barn."

After a turbulent decade of racing, Felix still believed that Zippy might race again: "He's still strong for a horse his age." Of course, having been pinned to the wall occasionally, Felix knew Zippy's strength firsthand.

Although he could have used the money, Felix was dead set against selling Zippy or any of his other horses, a real problem in a business where most trainers traded their underachieving prospects like baseball cards. When it came to Zippy's ornery nature and abysmal track record, few doubted the owner when he said, "If this horse was in somebody else's hands, he be dead by now." With any other owner in thoroughbred racing, this horse would have likely gone to auction and then to a processing plant north or south of the border.

Although Emily and Felix had been in the thoroughbred horse business almost all their lives, for them it had never been a matter of business. They had sold a few horses, but only to people they knew, horse people who shared their love for these beautiful beasts.

"We keep the horses Felix buys. We take care of our horses," Emily said, without having to add that a lot of other owners do not. The quick-flip sellers of thoroughbreds who buy low and sell a little higher after the horse has had a promising race or a strong time trial are called "churners." The Monserrates, all four of them, were definitely not churners.

"One week after we had Zippy Chippy, I knew Felix would never sell him, as bad a horse as he might be," recalled Emily.

"No, he was ours for good, plus . . . well, he wasn't all that sellable, to be honest with you."

Maybe not back in his racing days, but now, with all his hard-earned notoriety, Zippy Chippy, who had somehow escaped all those claiming races, was very "sellable." Oh, the irony of it all.

The great horses, from Secretariat to Seabiscuit, retired in ankle-deep Kentucky bluegrass, frolicking for the cameras and procreating their brains out on the off chance they might sire another hall of famer. But where do the ordinary horses go? The lame-gamers and last-placers and not-so-hots whose names nobody can remember a week after their last trip around the track? Sadly, these "orphans of the oval" have no value to racetracks or owners once their careers are over.

Such horses "go to glue," as Felix once said, with the despair shared by every backside worker who has seen firsthand the sweat, the struggle, the gallant efforts these animals have given to their years at the track abandoned quickly once their earnings end. Zippy filled up a lot of race cards in his time. A hundred, to be exact.

A few discarded thoroughbreds might earn their keep as show horses or riding horses. Fewer still are the lucky ones who become pets of big-hearted rural landowners or helpers at equestrian centers. The situation has become so dire that some old horses go to rescue and retraining farms where they are cared for by prison inmates. (They're keeping Zippy away from this program, because frankly, the really hardcore criminals wouldn't stand a chance!)

After years of dithering about Zippy's future, Felix received a novel proposal from Michael Blowen, founder of Old Friends Equine, a retirement home for unwanted thoroughbreds. Michael's rescue operation, located on the outskirts of the small town of

Georgetown, Kentucky, not far from Lexington, is a model sanctuary for over the hill stallions and unmemorable mares who left their hearts out on the track. Old Friends now cares for about one hundred and fifty-four retired racers, who cost about $2,500 each in annual care. In their prime, these same horses earned a combined total of more than $90 million for their owners.

Michael made the offer to purchase Zippy Chippy after he set up a second farm, Old Friends at Cabin Creek, near Saratoga Springs, New York. The plan was to use Zippy as the retirement home's poster boy and, naturally, its main attraction. With a million dollar operating budget to care for his growing brood of abandoned horses, Michael needed a familiar face for fundraising campaigns and a well-known ambassador to promote the humane treatment of old racehorses. He needed America's most famous also-ran. He needed Zippy Chippy.

It was a brilliant marketing strategy to build on Zippy's celebrity status and use him as a kind of Walmart greeter at Old Friends at Cabin Creek, where he would attract fans of horse racing to come and meet yesterday's warriors. Merchandising Zippy Chippy memorabilia would earn funds to support the retirement and care of horses at both of Michael Blowen's retreats.

"I guarantee you that within a year, Zippy Chippy will earn more in retirement than he did on the track," said the man who was once the film critic for the *Boston Globe*. First Felix and now Michael — when it comes to optimists, Zippy seems to attract them like a magnet.

"We all told him," said Marisa of her father. "Me, my mom, my brother, everybody, told him that Zippy Chippy going to Cabin Creek would be the best thing that could happen, but . . ."

Felix's immediate reaction was adamant: "Sell the Zippy horse? No way, Jose!" In his head, he knew that the sale of his buddy to this retirement farm was the best possible option for everyone involved. Zippy would be a happy retiree, romping in the spacious pastures on the outskirts of Saratoga Springs, three hours down the thruway from his Finger Lakes farm where the Monserrates could easily visit him. Above all, he knew the $5,000 sale price Michael was offering would go a long way to help keep his stable of horses operating. In keeping with his luck-less history as a trainer, in the two years following Zippy's last race, his other horses had presented him with fifty-four losses in a row. Coming up to seventy years of age, Felix did not have a whole lot to show for a half century in the racing game. Still, in his heart, he held on: "I love the Zippy horse. He's been family for a long time. I don't want to lose him. There is only one Zippy Chippy." And with the Zipster permanently snipped, there could never be another. He could never assume the role of a breeder. Traditionally, studs and mares produce foals that are destined to enrich thoroughbred racing, not vaudeville.

After several months and many changes of heart, Felix finally did the right thing by handing over his horse and halter to the gentle folks at Cabin Creek, where Zippy would do what he was born to do – act up, run around in crazy circles, eat treats, and pose for lots of photographs. His role would be to star in the Cabin Creek seniors' brigade, which included such fine stakes winners as Thunder Rumble, Will's Way, Cool N Collective, Midnight Secret, and Moonshadow Gold.

In the early spring of 2010, after the longest three-hour drive of his career, Felix pulled into the driveway of Old Friends at Cabin Creek with Zippy in tow. After Zippy was backed out of his trailer, he took off running – "No, no, that way, Zippy. That way!" – over the rolling hills and green pastures of his new fenced-in home.

Zippy was suddenly separated from the loves of his life – Marisa, Emily, and of course Felix, his favorite punching bag. Adored by hordes of fans, Zippy had thrived as the center of attention throughout his ten-year career, but he had shown disdain for the other horses, those speedy elitists who had barred him from the victory club. Now, here at Cabin Creek, he was surrounded by them – stakes winners and champions alike.

At first he preferred to stay outside alone, refusing to be groomed. "It took a few days for him to get used to my voice," recalled JoAnn Pepper, who operates the equine nursing home along with her husband, Mark and son, Cody. "You know, to figure out who was the boss." (I'm guessing – *him?*)

But then Zippy's life took a sudden turn for the best. He fell in love. It was platonic, of course, and after a soft nose touch, some serious sniffing, three nudges, a bump, and two approving neighs, Zippy Chippy and a stocky, capable racer by the name of Red Down South became pasture pals for life.

"Right there," said JoAnn, pointing to what is now the farm's logo, a photo of Zippy and Red meeting for the first time and gently caressing each other's snout as if they were shaking hands. "In that moment they became best buddies forever."

The Peppers live at the top of a hill that looks out over the beautiful barn where over twenty retired racehorses reside. The barn is made of pine, with multiple peaks and a long front porch, and the stables are both huge and homey. The ninety-two-acre property is ringed by thick stands of leafy maples, and each retired resident has his own large, fenced-in paddock, with room galore to run and play and roll around in the dirt.

Their paddocks separated by only a wooden fence, Thunder Rumble and Will's Way boarded side by side. Both were champion high-stakes speedsters who had each won Saratoga's prestigious

Travers Stakes. They were great pals in retirement, yet once in a while, at some mutually agreed-upon signal, Thunder Rumble and Will's Way would suddenly take off, running at full tilt the length of their fields, reliving their greatest triumphs just for the pure, unadulterated fun of it all. Free at last at Cabin Creek.

During the busy summer meet at the nearby Saratoga Race Course, almost one thousand people a week come to visit the great racehorses of the past, especially the Not-So-Great One. "Oh, swell," they say, coming down the path to the pens. "Okay, there's Funny Cide and Behrens, but where's that Zippy Chippy horse?"

Most of these grassy, half-acre, square pens have shade trees. All have open protective sheds, or "run-ins," where the horses go to feed and steer clear of bad weather. But only one is home to two geldings, and that's where Zippy Chippy and his best friend for life, Red Down South, can be found. Protective of each other, they are absolutely inseparable. When he was about to leave on a summer road trip to the Old Friends farm in Kentucky, Zippy flatly refused to board his traveling trailer. Not two or twelve handlers were going to force him in. He threw a bloody fit, bucking and bolting until the only thing they could do was walk him around to try to calm him down. But when he saw Red Down South enter the trailer, Zippy hustled up the ramp all by himself.

"They do everything together," said JoAnn. "Zippy's getting a little arthritic, and I think he prefers to stand around. But Red keeps him moving, keeps him walking. And that's good for both of them." After three deaths during the long, cold winter of 2015, Zippy is now the farm's elder statesman.

On a hot and sunny day in July 2010, Old Friends at Cabin Creek officially became "the Bobby Frankel Division," after the legendary New York trainer who died too early in life. It was also Zippy Chippy's debut as the farm's most famous retiree, and five hundred people showed up for the outdoor dedication ceremony. And there he was, the "Cad of Cabin Creek," in all his goofy glory: eyes narrowed and looking for trouble, with his scraggly tail flipping behind a well-rounded middle. Odd that infamy had trumped fame on this auspicious day, with all the great retired racehorses watching Zippy Chippy's ceremony from their respective pens.

Listed on the program as Zippy's former owner, Felix Monserrate was right there beside him. Proudly, they posed for photographs, enjoying casual banter with fans. In the shade of the barn's large, peaked entrance, a winner's circle had been created with flags and flowers and bales of hay. Waiting for them inside was a lush and fragrant bed of roses, the symbol of victory used to adorn winners of the Kentucky Derby. This was special, a haloed place of triumph that Zippy and Felix had never gotten to enjoy together in their ten years of trying.

A quick burst of rain earlier had left a rainbow arching over the farm and the surrounding woods. Horse lovers and handlers stood to the side or sat on folding chairs as Old Friends founder Michael Blowen addressed the crowd. Shorts, ball hats, and suspenders made up the dress code of the day. All smiled, a few sipped beer from plastic glasses, and most snapped as many photos as they possibly could of this triumphant reunion that would never be repeated. Off in the distance, horses vocalized their displeasure at being ignored. Felix held Zippy hard and tight to his body, knowing full well the horse was capable of turning this wonderful celebration into something that would end with sirens and a tranquilizer dart. Zippy was restless, constantly bellowing at Red Down South, whom he could clearly see in their fenced-in field a hundred yards away.

It was a significant, almost historic moment when Felix Monserrate led Zippy Chippy into the Cabin Creek winner's circle.

After a hundred classes at the school of hard knocks, they were finally being recognized with an honorary degree. All went well for about five minutes of this barn-style pomp and circumstance, until Zippy had had enough. One last shout-out to Red that he was coming home, and Zippy proceeded to kick down the sign reading CABIN CREEK WINNER'S CIRCLE. Then he gave Felix a sideways glance as if to say, *I don't want to win that way. Not on a photo op.*

In what amounted to a noisy wake-up call to those gathered in fantasy farmland, Zippy reminded them that there were more important things in life than winning, and one of them was getting back to Red Down South at precisely the same time that the guy with the floppy hat and the armload of carrots arrived at their pen. *Don't eat 'em all, Red!*

And then Zippy took to swaying and jerking Felix around. His behavior was so bad, some in the crowd thought he might be staging a comeback.

The Zippy and Felix Show was back on the air for one final episode. Displaying the infamous poor conduct that had gotten him banished from racetracks and exercise barns, the grumpy gelding was quickly escorted out of the winner's circle before he could actually destroy it. Mission accomplished, he looked rather regal as he was led back to the open-air stall he shared with Red, where they could resume their usual nickering and snickering and pressing their heads lightly together. The boys were reunited at long last. With this defiant act, in what might be the lasting image that underscores his legacy, Zippy Chippy was now banned from his very own winner's circle.

As the ceremony concluded, people shook hands and exchanged addresses and pleasantries before sauntering off with their photos and Zippy Chippy ball caps. The Peppers picked up the pieces of the sign along with their best intentions, and you could almost hear Walter Cronkite say, "And that's the way it is."

They make for an interesting pair of bedfellows, these two, the deep-brown Zippy and the chestnut Red Down South. Nine years the younger, Red has done something his pen-mate could only dream of: win a race. He only won twice in thirty-two starts, but he finished in the money often enough to earn a total of $116,650, and $3,645 per outing (Zippy's career total was $30,834.). And yes, I'm sure Red lords that over the Zipster every chance he gets. I can just imagine Red Down South standing in front of Zippy and pawing the ground 30,834 times, then falling down laughing.

With his sunny disposition, Red has a calming effect on the rambunctious Zippy, keeping his buddy in line. On the day I was visiting them in their paradise paddock at Cabin Creek, Zippy did something stupid that nobody noticed, and Red promptly bit him in the ass. After sulking under a shade tree for a while, Zippy came back to Red, all playful and loving again.

The summer after they met, Zippy and Red went on the road, spending a couple of weeks at Michael Blowen's Lexington farm, prancing around the property and showing off for visitors. Never more than a few feet apart, these two sassy seniors would race each other over and around the soft Kentucky knolls and then pull up to the fence, where well-wishers pushed treats into their faces.

There's a home video of the two of them, taken while they were relaxing at the Lexington farm. Their heads are bobbing up and down in anticipation as a guy approaches with his hands full of carrots. As he offers them up and across the top rail, Zippy's head recoils, while Red Down South leans in and demolishes the food, green stems and all. Astonished, the guy in the video turns to his wife, who's doing the filming, and says, "Jesus! Zippy doesn't even want to come first at eating!"

On the day of her visit, Pam Machuga, a fan of the Zipster, expressed great admiration for the two horses smiling at her from a distance. "These horses deserve respect. Work hard your whole life, this is what you should get — a big pasture with lots of love." Standing apart from a tour group that had just arrived to fawn over Zippy and then Red, the longtime fan of horse racing added, "Think about regular, everyday people in life. We don't always win, but we can at least get back up and keep going."

This picture is not lost on Michael Blowen. "I think more people can identify with a horse that loses all the time than a horse that wins all the time," he said. "Because there are more losers in the world than winners."

Michael Blowen's confidence in turning Zippy Chippy's fame to fortune has paid off quite well. Funny Cide, who would eventually visit Zippy at Old Friends, earned $3.53 million in thirty-eight races. By contrast, Zippy earned perhaps $80,000 during his career, from second- and third-place finishes, a couple of sideshows, some celebrity appearance fees, and a movie option. So Michael Blowen's bet on Zippy's earning power was certainly ambitious. Having missed the exalted Triple Crown by a loss in the Belmont Stakes, Funny Cide may be the greatest horse ever to come to Cabin Creek, but make no mistake about it: the sounds of the cash register and the size of the souvenir bags leave little doubt that the infamous imp Zippy Chippy is the star of this show.

Zippy's never-give-up attitude finally paid off in the end. He is the undisputed leader of the pack at Old Friends, and he is now helping pay for Red Down South's upkeep. As a matter of fact, Zippy's huge popularity with visitors to Old Friends is helping raise the funds to care for all the great horses boarding there. Incredible but true: Zippy the Clown is now supporting the entire circus.

In the end, Michael Blowen made the smart choice, and Felix Monserrate eventually came to a wise decision – Zippy Chippy was put out to pasture for what were to become the best years of his life. Fittingly, he earned the gold standard of retirement packages: room to roam, a buddy to play with, lots of visitors to fawn over him, and yes, carrots. A dignified retirement at the end of a courageous career was what everyone wanted for Zippy Chippy. And that he has in spades.

The prediction of Michael Blowen, the guardian angel of old, discarded horses, quickly became a marvelous reality. As Zippy's fame continued to flourish after his landmark one hundredth race, his faithful followers grew in numbers and displayed their loyalty in cash. A thousand people a week, and sometimes three hundred a day, come to pet him, feed him, buy his monogrammed merchandise, and pose for pictures worthy of their wallets. Yes, Zippy has earned more, much more, in retirement than he ever did racing.

Besides the caps, T-shirts, and lucky charms, the best-selling Zippy souvenir is a coffee mug. Below a cartoon of Zippy Chippy screwing up a race are the words that sum up his career, words that will serve him well as an epitaph, and words we all could live by. Under the comical sketch of the silly, galloping Zipster are the words WINNERS DON'T ALWAYS FINISH FIRST.

BETTING ON THE PONIES:
THE ULTIMATE CHARITY AUCTION

When I was twenty years old, I used to hang around with the wrong crowd. His name was Carvalho. He was older than me, shorter than me, and smarter than me, and one summer he introduced me to the track.

As a university student, Carvalho had a summer job as a Canadian customs officer at the Peace Bridge, which connects Buffalo, New York, to Fort Erie, Ontario. When American owners and trainers brought their horses to race at Fort Erie Race Track, they had to first get past Carvalho. Government paperwork could take a few minutes or a few days, he'd say – what did they have in the way of betting tips?

As a university student, instead of taking a summer job, I started a company in which I grossly underpaid high school students to paint houses. It was like a sweatshop operation, except they toiled out in the fresh air. I'd work with them in the mornings, then go to Fort Erie Race Track in the afternoons to bet the horses on which Carvalho had been given tips. We seldom won a race.

But Carvalho had a "system," and as he explained it to me, you had to stick to the system because it would pay off sooner or later. "Later" for me was September, by which time I had transferred all the profits from my painting business to the Fort Erie Race Track. I spent that following year operating a spark-splashing swing grinder at Atlas Steels in Welland, Ontario, to make enough money to go back to university.

I mean, losing was one thing, but we once bet on a horse that went sideways across the track and up to the grandstand, at which point his jockey yelled into the crowd, "Which way did they go?" I tell ya, we bet on a horse that was so slow, his jockey carried a change of underwear! We were so good for business that if I wasn't at the betting window for the first race, the racetrack would send a hired car to my house. Seriously, it's true what they say – a racehorse is an animal that can take a thousand people for a ride, all at the same time.

And Carvalho? Like one of those amazing little ironies you read in *Ripley's Believe It or Not!*, he got a job as a paid tout, a handicapper of racehorses. That's right, the guy whose luckiest day at the track was when he met somebody who lived on his street so he didn't have to hitchhike home got a job in which they paid him to give advice to bettors. He wrote a column for the *Daily Racing Form*, the bible for North American pony players.

But Carvahlo, he was funny. We'd go to the track together on weekends and in those days, Fort Erie Race Track charged an admission fee, except those who came late, say after work, could get into the seventh and eighth races for free. One day, tapped out after the seventh race, we were walking through the parking lot, pissed off and not speaking to each other as usual. Carvalho was slapping his thigh compulsively with that day's program, which had cost two bucks to buy. An American in a new Cadillac pulled up beside us, rolled down the window, and said, "Hey, buddy, do you mind if I have that program?" Instantly, I knew this wasn't going to end well for the moocher.

Carvalho gave the car a long look, from the gleaming hood ornament to the shiny chrome back bumper, and finally said, "So how'd you pay for the Caddy? Collectin' fuckin' pop bottles?"

We carried on toward my car and said nothing to each other for, oh, about six full seconds. Then I laughed so hard I really thought I'd pulled something near the base of my spleen.

Lesson learned: No horse can disappear around the far turn faster than the money you bet on him. Knowing that you'll lose it, take no more than twenty or forty dollars to the track, and have a wonderful afternoon playing with the ponies.

TWENTY-SIX

For when the One Great Scorer comes to write against your name,
He marks — not that you won or lost — but how you played the game.

Grantland Rice, "Alumnus Football"

O h, what a career the Zippy horse had: one hundred races, eight second-place finishes, twelve thirds, a whole bunch of fourths, four owners, four trainers, thirty-four jockeys, ten racetracks, one ball field, two harness tracks, a one-vehicle demolition derby, and total earnings of $30,834 on the track.

Tack on his new friend for life and stablemate Red Down South, and now two adoring families who love him dearly, and you've got a horse that could have costarred with Jimmy Stewart in *It's A Wonderful Life*. (Although there's little doubt in my mind that after spending time with Zippy Chippy, George Bailey would have jumped off the bridge over Bedford Falls, mercifully bringing that movie to an end a full hour earlier.)

And how did he do it? Cleanly — no drugs. The hard way, with not even a little help from his faster friends, who once in a while let him come close to winning but never allowed him to seal the deal. Zippy did it with dogged determination — fifty losses would have been more than enough to break down a normal thoroughbred. He did it with courage — not one horse in racing's Hall of Fame could endure ten straight losses, let alone ten times that many, and keep on high-stepping onto the track, ready to rumble. And he did it with a lot of crashing and bashing noises. When Zippy entered a barn, anyone who had anything to do with exercise or discipline got extremely nervous.

People say life is unpredictable, but that's putting it mildly. Life can be downright diabolical. Did you ever think you would see the day when a horse who lost one hundred races would go down in history as a genuine folk hero, while a guy who won seven Tour de France titles will forever be remembered as a liar and a cheat?

"He was an honest horse," remembered sports columnist Bob Matthews of the Zipster. "I didn't bet on him, but he ran hard. He gave you an honest effort every time out."

Every day there's the temptation to cut corners, juice the results, spin the truth, double dip, and fudge, just a little. Don't. Zippy Chippy never did, and someday, I believe, he will be in the Hall of Fame. Maybe not the official Hall of Fame in Saratoga Springs, New York, but certainly in America's Underdog Hall of Fame, located in the hearts of all of us who try and fail and live to try another day.

The media had a field day with THE CHAMPION OF FUTILITY and THE GOLD MEDALIST OF MEDIOCRITY and ZIPPO! NINETY AND NAUGHT — a lot of deflected sticks and stones, as far as Zippy was concerned. If you scanned a list of every reporter who came up with a clever Zippy Chippy putdown, you would not recognize even one of their names today. Call it fortuitous or even serendipitous, but the best thing Zippy Chippy ever did was never win a race. If he had won one or even two races, he'd have been known as a "nag." A win would have only served to blemish his perfect record. With his unbroken losing streak, Zippy is special – a beautiful, lovable, cantankerous oddity, a professional plodder, a hero to those who may hit rough times but always find a way to better themselves. The believers, they were the ones who bet on him and kept the tickets in order to remember why.

He certainly was not the world's slowest racehorse, not by a long shot. The aforementioned English horse Quixall Crossett racked up 103 losses in his career, often finishing a race when it was getting dark. Japan's Haru-urara topped that by two with 105 consecutive losses. And a Puerto Rican horse by the name of Dona Chepa lost a mind-boggling 135 races. She truly did earn her nickname, "the Hobby Horse," like the mechanical one that gives toddlers a bumpy ride in front of the supermarket.

Zippy wasn't even the slowest American thoroughbred ever. Thrust put up bigger numbers: 105 losses back in the 1950s. Somehow, all those sportswriters giving Zippy credit for being the "losingest" horse in North America had overlooked Thrust. They had followed the lead of sports columnist Bob Matthews, who, looking back, says simply, "Google got it wrong." So did *Guinness World Records*.

But none of these also-rans ass-kicked and head-butted their way into thoroughbred racing's Hall of Infamy. Not the way Zippy did. In Britain, Quixall Crossett never lost a race to a cricket player. In Puerto Rico, depressed as she might have been, Dona Chepa never ate a box of cheese-filled *quesitos* all by herself. And Thrust never took a curtain call out of the chute while the rest of the horses disappeared around the near turn.

Namewise, he was hardly zippy, but when you total up all the bruises, bite marks, broken equipment, and dented trucks he left in his wake, this horse sure as hell was chippy. And, okay, oddly enchanting, with an attitude that would make a mule seem obedient. Zippy bit, bucked, kicked, and dwelt his way through a remarkable career until he earned — with no small amount of hubris — the right to be called the World's Worst Racehorse, a banner Zippy Chippy will wear proudly up until his last day in the pasture. No horse can ever lay claim to that title, at least not while winning over as many supporters along the way.

Zippy's ten-year career as a thoroughbred racehorse was a Herculean quest to excel, to do his best despite the odds, which were always stacked against him. More workhorse than racehorse, more warhorse than exercise pony, Zippy Chippy challenged life head-on and took on all the tight curves and high hurdles that came with it. And now, romping around the big green paddock with his new best friend, both of them dropping to their knees and rolling around in the dust and dirt before galloping down the pasture's edge, he has ultimately won the stakes race of his life. Today, the unlucky gelding that the media often called "the little horse who can't" is this close to getting an appointment secretary. Zippy was never a champ, not nationally and not even at local fairgrounds. He was, however, a world-class scamp. In a world woefully short of eccentrics and real characters, this horse more than filled the bill for those of us who believe boredom is one of life's mortal enemies.

Survival with a splash of fun – that was Zippy's recipe for success. In racing, defeat was not the outcome this horse sought, but neither was it his life's undoing. Not to have tried time after time, that would have been his downfall. Failure is not a pratfall, the inelegant act of falling down in the face of adversity. Failure is not getting up to fight, again and again, in the end knowing you've done your absolute best, leaving the rest to fate. For that alone he can never be forgotten, and long after the remarkable races of other, more successful horses fade, Zippy Chippy will be remembered.

Above all else, Zippy Chippy was an artist. His self-portrait displays strong strokes of defiance and tenacity, but take a few steps back and you see that the big picture sparkles with life, dazzles with revelry and draws love from those around him. Zippy Chippy was the center of his very own weird and wonderful universe.

At one juncture of his storied career, Zippy Chippy was almost the star of his own movie. On a five-year film option offered by that L.A. screenwriter/producer, Felix had received about $40,000 for the rights to Zippy's story, which he always believed would one day be made by Disney. I have seen the filmmaker's "teaser" video and the photography is excellent, with streaks of gold from a setting sun spilling through windows and cracks. A dozen other horses are heard neighing contentedly in shed row stalls as the star of the show is led out of his pen and down the concrete walkway. They stop. Marisa fetches a box of grooming products and begins primping and fussing over Zippy. Felix is holding Zippy on a tight leash, obviously suspicious that this is all going too well. Zippy is cooperating like he fought to get the part in casting, and then . . . without warning or malice aforethought, Zippy rips a really loud fart. It's the kind of noise usually preceded by lightning and followed by heavy rain, and I'm thinking, *Good Lord, starring in the film is not enough for this horse. Now he wants creative control!*

Zippy Chippy was a horse that simply could not live with success, but strangely enough, in the end it came to him anyway. We live in a world inhabited almost entirely by great attempters. We try and try and try our best, and then we do a little victory dance. Our triumphs are small, our celebrations personal, and that's how we slowly but surely build better lives inside a cold and bitter world. Small steps, one foot after the other, steady and determined down the hard but right path.

So if you were the kid who got picked last for the team — or, worse (and none of us today are proud of this), the fat kid we sent out onto Mud Lake before the hockey game started in order to test the thickness of the ice, or the girl who couldn't get a date for the prom, or the student who died a thousand deaths standing dumbstruck at the blackboard in front of the class, or the idiot who rubbed his contact lenses after cutting up crazy-hot chili peppers for the pizza when he was stoned and in college (sorry, sometimes I still tear up for no apparent reason!), or the person who got picked on, criticized, beat up, and centered out — here then is your poster boy, Zippy Chippy, America's lovable loser. This was the horse who showed the world that no matter how impossible things seem at the time, you can still come out alive and well down at the other end. Try hard and do good and there's a cool green pasture waiting for when you finally get off that treadmill — as good a reward as any of us can expect.

America, it is said, is the land of second chances. Zippy Chippy proved that America is a country of eternal hope, offering up ninety-nine second chances as long as you're willing to try. As the fame game flourishes in social media and on TV, more of us are meant to feel like losers every day. There's no doubt that the lives of the rest of us are a lot closer to the Zippy Chippy model than that of Secretariat, Man o' War, or Northern Dancer.

Oh yeah, the world will most definitely remember Zippy Chippy, with his perfect record of one hundred losses and his heart the size of that '88 Ford he was traded for, and we will be better for the lessons he taught us in living and striving and giving our all. Sometimes just getting through a rough day takes everything you've got. Following the Zipster's lead and his take on life might just be our best shot. In the end, Vince Lombardi, the legendary coach, came to believe that a winner was not necessarily the man photographed holding the trophy over his head or the woman wearing the finish line across her chest. In the end,

Lombardi believed that it was the one who worked tirelessly, relentlessly, unflinchingly for a good cause and the betterment of all those around him. In the end, Lombardi was often heard quoting these lines from "Thinking," a poem by the little-known Walter D. Wintle:

> Life's battles don't always go
> To the stronger or faster man.
> But sooner or later the man who wins
> Is the man who thinks he can.

HARU-URARA FOR ZIPPY CHIPPY
AND HIS DOUBLE IN JAPAN!

Trouble doubled: Zippy Chippy had a doppelganger. Zippy's track twin was a Japanese horse named Haru-urara. By the time Zippy registered his one hundredth loss, the eight-year-old mare from the northern island of Hokkaido had clocked in at 106 straight misses. Okay, so she was more productive than Zippy. It's that relentless Japanese work ethic, I tell you!

Her name in English was Glorious Spring, and she became the undisputed darling of the Japanese media. Her story of athletic artlessness grew to legendary proportions in the Land of the Rising Sun. Workers all over the country bet on Glorious Spring, hoping the losing tickets would serve as lucky charms. A crowd of 13,000 fans attended one of her last appearances, and five hundred lucky Haru-urara horsetail souvenirs sold out in less than three hours. At an end-of-the-season ceremony at the Kinki University (folks, I do not make this stuff up!) – affiliated with Hiroshima High School, the principal talked about Haru-urara and Zippy Chippy. "Despite their lengthy string of failures, they were popular," he said. "Please cherish your individuality, don't give up your dreams, and work hard to achieve them." Japanese Prime Minister Junichiro Koizumi cited the filly as "a good example of not giving up in the face of defeat."

There have been poems written and songs sung about Haru-urara, with a movie deal underway. According to a piece in *Newsweek* magazine, the horse had been "inundated with food, fan letters and even cash." (Wow! All Felix Monserrate ever got was a nip on the neck and a steep bill each month from Farmington Feed and Seed.)

In the midst of a sluggish economy, Zippy's counterpart became a major cult figure as millions of Japanese equated the horse's shortcomings with their own financial hardships. They tucked her losing tickets away in sacred places, believing their blessings would ward off bad luck and help them keep their jobs. In their slow economy, the Japanese rallied around this slow horse, and yes, the nation's finances did improve. (Why didn't we think of that? Instead of, you know, bailouts?)

At these two horses' peaks, which were really their lows, racing fans and sportswriters in both countries championed the idea of a match race between Zippy Chippy and Glorious Spring. Yeah, an "our loser is worse than your loser" kind of contest. Such a match race would be a very bad idea. Think about all that courtesy Zippy Chippy showed to male horses by letting them go first out of the gate, the chivalry that got him banned from Finger Lakes. Can you imagine the kind of gallantry he would offer a damsel in the stretch?

Hail Haru-urara! Long live the Zipster! And may these beautiful losers never meet, because if they did, the unthinkable would become the inevitable, and one would have to win. The silver lining to all this doppelganger business was that Felix Monserrate had never heard of comedian Steven Wright, who said, "If I ever had twins, I'd use one for spare parts." I mean, he did want Zippy Chippy to go on racing forever!

TWENTY-SEVEN

Winning isn't everything. Period.

Consider for a moment two great golfers: Tiger Woods and Jim Nelford. You've heard of Tiger Woods, who despite his scandalous meltdown years ago continued to be one of the most exciting golfers in the game. An elegant and powerful athlete, Woods lived by the words "Winning isn't everything; it's the only thing."

Intense, obsessed, and motivated to win at all costs, Tiger Woods referred to the golfer who came in second in a tournament as the "first loser." Really? By extension, then, every Olympic podium would feature the gold-medal winner flanked by tarnished silver and rusted bronze.

You might not have heard of Jim Nelford, who was born in Vancouver, British Columbia, and had a stellar amateur career. Considered one of the best ball strikers in the game, he made his mark on the PGA Tour when he finished second after Fuzzy Zoeller at the 1983 Sea Pines Heritage Classic at Hilton Head, South Carolina. The following year, at the Bing Crosby Pro-Am, Nelford was ready and more than able to be crowned king of "Crosby's Clambake." A helluva golfer, Nelford had the Pebble Beach, California, tournament all but locked up and in his bag, with one hole to go. With the clubhouse lead, he watched

Hale Irwin, the only golfer on the course who could beat him, dump his drive on the eighteenth hole into the seaside rocks below the fairway. For Nelford, Irwin's suddenly disastrous predicament was the moment in which the brain switches from anxiety to relief to "Who do I need to thank?"

But wait! Irwin's errant drive did in fact hit the rocks along the shore of the Pacific Ocean, and then . . . defying logic, and the naked eye, it bounced back onto the fairway. With blessings aplenty, Irwin then nailed the flagstick, leaving his ball five feet from the cup. Many who witnessed those shots believed it proved once and for all that God really is American. Somehow, Hale Irwin had manufactured a birdie on the eighteenth, forcing a sudden-death playoff, in which he defeated the still-stunned Jim Nelford.

Having watched his greatest personal triumph disappear in a fraction of a second, Nelford was utterly devastated and broke down in front of reporters at the airport. For Jim Nelford, it seemed things could not possibly get any worse. But wait! A year and a half later, a waterskiing accident nearly killed him and left his right arm severely damaged after it was sliced by the blade of a propeller. Doctors concluded he would never swing a club again.

Cut down in his prime, did Nelford look upon the debacle at Pebble Beach as a curse in some sort of career-ending conspiracy? No, though many of us would. Instead, he went through prolonged and painful rehabilitation until he finally made it back to the top of the game. With his arm bolstered by pins and screws, covered with scars and skin grafts, the man slowly and painfully earned his way back onto the PGA Tour.

He would never win a PGA tournament; that ridiculous twenty-yard bounce up and off the rocks at Pebble Beach had ended his best shot at a title. Still, during a highly successful career, Nelford won the Canadian Amateur Championship twice. He once beat the great Jack Nicklaus in an exhibition match. With Dan Halldorson, he won the World Cup of Golf in 1980 in Bogotá, Colombia. Once a TSN golf analyst, still a player, and a devotee of the game forever, today Nelford derives great satisfaction from teaching. In 1992 the Golf Writers Association of America presented Jim Nelford with the Ben Hogan Award for staying active in the game after such a devastating injury. Haunted by nightmares of careening golf balls and crashing boats, this guy definitely is not.

At his Canadian Golf Hall of Fame induction ceremony at the Glen Abbey Golf Club near Toronto in 2013, Nelford talked about the love he has always had for the game, as well as the rewarding career it gave him. He also challenged Tiger Woods to a one-on-one match of words.

"I don't agree with Tiger Woods," he said. "Second place isn't first loser – it's the silver medal, and there's a bronze medal and then there's participants. In this era we put so much emphasis on winning, winning, winning, and everybody that doesn't win is a loser. That's a horrible thing to tell our kids. No, you're competing. You're doing the best you can. It's a long journey, and enjoy that. You're a winner because you're out there doing it."

Arrogant winners put themselves above the game – and then out of it, once they suffer a loss they cannot handle. At the moment, Tiger Woods has missed the cut in three of his last four major tournaments, including the just completed British Open. When a reporter asked the thirty-nine-year-old if retirement might be in his future, Woods shot back: "I don't have an AARP card yet!" That would be the American Association of Retired Persons, who returned his shot with a hole-in-one tweet: "Tiger Woods. It's better to be over fifty, than it is to be over par." Ouch!

Not the stars but the stayers and the plodders, the Jim Nelfords and the Zippy Chippys, reap riches from their sports because they worship the game itself and not necessarily their place within it. There's an awful lot more to be gained from feeding off playing the game with teammates than from drinking from the cup all alone. Real success comes from playing the game, not from laying claim to the trophies and record-setting stats it offers.

Displaying great modesty, Nelford concluded, "Embracing the journey is more important than the details of the destination, even when you happen to arrive at a hall of fame." Golf has shaped Jim Nelford's life, but it's his good-natured and relentless competitive spirit that defines who he is: a hall of fame golfer and a very happy man. Who would you like to instruct and mentor your kids in golf, or even in the greater game of life? Tiger Woods or Jim Nelford?

Celebrity and winning being the tenets by which we measure success today, Jim Nelford will never be inducted into the World Golf Hall of Fame in St. Augustine, Florida. Maybe, just maybe, he should be. And that is precisely how Old Friends farm sums up the life, career, and retirement of the remarkable Zippy Chippy: Winning means way more than coming in first.

"THE REAL DEAL": A TITLE ABOVE
HEAVYWEIGHT CHAMPION

You hear it a lot in sports and life, the high compliment of being "the real deal," a person who is genuine, honest, and worthy of serious regard.

Michael Gerard Tyson was a fearless and destructive boxer, the youngest-ever heavyweight champion of the world. Referred to as "the baddest man on the planet," as a person Tyson was a plug. It's believed that "Iron Mike" – "I'm on the Zoloft to keep from killing y'all" – may have had anger issues. Volatile and erratic in and out of the ring, Iron Mike was never a threat to win the title of Sportsman of the Year. "I try to catch [other boxers] right on the tip of the nose," he once said, "because I try to push the bone into the brain." Living a lopsided life – an almost invincible fighter by night, a villainous human by day – Mike Tyson was not the real deal.

By contrast, undisputed world champion Evander Holyfield was not just a great boxer but also a gentleman, calm and quiet with a self-deprecating sense of humor. So much so that his nickname was actually "the Real Deal."

On November 9, 1996, Holyfield fought Tyson for the first time, and as the 25–1 underdog surprised everybody but himself when he defeated "Iron Mike" with a technical knockout in the eleventh round. In a rematch the next year, a desperate Tyson bit Holyfield's ear in the third round. The referee was about to disqualify Tyson, but Holyfield didn't want to win that way and the fight continued. Incredibly, Tyson then bit Holyfield in the other ear and spit a chunk of his flesh onto the canvas. This time the referee disqualified Tyson, who, fearing he'd get his ass kicked again, had actually planned this exit strategy. After this childish, insane act, Tyson's former trainer called him "a very weak and flawed person."

At a speaking engagement shortly after what became known as "the Bite Fight," Holyfield got to the podium after the MC ended his generous introduction with, "Ladies and gentlemen – the Real Deal."

Holyfield's first words into the microphone were, "Hey, did that guy call me 'the Real Deal' or 'the Real Meal'?" Tyson versus Holyfield, cannibal against character. Holyfield retired on his fiftieth birthday, showing great respect for the sport. "The game has been good to me," he said, "and I hope I have been good to the game."

Except for the "serious regard" part, Zippy Chippy possessed all the admirable qualities of someone who's the real deal. Okay, there were some pretty crazy stunts, and a few very dramatic acts of defiance, and that truck he tried to total, and . . . let's just refer to Zippy Chippy as "the Real Heel" and leave it at that.

TWENTY-EIGHT

Life Lessons the Zipster Taught Us

Unhappy? Seriously, quit your day job! In 1979 I was living on the coast of southern Spain, in a small villa above the town of Mijas, near Málaga. Off in the distance the Mediterranean Sea shimmered in deep turquoise, and beyond that, on a clear day, you could see the snow-capped High Atlas Mountains of Morocco. My rent was less than four dollars a day, and I was making eight dollars an hour teaching tennis at the three-star Hotel Mijas. Champagne cost only a few *pesetas* more than a bottle of water. I was trying to become a writer. I had just resigned as a salesman from the 3M Company. Life was good.

After my morning lessons, I'd sit in the square drinking *agua con gas y limón,* watching the town slowly slip into a coma called siesta. Among the African wood carvers and Moroccan jewelry makers selling their wares on the sidewalks was a Dutch artist whose work I did not think was very good. His paintings were all too bright, with square houses and stick-people figures – a genre of artwork common in Holland, and on refrigerator doors everywhere. I'm sure more than one tourist or local walked past his display and whispered that tired and contemptuous cliché, "Don't quit your day job."

He had only four months left, he told me, to realize his dream of becoming a full-time, working artist. Otherwise, he would have to return to his well-paying position as an art designer for a large printing company in Amsterdam. He tolerated his regular job, but he wished with all his heart to be known as a painter. He yearned to be his own man, not someone else's department head. He refused to assume the title of painter until he was able to actually make his living from his work. This stint in Spain was his last shot.

As his departure day neared, I noticed he was looking a little more desperate – unshaven, clothes rumpled, hair much longer than when he arrived. He had moved a couple of times into cheaper digs.

"I've never been happier in my life," he assured me, and his beaming smile confirmed it. For the moment, he was sustaining himself by the strokes of his brushes. Two commissioned portraits had come his way – not his specialty, but art all the same. He was scraping by, from hand to canvas to mouth. Finally, he was making a living from his own creativity and hard work rather than at the orders of others. Every day, in small ways, he was earning the right to call himself a painter. He had dared to make a lunge for the Holy Grail, and the world around him was finally cooperating, albeit reluctantly.

When I left at the end of the summer to return to Canada, he was still there, still hanging in, a month past the one-year deadline he had set for himself. And happy. I finally broke down and bought one of his paintings and gave it to my landlady as a going-away gift. *Good for you, Dutchy*, I thought as I buckled up my seatbelt for the flight from Málaga to Montreal. Then I put a pen to my Iberia Airlines boarding pass and wrote, "Dutch painter – It is better to fail at what you love than succeed at what you do not."

If you've been thinking about leaving a lucrative position in order to fulfill the dream that's been in your heart for what seems like forever, and, most importantly, if this daring move does not put in jeopardy those who rely on you for income and support, then you should really take the leap. Seriously, quit your day job and do it before it's too late. I did. In 1978, I was a salesman for the 3M Company in Burlington, Ontario, when my boss, a good friend and a Brit by the name of Richard Smythe, fired me. The company was divesting itself of sales and service employees and replacing them with store-front dealerships. Because I was no longer an employee, Richard then offered me a dealership. The plan was to split Canada in half, I'd own a dealership in Toronto and he'd operate one in Vancouver. "Millionaires in five years," Richard assured me.

I turned the offer down and set off to Europe to become a writer, a life-changing decision. Richard and the Toronto guy became millionaires in three years. But that guy, the one who took my place? He didn't start his career picking and carrying grapes in Burgundy and celebrating in Spain over his first pub-lished piece. He didn't make his money at ten cents a word teas-ing his wee Irish mother in a book and documenting the weird world of his unfaithful dog Jake or spending three summers at racetracks and hanging out with Zippy Chippy. I did and loved it all. Money is what you need to pay the bills and cover a reasonable lifestyle. Zippy got that.

Not always focused on winning, Zippy had a lot of opportu-nities to think about other things on all those trips around the track. Here, then, are the life lessons Zippy Chippy passed on to all of us.

- Life is like a horse race – the bell rings, we're off
  and running, and before you can blink, you're at the
  finish line. Make the trip the way Zippy did – slow but
  sure, and looking around at what all the others miss. In
  short, take the long way home. The end of the journey
  comes way too soon.

- As Zippy demonstrated time and time again, never bite
  the hand that feeds you. Bite him in the back. That way
  he can still fix your supper.

- Chase your dreams relentlessly, unflinchingly, the way
  Zippy Chippy chased a thousand horses around and
  around a track, believing he would win one day.

- Never give up. As Zippy might say, *Oh man, I got horses
  in front of me, horses behind me, and a horse on each side of
  me. Boy, am I going to tuck into the ol' feed bag when this day
  is done.*

- See all the way down the track to the finish line. You
  struggle and stumble, you compete and get beat, and
  what? You're losing sleep? Pull . . . eese! You're alive
  and kicking, and if you weren't, you wouldn't be on
  your feet. There are a whole bunch of people your
  age who should be alive, but they aren't. You are.
  Appreciate the basics – lungs, legs, and brain still
  working – feet, don't fail me now! Get back in the race
  and finish it as best you possibly can. Go slow. Get it
  right. It takes as long as it takes. Seek serenity. If slow is
  sublime, then quiet is exquisite. Create your very own

little corner of tranquility and retreat there as often as you can.

- Life is not a beach, it's a bitch, and sometimes "losin' real close" is plenty close enough.

- Remember, when Zippy dwelt, Felix explained that he was just letting the other horses go ahead of him. Courtesy and respect are very much in demand these days. Also, opening the door for others leaves you with the option of locking the bastards inside.

- Do not take failure to heart. Failure is not coming in second. Failure is refusing to show up for the next race to give yourself a chance to come in first.

- Never, never — as ornery as they might be at an early age — have your children gelded. That's just wrong.

- Be frugal with yourself, the way Zippy was with wins. Be generous to others; they probably need the rewards it brings more than you do.

- Win if you can, fail if you have to, but have fun. Kids do not have a monopoly on play time.

- Remember Casey Stengel's secret to good management: "In any group, you've got those who love you, those who hate you, and those who are undecided. The key to leadership is to keep the ones who hate you away from those who are undecided." That's why racehorses are separated by stables.

- Straighten up and fly right. Zippy may have lost one hundred races, but he never once got lost out there or tried to take a shortcut. "Find yo purpose and hang on."

- Give yourself small rewards for little victories. Eventually you'll carry the day, the way Zippy earned his platinum retirement package, and *Pop!* goes the cork on that cold bottle of champagne. (Do not spray it. Sip it!)

- Loyalty is the essence of love and life. During their careers, Felix could never part with Zippy, and in return, Zippy gave Felix more losses than he had given all of his previous trainers combined. It's the thought that counts.

- Be the first to congratulate a rival for winning. Zippy would have done that, if he wasn't so damn far back all the time.

- Be strong enough to face the world each day and smart enough to know there's always tomorrow. Be foolish enough to believe in miracles. Be wise enough to know miracles come with calluses and lower back pain.

- If you think you are a loser, you are. But remember, Zippy Chippy lost one hundred races in a row to make you, by comparison, look like a champion. Someday he will die for our misguided vanity.

* You could do a lot worse than patterning your life after the fun-loving and tenacious Zippy Chippy. But if you notice a guy following you around with a shovel, you've gone too far.

* Horses live in packs and talk to each other constantly. (There is no proof whatsoever that Zippy taught the others how to curse.) Surround yourself with good people, and you almost can't help but become one.

* Look out the window. At nothing. Daydream. It's time well spent. I've had a great life, and I've carved out a pretty good career from making fun of my ex-brother-in-law, my pets, and my wee Irish mother. She became furious when she saw the working title of my book about her life: *All Humor Needs a Victim and Your Mother Should Come First*. So I changed the title to *Margaret and Me*, because at eighty-nine years of age, she could still get a lawyer! At least two of my report cards from my early days of public school had comments like, "If William spent half as much time studying as he does gazing out the window, he would be an A student." Sorry, Mrs. Leach, but A students become accountants; daydreamers become lovers of life. My mother always smiled at me before she signed off on those report cards.

* Pack little, read lots, walk everywhere you can. (Okay, that's my lesson in life.) Live lightly and remember the

words of the great comedian Red Skelton who said, "You might as well laugh, nobody's getting out of this one alive."

• Most important of all, be yourself. There is and forever will be only one Zippy Chippy. Like thumbprints and snowflakes, you are uniquely you. And we are all more like Zippy than we would care to admit.

All together now: "Life's battles don't always go to the strongest or fastest man. But sooner or later THE MAN WHO WINS IS THE MAN WHO THINKS HE CAN!"

TO DO JUST ONE THING,
BETTER THAN ANYBODY ELSE

Although Zippy Chippy could do one thing very well – lose – he rarely lost in the same way twice. On many days, his unique outings were more exciting to watch than the easy wins of other, more talented horses. But his consistency – the harmonious and principled application of continuous and non-successful effort – this was his gift and greatest strength. Skeptics may certainly doubt his skill, but never his will. Never a "die-er," always a "tryer," the Zipster was a trooper through and through.

If Zippy had quit at fifty losses, or even sixty-five, his record would have been described as awful and no one would remember his name to this day. But instead he pushed on, he raced every chance they gave him, he honed his skills at not winning, and therein lies the beauty of his record: upside-down excellence in the face of recurring defeat. Now the sole holder of the title of the World's Worst Racehorse, Zippy took his profession seriously.

The importance of such noble effort was once beautifully articulated by the Reverend Martin Luther King Jr.:

> If it falls to your lot to be a street sweeper in life, sweep streets like Raphael painted pictures. . . . Sweep streets like Beethoven composed music. Sweep streets like Shakespeare wrote poetry. Sweep streets so well that all the hosts of heaven and earth will have to pause and say, "Here lived a great street sweeper who swept his job well."

Looking back on Zippy's career, we can safely say, here ran a horse that lost races like no thoroughbred ever could. A job well done, Big Ears. Martin Luther King Jr., the poet. Zippy Chippy, the poet in motion. Okay, then: slow motion.

POSTSCRIPT

As a hiker and frequent visitor to the trails around the Finger Lakes – and, okay, the bars – I had heard of Zippy Chippy, local hero and classic crazy-ass racehorse. I loved the story and immediately contacted Felix Monserrate, the long-time owner and trainer of Zippy Chippy, about the idea of writing this book. He was only too glad to meet with me near his home in Farmington, just a mile from the Finger Lakes Racetrack.

Despite being sixty years removed from Puerto Rico, Felix still had an accent, and as he rattled off driving directions over the phone, I was scrambling to write them down: Exit 44, second light on Route 96.

"Maddono's," he kept saying. *No fool, Felix*, I thought. *I get the interview and he gets an expensive lunch at some high-end ristorante called Maddono's.* After two U-turns, I finally noticed the McDonald's on the corner, right where he said it would be.

When Felix was late, I approached the kid at the counter to ask to use a phone.

"Help ya?"

"Yeah. I'm here to see a man about a horse, and . . ."

"Down the hall and on the left. Next!"

When the payphone didn't work, I went back to the counter and asked if there was a cell phone I could use to call the guy with the horse who was late.

Handing me a phone, he said, "Don't call Canada."

"How'd you know I was Canadian?"

"You've thanked me three times already, and you haven't even ordered anything."

So far this wasn't going so good.

Felix finally walked into the fast food joint, and from the reaction of that day's clientele, I can tell you that in that part of New York State he's more popular than "Ronno Maddono." Everybody recognized him, and he took the time to talk to them all.

Felix showed me his favorite Zippy Chippy memento, the scar on his back from the horse's teeth. We got along like two kids at camp, and I walked away with his oversized white plastic satchel full of Zippy Chippy clippings, racing programs, and posters.

After interviewing the trainer, I went next to meet the trickster at Old Friends at Cabin Creek, near Saratoga Springs, New York. There the legend stood with his head resting on the top of the fence, staring at me like, *What kind of a jerk comes to see me without a bag of carrots?* With camera in hand I walked up to this ruggedly almost-handsome beast with the head that looks like it's made of granite and said, "Hey, Zippy. I'm the guy that's writing your life story." Apparently I make a lousy first impression, because he stuck his one-and-a-half-foot-long tongue out at me and snorgled.

Zippy, you ungrateful bastard, I love ya. I really do.

Although Zippy Chippy survived the brutally cold winter of 2015 to become Old Friends farm's elder statesman, Felix Monserrate passed away in late spring of pneumonia complicated by heart problems. He was seventy-two. A small man who walked tall, he will be deeply missed by his family and fondly remembered by fellow horsemen. Like Zippy's incredible career of one hundred races, this book would also not have been possible without the patience and participation of Felix Monserrate.

William Thomas

ACKNOWLEDGMENTS

First and foremost, I want to acknowledge the participation and assistance of Felix Monserrate, who trusted me with his collection of souvenirs and scrapbook material. He also trusted me to tell this story, which I hope will serve as a final tribute to a sweet man and a dedicated horseman. Felix Monserrate died in June of 2015, before this book was published. Thanks go to his daughter Marisa for the many conversations and emails, and for the time we had at the track. Thank you, Emily Schoeneman, for your time between hot-walks, and to Felix's extended family: Orlando, Odalis, Myra, Eileen, Edgar, and Karen.

At Finger Lakes, jockey Pedro Castillo and farrier Chris Roncone were very helpful. Big hugs of thanks go out to Kim DeLong, Administration Manager, Delaware North at Finger Lakes Gaming and Racetrack; and Sandy Stanisewski, the last racing director at Northampton's Three County Fair. Much gratitude to Judy Peck Laplante, Zippy's biggest fan. In Rochester, thanks be to promoters like Dan Mason and John Blotzer of Red Wings Baseball, as well as Todd Haight at Batavia Downs Raceway.

Special thanks go to two successful sports icons, ESPN's Tony Kornheiser and golfer Jim Nelford, for their blessings in putting their words on these pages. I appreciate the assistance of Jim's friend and co-author Lorne Rubenstein. And to two great guys and trusted writers, Rochester talk show host Bob Matthews and L.A. scriptwriter Dave Latham — it was good to have you both in my corner. Too few words of Kentucky's Poet Laureate Frank X Walker grace these pages; "Praise Song" is the most inspirational poem I have ever read. Notes by friend and reader Heather McArdle moved the manuscript to a better draft. To Barb "I need another copy of the manuscript in five minutes" DeGuerre of Business Express: Quit closing up the shop when you see me coming.

A tip of the hat to Steve Bradley and Kevin Oklobzija at the Rochester *Democrat and Chronicle*, as well as Sarah "Skippy" Moon at Finger Lakes Community College. Old Friends farm – Michael Blowen, JoAnn, Mark, and Cody Pepper, and photographer Connie Bush – thank you for your enthusiastic support. Zippy's previous trainer, Ralph D'Alessandro, and first owner Charles "Bill" Frysinger were patient with my calls.

Simply put, this book does not happen without Scott Sellers, my publisher and publicist at Penguin Random House Canada, who loved this story from minute one. Thank you Don Bastian, who I can always count on for sage advice. To my editor at McClelland & Stewart, Bhavna Chauhan: Thank you for your guiding hand and your patience.

And a salute to the tote board for my track buddies Al Dicenso and Dan Patakfalvi who did nothing whatsoever to help me with this book.

ZIPPY CHIPPY

Foaled: April 20, 1991, at Capritaur Farm in Upstate New York

Sire: Compliance *Dam:* Listen Lady *Damsire:* Buckfinder

Sex: Gelding *Color:* Brown
Breeder: Capritaur Farm
Owner: Felix Monserrate
Major Wins: None

Zippy Chippy's Pedigree: Ben Brush, Buckpasser,
Busanda, Bold Ruler, Count Fleet, Man o' War,
Nasrullah, Native Dancer, Northern Dancer, Round Table,
Tom Fool, War Admiral, and La Troienne

CAREER STATISTICS

Starts: 100 *Firsts:* 0 *Seconds:* 8 *Thirds:* 12
Earnings Per Start: $308 *Career:* $30,834

///

Belmont Park	9/13/1994	8th		Finger Lakes	12/9/1994	3rd
Belmont Park	9/23/1994	3rd		Finger Lakes	12/13/1994	5th
Belmont Park	10/1/1994	4th		Aqueduct	12/29/1994	7th
Belmont Park	10/6/1994	3rd		Aqueduct	1/8/1995	10th
Belmont Park	10/14/1994	10th		Suffolk Downs	1/23/1995	5th
Aqueduct	10/28/1994	9th		Suffolk Downs	2/15/1995	12th
Aqueduct	11/16/1994	8th		Suffolk Downs	3/10/1995	8th
Finger Lakes	11/26/1994	4th		Suffolk Downs	4/12/1995	4th

Suffolk Downs	4/19/1995	8th	Finger Lakes	8/26/1997	5th
Suffolk Downs	4/28/1995	3rd	Finger Lakes	9/4/1997	4th
Finger Lakes	5/23/1995	4th	Finger Lakes	9/14/1997	6th
Finger Lakes	6/3/1995	4th	Finger Lakes	9/27/1997	4th
Finger Lakes	6/16/1995	6th	Finger Lakes	10/5/1997	7th
Finger Lakes	7/6/1995	3rd	Finger Lakes	10/10/1997	4th
Finger Lakes	7/29/1995	5th	Finger Lakes	10/18/1997	5th
Finger Lakes	8/8/1995	3rd	Finger Lakes	10/21/1997	5th
Finger Lakes	8/20/1995	5th	Finger Lakes	11/2/1997	3rd
Finger Lakes	8/30/1995	7th	Finger Lakes	11/12/1997	8th
Finger Lakes	9/10/1995	6th	Finger Lakes	11/16/1997	4th
Finger Lakes	9/23/1995	2nd	Finger Lakes	11/24/1997	10th
Finger Lakes	10/3/1995	2nd	Finger Lakes	11/30/1997	2nd
Finger Lakes	10/13/1995	7th	Finger Lakes	12/2/1997	4th
Finger Lakes	10/16/1995	7th	Finger Lakes	4/3/1998	4th
Finger Lakes	10/22/1995	5th	Finger Lakes	4/8/1998	4th
Finger Lakes	11/3/1995	7th	Finger Lakes	4/14/1998	2nd
Finger Lakes	11/14/1995	6th	Finger Lakes	4/25/1998	2nd
Finger Lakes	11/21/1995	5th	Finger Lakes	4/27/1998	7th
Finger Lakes	11/26/1995	2nd	Finger Lakes	5/5/1998	5th
Finger Lakes	12/4/1995	6th	Finger Lakes	5/15/1998	7th
Finger Lakes	7/6/1996	4th	Finger Lakes	5/23/1998	3rd
Finger Lakes	7/15/1996	5th	Finger Lakes	5/30/1998	4th
Finger Lakes	7/20/1996	6th	Finger Lakes	6/13/1998	7th
Finger Lakes	7/27/1996	7th	Finger Lakes	6/23/1998	7th
Finger Lakes	7/30/1996	6th	Finger Lakes	7/6/1998	5th
Finger Lakes	8/10/1996	5th	Finger Lakes	9/8/1998	9th
Finger Lakes	8/23/1996	4th	Northampton	9/5/1999	3rd
Finger Lakes	9/4/1996	7th	Northampton	9/1/2000	2nd
Finger Lakes	9/13/1996	3rd	Northampton	9/16/2000	3rd
Finger Lakes	9/23/1996	5th	Penn National	2/16/2001	7th
Finger Lakes	10/6/1996	9th	Northampton	9/9/2001	5th
Finger Lakes	11/6/1996	3rd	Northampton	9/15/2001	7th
Finger Lakes	11/16/1996	6th	Penn National	1/31/2002	7th
Finger Lakes	11/30/1996	6th	Penn National	2/28/2002	8th
Finger Lakes	12/2/1996	9th	Northampton	8/31/2002	7th
Finger Lakes	7/14/1997	8th	Northampton	9/8/2002	4th
Finger Lakes	7/22/1997	7th	Northampton	9/15/2002	6th
Finger Lakes	7/27/1997	7th	ThistleDown	4/16/2003	8th
Finger Lakes	8/1/1997	6th	Northampton	9/6/2003	2nd
Finger Lakes	8/10/997	7th	Northampton	9/4/2004	7th
Finger Lakes	8/17/1997	6th	Northampton	9/10/2004	8th

THE LAST WORD

If you've ever enjoyed a horse race or even this book, if you've ever been impressed by the beauty of these muscled and elegant beasts, if you've ever spent even a little time with a horse and come away feeling better, then please, support the Old Friends Farms. Michael Blowen and the Peppers are the caretakers of these magnificent creatures who, after their working days are done, remain helpless and homeless.

As charities that help our four-footed friends go, Old Friends is one of the best and most deserving of your donation. Not only would you be helping to make a comfortable life for the ex-champions and also-rans, but you would be helping these farm operators expand their facilities to bring more aging thoroughbreds in out of the cold.

I won't even mention the alternative option to a retirement; it is far too painful a thought. Please give what you can to yesterday's heroes, who without Old Friends would be in dire straits. Think of it as placing a bet on Zippy Chippy, only this time you win!

Donations — via PayPal, check, or
credit card — will be ever-so-thankfully received at:
Old Friends Farm for Retired Thoroughbreds
1841 Paynes Depot Road
Georgetown, Kentucky 40324
Telephone (502) 863-1775

and/or:
Old Friends at Cabin Creek
483 Sandhill Road
Greenfield Center, New York 12833
Telephone (518) 698-2377

A NOTE ON THE SOURCES

While most of the information presented in this book was obtained from interviews with the aforementioned participants and original research, several sources and publications provided background material that proved most useful in this project including:

Seabiscuit: An American Legend
by Laura Hillenbrand (Random House, 2001)

The Horse God Built:
The Untold Story of Secretariat, the World's Greatest Racehorse
by Lawrence Scanlan (Thomas Dunne Books, 2006)

The Ghost Horse: A True Story of Love, Death, and Redemption
by Joe Layden (St. Martin's Press, 2013)

Northern Dancer: The Legendary Horse That Inspired a Nation
by Kevin Chong (Viking Press, 2014)

An Unbroken Line
by Peter Gzowski (McClelland & Stewart, 1983)

Voices of the Game:
The First Full-Scale Overview of Baseball Broadcasting, 1921 to the Present
by Curt Smith (Diamond Communications, 1987)

Mike Moran, sports editor of the *Daily Hampshire Gazette*, kindly offered copy he'd written about Zippy Chippy and provided columns filed by previous writers, including Scott Cacciola, Andy Walter, Lou Carlozo, and David Abramowitz.

In addition to these newspaper articles, the columns of Bob Matthews in the *Rochester Democrat & Chronicle* that really got the Zippy Chippy story rolling across America were entertaining and helpful. Additional articles I referenced would include: "Our Hero: Mr. Potato has the right stuff" by Jason Stark (Baseball America Online); "HORSE RACING – Races Make Return to Fairgrounds" by Bill Mooney (*The New York Times*, 2001); "Catching Up With A Lovable Loser" by Bill Littlefield (*Only a Game*, National Public Radio); and, "Puss N Boots: Splishin' And A-Splashin'" by Nick Cota (Trackside with Trackman).

The following issues of *People Magazine* were also helpful: May 8, 2000 ("Running Joke") and December 25, 2000 ("Short On Horse-power.")

Always at my fingertips were the information bases of Google, Wikipedia (yes, I do send money!), *The Blood-Horse* magazine, and especially Equibase.

PHOTO CREDITS

Page 1
Team Monserrate: photo courtesy of Emily Schoeneman
Racing's Biggest Loser: photo courtesy of Emily Schoeneman

Page 2
Zippy Chippy, Milton Delvalle, Felix Monserrate: photo used with
    permission of the *Philadelphia Inquirer*
Zippy biting pants: photo credit to Connie Bush

Page 3
Zippy grazing in the field: photo courtesy of Emily Schoeneman
3 County Fair flyer: courtesy of Emily Schoeneman

Page 4
Pedro Castillo and Zippy Chippy: photo courtesy of the
    Rochester Red Wings
Felix and Zippy Chippy: photo credit to Emily Schoeneman

Page 5
Jorge Hiraldo and Zippy Chippy: photo courtesy of the
    Rochester Red Wings
Zippy Chippy at Northampton Fair: photo courtesy of Emily Schoeneman

Page 6
Zippy Chippy and Michael Blowen: photo credit to Old Friends at
    Cabin Creek
Old Friends at Cabin Creek: photo credit to Connie Bush

Page 7

Zippy Chippy and Red Down South touching noses: photo credit to
    Connie Bush

William Thomas and Zippy Chippy: photo credit to Monica Rose

Zippy and Red: photo credit to Old Friends at Cabin Creek

Page 8

Marisa in the feed bucket: photo credit to Emily Schoeneman

Marisa and Felix: photo credit to Emily Schoeneman

Marisa Monserrate: photo courtesy of Emily Schoeneman

ABOUT THE AUTHOR

William Thomas is an author, scriptwriter, and nationally syndicated humor columnist. He is the author of ten books, including the runaway bestseller *The Dog Rules — Damn Near Everything!* William's work was included in the *Great Canadian Anthology of Humor* along with fifty of the best humor writers in Canada. www.williamthomas.ca

A NOTE ON THE TYPE

The body of *The Legend of Zippy Chippy* has been set in Perpetua, a typeface designed by the English artist Eric Gill, and cut by the Monotype Corporation between 1928 and 1930. Perpetua (together with its italic partner Felicity) constitutes a contemporary face of original design, without historical antecedents. The shapes of the roman characters are derived from the techniques of stonecutting. Originally intended as a book face, Perpetua is unique amongst its peers in that its larger display characters retain the elegance and form so characteristic of its book sizes.